DESIGN TRANSITIONS

Joyce Yee
Emma Jefferies
Lauren Tan

DESIGN TRANSITIONS

Joyce Yee
Emma Jefferies
Lauren Tan

Published in 2013 by

BIS Publishers
Building Het Sieraad
Postjesweg 1
1057 DT Amsterdam
The Netherlands
T (31) 020 515 02 30
F (31) 020 515 02 39
bis@bispublishers.nl
www.bispublishers.nl

ISBN 978-90-6369-321-3

ACKNOWLEDGEMENTS

An idea usually arises from a question. The question, 'How is design changing today?' did not form overnight, but rather built up slowly and solidified through discussions and encounters with colleagues and peers. It is a question that has driven us to search for answers around the world, both physically and virtually, and to experience dynamic conversations with insightful and enlightened individuals.

This book would not have been possible without the generosity of these individuals, and many others to whom we wish to extend our thanks:

- To all the designers and practices that generously gave up time to share their stories with us, providing us with valuable insight into the transitions happening in design practice today.
- To all the individuals who contributed to our list of the world's most admired design companies, enabling us to capture these as-yet undiscovered stories.
- To our editor Louise Taylor, who helped transform our text into a fluid and engaging narrative.
- To our website designer Vicky Teinaki, who provided us with a platform from which to share our stories as soon as they were captured.
- To our publisher Rudolf van Wezel, who had faith and gave us the freedom to shape this book around our vision.
- To our colleagues at the Design School at Northumbria University, who not only provided generous institutional support in the production of this book, but also opened many exciting doors for us thanks to their international connections.
- And finally, to Tim Brown, CEO and President of IDEO, who took time out of his incredibly busy schedule to provide a thoughtful and perceptive foreword to this book.

Finally, on a personal note:
To Ray, thank you for your love, patience and support throughout the making of this book. Your critical insights have been invaluable. To my family Sze Mun, Yoke Sum, Rodney, Ivi and Ethan, thank you for giving me the opportunity to experience life outside of design. I love you all. Finally to my co-authors Emma and Lauren, it's been an inspiring and unforgettable journey. Let's do it again!
Joyce Yee

To my partner Stu, my family Angela, Hugh, Mark and Pam and all of my friends – thank you for your love and support. To DesignThinkers Group in The Netherlands, Voël in Brazil and Idiom in India – thank you for the opportunity to realize my dream of an International Design Walkabout, and thanks also to all the individuals who shared their design insights along the way. Joyce and Lauren, I'm honoured to work with such incredible minds – and congratulations to Joyce on the design of the book.
Emma Jefferies

To Geoff Miller, my husband, who never ceases to support and encourage me throughout life and my design career, and with whom I now share our beautiful new daughter Lily. To my family – Chris, Patsy and Melissa, who are always there to love, support and lend a helping hand whenever I need it. And finally to Joyce and Emma, for inviting me on the Design Transitions journey, bringing new experiences and encounters I could have never imagined.
Lauren Tan

I. CHANGING PRACTICES

II. NEW TERRITORIES

CONTENTS

III. VIEWPOINTS

SUMMARY

FOREWORD

Design is what we do to shape the world around us. Hence, as advances in technology and knowledge cause that world to change so the methods by which we design must also change. The industrial revolution enabled a considerable proliferation of new design practices, ranging from commercial graphic design and design for film and television to industrial design and transportation design. The signs are that the post-industrial information age will produce a far greater expansion. Already we have seen the emergence of interaction design, video game design, design of data, service design, design strategy, design innovation, social design and design futures.

New disciplines emerge alongside the latest developments in science and technology. Bio-design has established an early beachhead under the guise of bio-mimicry, but this is surely just version 1.0. Already designers are working alongside synthetic biologists to explore what it means to design with DNA. Similarly, the emerging 'Internet of Things' is creating new opportunities for designers to combine the design of the physical and digital in new ways, with the likely result being that some other kind of new design discipline will emerge.

In addition to what we are designing, it is important to consider the changes in how we are designing. My colleague Jane Fulton Suri talks about the changing relationship between designers and users in terms of designing *for*, *with* and *by* users. Traditionally designers, like architects before them, took responsibility for designing on behalf of users. In some cases there was no attempt to 'know' the user, but rather a belief that the designer's job was to interpret the world on that user's behalf – often, in effect, designing for themselves. This strategy can be successful when applied to relatively simple questions. The design of a glass, a toilet brush, a chair, or a building can be quite amenable to this approach. But it was the emergence of more complex design problems, in particular intelligent products and computer-based systems, which forced a reconsideration. Some designers, including my mentor Bill Moggridge, began to see the importance of a deeper understanding of the user. Instead of relying on traditional market research, they embraced ethnographic forms of enquiry and got out into the field, working with users as an inherent part of their design process. This approach became a founding principle for many of the new design disciplines, such as interaction design and service design which both have deep research and collaboration with users at their core.

We are now in the very earliest phases of the next big transition from designing *with* users, to designing *by* users. The democratization of many steps in the 'design supply chain' is opening up access to design in ways that force professional designers to reconsider their role. Crowd-sourced design tools such as Quirky, Threadless and Open IDEO allow many more people to participate in the design process. Crowd-sourced funding from the likes of Kickstarter and Indiegogo mean that anyone can fund a project. 3D printing and other 'Maker' technologies take manufacturing and production from those privileged with scale and capital, and give it to anyone with a few hundred bucks and access to a maker space. Through these and other breakthroughs, it is likely that in the future we will see unprecedented participation in design from a diverse population of users, and from wide ranging parts of the world. Professional designers are no longer a protected priesthood with sole access to the knowledge and tools of the trade. Perhaps they will instead become curators of this new design landscape, or discover new and unique contributions to make as thoroughly trained and deeply experienced practitioners.

What is surely true is that there is, and will be, no single recipe for good design practice. Earlier strategies of designing *for* and *with* users will remain as relevant approaches in the right circumstances, but in a time of ever-increasing complexity designers must face the ongoing challenge of questioning and evolving their practice. If, as might be argued, many of the most intractable problems facing society are a result of the design of systems emerging from the industrial and consumer revolutions, then we have a responsibility to redesign those systems to meet the needs of today. The methods by which we design and construct the 'manufactured' world around us form one of those systems, and examples of interesting new approaches continue to present themselves – but there is still more to be done. Perhaps the most interesting creative opportunity for design today is to redesign the very nature of design itself.

Tim Brown
CEO & President, IDEO
San Francisco
July, 2013

INTRODUCTION

Change is the very nature of design, an essential part of its DNA. Design practices are shaped by shifting societal, economic, political and ecological needs, and designers themselves thrive on the search for new and more innovative solutions, projecting into the future in order to challenge the status quo. Design responds continually to change – and so design itself must change continuously.

Design Transitions presents 42 unique and insightful stories of how design is changing around the world. Twelve countries are represented from the perspectives of three different communities: design agencies, organizations embedding design; and design academics.

Since change has always been a defining characteristic of design, why focus on it now? What makes the current transitions within design practices so important? Climate change, depleting global resources, global financial crises, the rapid pace of technological change and emerging social activism are forcing us to reconsider the way we live. Businesses are struggling to remain economically viable in these circumstances, and are increasingly turning to design in search of fresh approaches that will help them to face the unforeseeable future. A new generation of designers are taking the lead in addressing these challenges, moving away from the design of objects and into the design of services and experiences, in the process expanding their sphere of professional responsibility to include leadership, policy, strategy and the shaping of positive social change.

Our approach

Our goal in writing this book was to explore the question 'How are design practices changing today, and where are they heading in the future?' As design practitioners and researchers we have witnessed for ourselves how design is moving into new areas, and in this book we wanted to explore these changes through the eyes of other designers. We have captured the as-yet untold stories of a wide range of design practices to paint a rich, pluralistic and truly global picture of where design is heading.

The stories and viewpoints captured here have been selected by the authors and also crowd-sourced from within the design community. Our selection includes a diverse cross-section of small practices and larger, more established organizations operating in both the developed and emerging markets.

Design Transitions is divided into three sections:
Section I: Changing Practices features 25 stories from design practices in a range of disciplines. There are two types of stories: longer case studies (six to eight pages long); and short snapshots (two pages). Some of these case studies focus on distinct transitions within design processes and approaches, while others describe changes in philosophy and values.

Section II: New Territories features five organizations introducing and embedding design approaches into their core practice and operations. These stories illustrate how design thinking and methodologies are moving beyond the boundaries of traditional consultancy models, and now have a new presence inside organizations such as large corporates and government departments.

Section III: Viewpoints features 12 interviews with leading design academics, offering additional insights and a critical perspective on the key themes that have emerged from our case studies and interviews.

Who is this book for?

The design community has become increasingly diverse, and a number of different audiences will find this book both an insightful read and a valuable reference.

Practising designers from fields such as interaction design, service design, product design, social design, visual communication, branding and innovation will find much that is enlightening and inspiring in the design philosophies, methods, tools and approaches revealed here.

Design educators and design students will find that these stories broaden their understanding of current trends and directions in the practice of design.

Design leaders will find great value in the deep insights this book offers into the culture of design, how it can add value to their organization and the way it is being practiced in both consultancies and in-house design teams. Collectively, the stories presented here build a convincing case for the inclusion of design as a core competency in any organization.

People who work with designers, such as business strategists, ethnographers, researchers, psychologists, engineers, project managers and marketing executives will all find this book a window into the world of design, its culture and methodologies.

For people with a general interest in design we offer a rare insight into the philosophy, cultures and approaches of design and designers.

Our hope is that readers will use this book as a starting point in their development of a new understanding of how design is practiced today, and where it is going in the future. Our aim is to leave you with an inspiring and expanded view of design, and to offer deep insights into the impact and value that design can bring in addressing the complex challenges of our ever-changing world. *-end-*

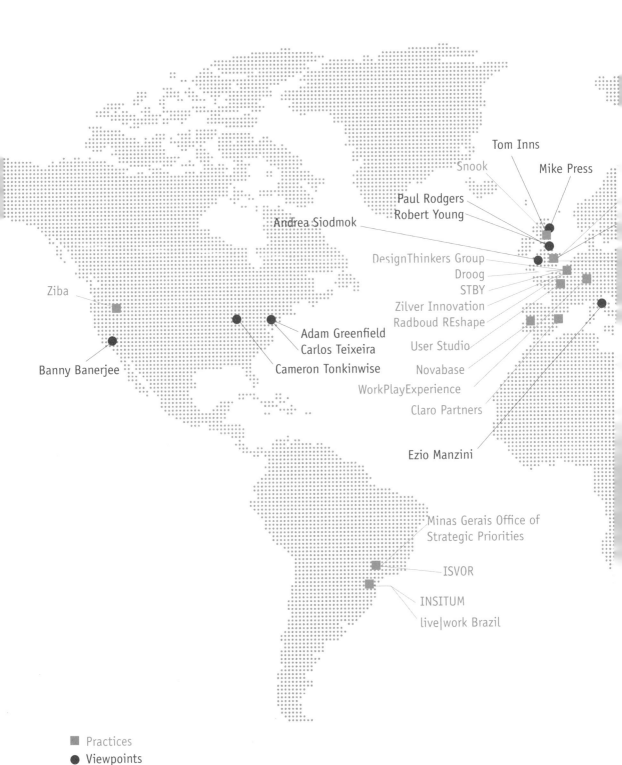

Tom Inns

Snook

Mike Press

Paul Rodgers
Robert Young

Andrea Siodmok

DesignThinkers Group
Droog
STBY
Zilver Innovation
Radboud REshape

Ziba

User Studio

Adam Greenfield
Carlos Teixeira

Novabase

Cameron Tonkinwise

WorkPlayExperience

Banny Banerjee

Claro Partners

Ezio Manzini

Minas Gerais Office of
Strategic Priorities

ISVOR

INSITUM

live|work Brazil

■ Practices
● Viewpoints

BERG
Fjord
FutureGov
Superflux
thinkpublic
Uscreates
We Are What We Do

Lucy Kimbell

Hakuhodo
Innovation Lab

Xin Xiangyang

frog Asia

designaffairs Shanghai

Idiom

PHUNK

Asilia

InWithFor &
The Australian
Centre for Social
Innovation (TACSI)

Optimal Usability

LOCATION OF
PRACTICES & VIEWPOINTS

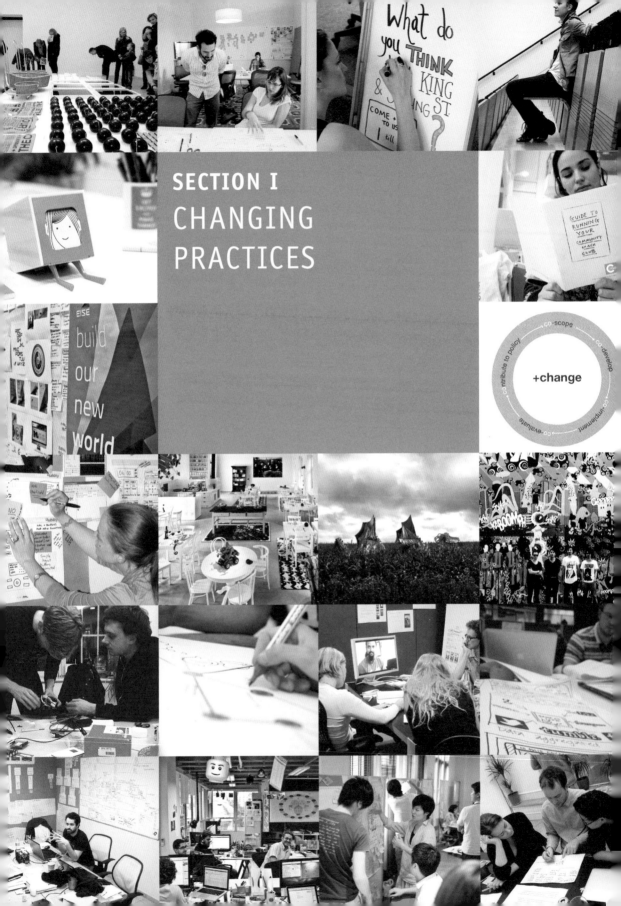

SECTION I
CHANGING
PRACTICES

Stories of how design practices are transitioning

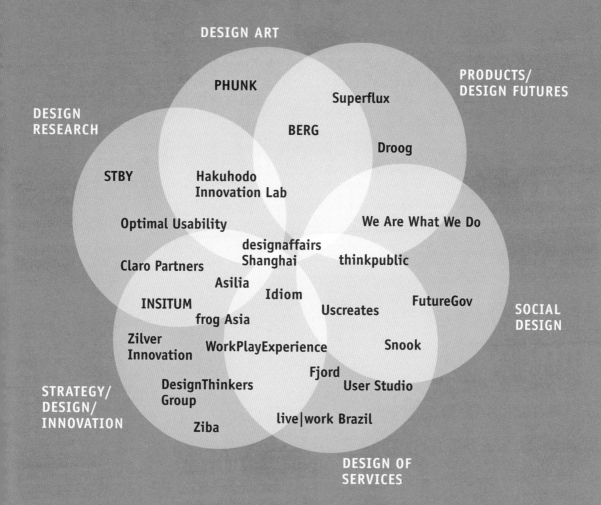

DESIGN ART

PHUNK

Superflux

PRODUCTS/
DESIGN FUTURES

DESIGN
RESEARCH

BERG

Droog

STBY   Hakuhodo
Innovation Lab

Optimal Usability

We Are What We Do

designaffairs
Shanghai   thinkpublic

Claro Partners

Asilia
Idiom

INSITUM

Uscreates

FutureGov

SOCIAL
DESIGN

frog Asia

Zilver
Innovation   WorkPlayExperience

Snook

STRATEGY/
DESIGN/
INNOVATION

DesignThinkers
Group

Fjord
User Studio

live|work Brazil

Ziba

DESIGN OF
SERVICES

DROOG

Amsterdam | www.droog.com

Continuously Challenging the
Business and Perceptions of Design

Droog's Transitions

The origins of Droog – A curatorial practice

Droog Foundation & Droog Collection

Collaborative practices

Experimenting with business models

Diversification of practice

Founded in Amsterdam in 1993 by curator and historian Renny Ramakers and designer Gijs Bakker, Droog creates cutting edge products, projects and events around the world in collaboration with designers, clients and partners. Droog is unique in their curatorial approach, initiating work that aims to challenge our perception of design. They pioneer new directions for design, and redefined notions of luxury and design through design classics like Rody Graumans' *85 lamps* and Tejo Remy's *Chest of Drawers*. Constant change and reframing are part of Droog's DNA – as demonstrated by the 2012 opening of Hôtel Droog, which turns the very concept of a hotel upside down. We spoke with Agata Jaworska of Droog Lab about why Droog continues to be one of the world's most influential design studios, and how it retains its relevance in a changing context.

A curatorial practice

Droog began in an intuitive way. Renny Ramakers, a curator and historian and Gijs Bakker, a conceptual jewellery and product designer began to notice a reactionary movement arising within the Netherlands. Renny and Gijs brought together designs that reflected this change, and presented their first collection at the 1993 Milan Furniture Fair. Within a design context characterised by formal, material and technical perfection, Droog's collection featured pieces of critical design such as Tejo Remy's strapped-up *Chest of drawers*, and Rody Graumans' loosely-bundled hanging light bulbs, *85 lamps*. This collection made a statement about the very act of designing through its improvised, straightforward yet playful use of readily available materials. These qualities led to the founding principles behind Droog, which are still based upon this model of curatorial practice – although the way they curate has continued to evolve. For example, after their 1993 success Droog returned to Milan in 1996 with Dry Tech, a very different collection based on a combination of high and low technologies that resulted from a collaboration with Delft University of Technology.

'Every product tells a story' is the slogan that underpins all of Droog's work. The studio celebrated its 20th anniversary in 2013, and continues to surprise and delight audiences by taking risks in new design territories. An important part of Droog's approach is using what already exists, but adding a twist – 'turning things upside down' and combining different worlds. Droog aims to rethink and reframe, not only the design outcome of a project but also every aspect of the way that project is undertaken. It does not conform to trends or seek to establish a 'Droog style', and this is one of the key reasons that Droog remains influential in the world of design.

Droog is a small team of around fifteen people, and that team can expand or contract depending on the nature of a project. This allows Droog to engage in a broad diversity of creative activities which are not bound by in-house expertise. A lot of what makes Droog work is their ability to pull together the right team for the right project. The boundaries around and within their team are never clear-cut and, as a result, its structure remains flexible. Droog sees this type of flexibility becoming increasingly relevant in the future

Chest of Drawers by Tejo Remy and the *85 lamps* by Rody Graumans, part of the collection presented by Droog at the 1993 Milan Furniture Fair

Droog Store in Amsterdam

Time is Life Carpet

when organizations will need to respond quickly to more challenging factors.

Droog Foundation and Droog Collection

Droog is comprised of two parallel entities. The first is the Droog Foundation, which was founded after the 1993 Milan Furniture Fair. Following their successful debut Droog began initiating experimental projects and accepting commissions from external companies. The second entity is Droog BV[1], which was set up in 2004 to develop, produce and bring Droog products to market as the Droog Collection. The Collection currently consists of around 200 products by more than a hundred designers, and is distributed through various channels including the Droog store in the heart of Amsterdam, the online Droog store (www.droog.com) and other international retail partners. Another entity, Studio Droog, was also established as an in-house design studio servicing the two entities of Droog Foundation and Droog BV, providing research and design development for all of their projects, products and events.

A collaborative practice

The Droog family grew further with the 2009 launch of Droog Lab, a collaborative design platform set up by Droog. Over the course of four years Droog Lab travelled to a number of countries with the aim of learning from diverse viewpoints and ways of living. Their series of projects aimed to understand and experience how different cultures live, in the context of a globalized era where brands have global penetration and cities are beginning to look more alike. There were nine project locations in total, each coupled with unique themes including copying in China, ambition in Dubai, the service economy in New York, consumption in Moscow and survival in the far North of Canada. Together with local partners and designers, the Droog Lab team developed projects that explored what could be learned from these very different societies.

Open House was the result of the New York Droog Lab project, undertaken in collaboration with New York City-based architectural practice Diller Scofidio + Renfro.

An important part of Droog's approach is using what already exists, but adding a twist – 'turning things upside down' and combining different worlds.

Clockwise from top left: *Saved by Droog* exhibition at Laboratory of the Future, *Full of Thoughts* cup and saucer by Annelys de Vet, 36 Imaginary Brands and Cellulose Station for the *Material Matters* exhibition in the Dutch Design Week

Open House is a movement in which suburban homeowners supplement their income and develop a new vocation by offering homemade services and facilities to the public. This project was inspired by the service-oriented mentality of New York City, and resulted in a one-day event in which visitors could participate in nine installations within houses, designed and executed by architects, designers and artists in collaboration with the homeowners themselves.

Another Droog Lab project, *Fantastical Investment*, was inspired by Russian habits of consumption ranging from the love of 'bling' to the love of literature. This project was conducted in collaboration with Strelka Institute for Media, Architecture and Design in Moscow, Daniel van der Velden of Metahaven design and research studio in Amsterdam, and a team of local Russian designers. The result was an imaginary luxury brand that acted as a vehicle for discussion on the co-existence of fiction and survival within a new vision of luxury. A number of prototypes were produced by Droog's product development team and exhibited as part of *Fantastical Investment*. One of these was *Time is life*, a 13-metre long carpet representing a person's life phases, which Studio Droog later turned from a piece of experiment R&D work into a new commercial product. The resulting carpet, named *All in One*, features multiple carpet pieces that can be arranged in different configurations. *All in One* is now available through the Droog store, and is also on display at Hôtel Droog.

Experimenting with business models
Droog has always been experimental and flexible in the way it runs projects. Recently, Droog has also been considering business models themselves as a form of design, and looking at new ways to prototype and test them out. One of the projects that led Droog to challenge and experiment with existing business models was their 2010 *Saved by Droog* project.

In *Saved by Droog*, Droog explored how dead stock could be re-appropriated in order to generate new income. This project was a direct response to the financial crisis of 2009, when many companies were declared bankrupt, leaving behind large amounts of unsold stock. Droog bought over 5,000 pieces of unused stock from liquidation sales and asked designers to consider them as raw materials ready for creative reinterpretation. The project resulted in 19 prototypes that were available for sale at the *Saved by Droog* exhibition in Milan in 2010.

The follow up to this project was *Up*, a platform and framework for redesigning products from dead stock. *Up* is an economic model in which unsellable products are redesigned and brought back into circulation. *Up* was presented at a symposium, generating discussions between designers, members of the public and companies about how the

idea could be taken forward. This was an investigative project, and some resulting of the products have been developed for market through the *Up* label and platform. One of the most successful *Up* products has been *Full of Thoughts*, a cup and saucer redesigned by Annelys de Vet.

Another example of Droog challenging the conventions around business models can be seen in the *Material Matters* exhibition, presented in collaboration with TD at the 2012 Milan Furniture Fair, and later at the 2012 Dutch Design Week in Eindhoven. *Material Matters* was a future furniture fair inspired by a speculative newspaper article. Economists and philosophers played with the idea of a future where income tax is partially replaced by a tax on raw materials, and asked the question: 'What effect would this have on society?' Droog researched a number of current initiatives, such as fishing plastic from the sea and making products out of the sand of the Sahara. In response they invented companies that would thrive in this new society, and created their contributions to a fictional future Milan Furniture Fair. In an example of how Droog projects tend to inform and contribute to their other work, the *Up* label was also featured as one of the 38 imagined future companies.

A diversification of practice
Droog always strives to be different, while ensuring that this is in response to changing context and is relevant to the current situation. The 2009 economic crisis led to structural changes in the marketplace, which in turn required changes to the way design businesses operated. Projects such as *Saved by Droog*, 2011's *Design for Download* and *Material Matters* in 2012 are a way to explore new models of design practice, and products

Hôtel Droog, Eat & drink at
ROOMSERVICE cafe

Hôtel Droog, Fairy tale garden, design by French
Designers Claude Pasquer and Corinne Détroyat

like the *Time is Life* carpet are a means of
conveying new ideas about design. For
example, *Time is Life* explored the need for
durable goods imbued with fantasy, which
becomes particularly relevant in times of crisis.

Droog is making its diverse activities more
visible to the public through the recently-
launched Hôtel Droog. The hotel is housed in
a 700m^2 17th century building and contains
the Droog store and office, a café, a range
of retail stores and a single hotel bedroom
that is available to rent. In true Droog style,
the concept of a hotel has been reversed
here – whereas a typical hotel is focused on
sleeping arrangements, at Hôtel Droog all the
other things a hotel has to offer have been
enlarged, emphasized and made central to
the experience. Hôtel Droog is a place where
anyone can stop for a drink, have a bite to
eat, shop for exclusive brands, gather beauty
advice, have a stroll in the garden, attend a
lecture – and even have a bed for the night.
The Hôtel brings together all of Droog's
activities under one roof; from curation to
product design, exhibitions and lectures,
enabling people to engage as and when
they choose.

Meeting the challenges of the future

To celebrate its 20th anniversary Droog
presented a range of new works, initiatives
and collaborations at the 2013 Salone del
Mobile in Milan, giving an overview of
Droog's current activities and the direction
in which it is heading. Aiming to raise the
level of discourse on the future of design,
Droog Lab visited the epicentre of China's
copycat culture – Shenzen – with the intent
of 'copying' China. The result was *The New
Original*, a collection of 26 works by Studio
Droog, Richard Hutten, Ed Annink, Stanley
Wong and Urbanus, with each work taking
the notion of copying as its starting point.
A selection of seven works from *The New
Original* were presented at Milan, along with
works by Studio Droog and deJongKalff that
reinterpreted centuries-old artworks with
contemporary shapes, techniques and materials
using the Rijksstudio collection – 125,000
digitized and free-to-use images from the
Rijksmuseum that had been made available
to the public.

Today Droog continues in its experimental
approach, exploring issues and elevating debate

through the use of design fiction. Another project presented at Salone del Mobile in 2013 was *Identity Land: Space for a million identities*, created in collaboration with Erik Kessels. *Identity Land* is an imagined society of a million identities unlimited by geographical boundaries, with propositions including a coin with a mirrored face that lets you see your reflection, a transparent flag and an anthem that combines all the world's anthems in one. The project was exhibited alongside a website www.identityland.net where people from all over the world could donate square metres of private space to form a global post-national nation. The site also contains downloadable tools for activism, and opportunities to join in the *Identity Land* conversation online.

Of all the diverse forms their work has taken, Hôtel Droog is perhaps the best example of the exciting transitions that have driven, and continue to drive Droog forwards. Bringing together the full range of Droog design activities within a single physical space, the experiences and opportunities encapsulated within Hôtel Droog truly represent the way that Droog has evolved over the last 20 years – and how it will continue to evolve in the future. ~end~

Notes
1. The term Besloten Vennootschap (B.V.) is the Dutch terminology for a private limited liability company.

Identity Land exhibition

Today Droog continues in its experimental approach, exploring issues and elevating debate through the use of design fiction.

BERG

London | www.berglondon.com

Making Pleasurable Inter-Connected Products

BERG's Transitions

From consulting to delivering products that illustrate strategy

Expanding the capability to build and prototype

Platform for connected products

Matt Jones is one of three partners in BERG, a design consultancy based in London that works with companies to research and develop technologies and strategy, by finding new opportunities in networks and physical objects. BERG specializes in product invention, working with technology and media companies across web, mobile, video and the Internet of Things[1]. We spoke about the importance of thinking through making, and how video has become a key tool for prototyping behaviours in internet-connected products. One of BERG's key transitions has resulted in improved access to manufacturing processes, and the availability of networked technology which has enabled them to bring their first internet-connected product, the *Little Printer*, successfully to market.

BERG's background

BERG is a design and invention consultancy, founded in 2005 when Jack Schulze and Matt Webb created a design partnership. I joined the partnership in 2009, and we then became BERG. We have since grown and there are now 15 of us, more or less an equal split between designers and technologists, and we have a strong emphasis on thinking through making, and investigating through material and phenomena rather than in a theoretical way. Half of our work is in consultancy for large corporations, where we offer research and development (R&D), concept invention and prototyping. The other half of our practice is in inventing and creating our own products that we sell directly to the public. Our most complex and ambitious product at the moment is *BERG Cloud*, a virtual platform for physically connected products. This was initiated in 2011 with the launch of *Little Printer*, our first connected product which is an internet-enabled device that prints a variety of content chosen through a smartphone. The interaction between our product development and our consultancy work has become a catalytic process for us. The things that we learn through consulting feed into our own products, and vice versa, and we are now able to speak to large corporations about actual products that we have successfully launched. We create evidence for our ideas through practice, rather than through theory, by experimenting with them ourselves at a smaller scale.

Our studio is full of generalists: either designers with a sense of curiosity and a penchant for technology, or technologists who have an eye for product, media and culture. We all get along, and the conversations that happen between us make for good outcomes in terms of design. We have specialists that we use a lot, such as animators, electronic engineers, data mining specialists, model makers and people with a technical or craft specialty. We have a great working relationship with these contractors, who we treat as part of our extended family.

BERG's philosophy and process

Our work is mainly driven by curiosity, and this is reflected in the diversity of our projects. We are a curious bunch of people, very interested in new technologies and how they might be used to create new experiences, pieces of cultural media, things in your home and things in your life. This curiosity that drives our activities is also what draws in our clients. They want us to bring that curiosity to bear on their company's technology, to find out where it could go and how it might do something quite unexpected, unusual, quirky or interesting.

We are a curious bunch of people, very interested in new technologies and how they might be used to create new experiences, pieces of cultural media, things in your home and things in your life.

BERG Cloud and *Little Printer*
1. *Little Printer* Packaging
2. *Little Printer*
3. *BERG Cloud* Bridge
4. The *BERG Cloud Remote* web
   app controls *Little Printer*
5. A *little Printer* delivery
   can be made up of several
   publications

We have our own underlying perspective, which is that we want to make these technologies more evident, legible, readable and playful so that people are not afraid to engage with them. Personally, I do not agree with hiding technology and making it disappear. I want to make technology evident, pleasurable and enjoyable so that people can truly master it.

We tend to have a small client base, companies we have built good relationships with and who have been working with us for some time. I would like to think that we have built up a lot of trust with our clients, and they usually approach us with ideas they want us to explore with them. We rarely get a brief or 'Request for Proposal' (RFP), and often the first step is just to have a conversation. People might contact us out of the blue, through our website or having seen our previous work. Matt Webb and I have also done a lot of speaking at conferences about design and technology, and often that is how people come to hear about

us. Our blog – where we publish our thoughts and talk about how we develop our own products – is another avenue. There are lots of different starting points, but generally people know we have a certain approach to exploring ideas and have seen what we have done in the past. That often becomes the starting point for a conversation about what they are interested in, and what BERG's viewpoint on that might be.

We always ensure we are able to work in a nimble way, to allow us to start making quickly. We do not have any account handlers or account management. Everything is done through the Principals of the company: myself, Matt and Jack. Our nimbleness is reflected in our early prototyping process, where we find out as fast as possible what works, what does not and what needs to be refined in order to discover where the value really lies. We are inspired by the Pentagram model, where each Principal leads a small dedicated team and continues to work closely with their client.

Staying close to the work in this way will be our key concern, if BERG continues to grow.

One of our key learnings as a practice is to always be building a platform – which means leaving behind a technique, infrastructure or apparatus for the next project. Although there is diversity in our portfolio there is also a thread and, more often than not, new projects stand on the shoulders of our previous work and build on the skills that we have acquired as individuals and as a collective.

From consulting, to delivering products that illustrate strategy

When we started out in 2009 there was a lot of emphasis on pure consultancy because our team was quite small. We focused on workshops, consulting and proposing directions which would then be implemented by a client's internal teams or other external providers. Once we started to grow we were able to build and prototype those outcomes ourselves, and demonstrate and interrogate those prototypes during our design process. As BERG expanded we were also able to increase our cycle of making, in order to critique what might be considered the more strategic design consulting. We were able to propose not only a strategy, but also a product that would illustrate that strategy in a concrete way. This is now our main offering and it results in concrete examples of products and services that we can place in people's hands, allowing them to speak about very abstract or futuristic things because we have made them physical and real.

Expanding the capability to build and prototype

One of the main changes in our practice is our increased capability to build and prototype as we have expanded. With more space, and more people with the right skills joining us, we've acquired more confidence in the way we do things. The biggest driver of change that we have seen has been the increasing accessibility of manufacturing processes and environments, which has enabled small practices to have a wider reach. This has come about due to the strategic decision-making of large technology corporations, who have made their manufacturing processes and environments cheaper and easier for smaller companies to access. As things get cheaper and more powerful over time, as described in Moore's law, we are definitely making the most of this more accessible and affordable technology. It has been a major transition that has had a huge effect on our practice, and it's a trend that looks set to continue.

It was much harder to achieve small-scale manufacture when we first started BERG, but we are now able to try things out for ourselves. This transition is perfectly illustrated by the difference between our first attempts at a physical product with *Availabot,* compared to our recent project *Little Printer. Availabot* was developed in 2006, and provided a physical representation of friends' presence in instant messenger applications. At that time *Availabot* did not make it to market, because we had very little experience of designing and engineering for manufacture and *Availabot* was on too

One of the main changes in our practice is our increased capability to build and prototype as we have expanded.

small a scale to be successfully manufactured. Six years on the world has changed, and there are now many more factories geared up for small-scale manufacture. New technologies have enabled the rapid prototyping of electronic and engineered components, and the emergence of a bigger shared knowledge base. It was a culmination of the experience gained from our past projects, emerging new technologies and the growing community of shared knowledge that made *Little Printer* possible, and as a result we were able to successfully launch this web-connected printer for the home in November 2011. *Little Printer* enables people to use their mobile phone to configure the type of information they wish to receive – for example tweets, news, calendar notifications, word puzzles and even messages from a friend's printer.

Another big change in our practice has been the increasing use of video to create prototypes.

We have found this to be very successful, because it can illustrate the behaviour over time of a product or service – and this is really important as the majority of today's products are now powered by software and so demonstrate behaviours. Video prototyping is essential for sketching behaviour, and we often use it very early on. My favourite way of using video is to take a photo, and then draw on top of it using an iPhone or sketchpad. Or we might video something with our iPhones, draw on top of the video and then show it to each other. This is a way of representing behaviours non-verbally, and within the first two weeks of nearly every BERG project you will find us creating really rough video prototypes or video illustrations.

We also use video prototyping to communicate complex ideas very quickly. One of the other great things about using video prototyping is that you get to the physics of a behaviour

1   2   3

BERG worked with Bonnier R&D to explore the future of digital magazines through the use of video prototyping. This work helped define the types of interaction in the Mag+ iPad app. Above are sample screens from the Popular Science magazine available through the Mag+ app
1. Popular Science contents page
2. Tapping the screen enables the reader to call up navigation tools to browse the issue
3. Online store includes promotional banner and editor-in-chief note

very quickly, which gives you a 'boundary object[2]' to discuss with collaborators. This was really helpful on the Mag+ iPad magazine project for Bonnier R&D, a digital media innovation company. On this project we used a lot of video prototyping early in our process in order to build credibility. We were able to quickly use these video prototypes to illustrate to the developer how we thought transitions in the videos should feel. This was a way of illustrating behaviour, animation and physics, and it was so much quicker to develop that way – which was really important because we had just 54 days to take Mag+ from a concept to an app available in the Apple App Store, in order to coincide with the iPad launch. We achieved this incredibly fast turnaround because we were able to translate concept video into code very quickly. In this way, video is an effective means of natively displaying behaviour and its physics in order to contextualize design systems and objects.

We also find video prototyping very useful as a means of communicating what we think the behaviour of a product or system should be. We recently collaborated with Ericsson to illustrate some very abstract concepts around home networking, and throughout the project video sketching was a key output. Video has this versatile ability to be both a project deliverable and an internal communication tool, enabling us to invite experts and the general public into a conversation about what we are designing.

Platforms for connected products

In 2011 we launched not only the *Little Printer,* but also *BERG Cloud.* This is a platform for designing, prototyping, manufacturing and selling connected products with embedded behaviours, quickly and cheaply. The driver behind *BERG Cloud* was

our need to make the design and manufacture of connected products much easier. We have removed a lot of the complexity involved in their development, making security, connectivity and communication between products in the household very quick and cheap. We have got this down to chip-level, and so now we are able to put these chips into lots of different products. *Little Printer* is the first connected product that we are producing ourselves, and there will be more to come. *Product 2* will be our next connected product, and in 2013 we hope to open up the *BERG Cloud* platform and let others use it to design, build and manufacture their own products on a small scale – just as we have done with the *Little Printer.*

What next for BERG?

We are doing a lot of consultancy work on the design of connected products, where product and industrial design combines with software and service design – and that is probably where our next stage of consultancy work will be focused. We hope to work on projects that give us the opportunity to consider the total experience of an object and the systems in which it is embedded, and to explore what this can deliver to the client. This is what we have done for ourselves with *BERG Cloud,* using our own product to try out a new approach that we hope will be valued.

In the future, connected products will become much less unique and just a part of everyday life. They will be unremarkable. We will have these products in our homes that communicate with us, and with each other, and that will hopefully become mundane but also pleasurable. People will want to buy them because they are appealing as well as functional. Technology should be something that people want to invite into their homes,

Technology should be something that people want to invite into their homes, that we buy because it is appealing and functional rather than something we have to post-rationalize.

that we buy because it is appealing and functional rather than something we have to post-rationalize. It should be a given that our technology works well – but it also needs to work with wit and with charm if it is going to be something that we are happy to have in our home for years to come. *~end~*

Notes

1. *The Internet of Things* is a term that was first used by Kevin Ashton in 1999, and refers to physical objects embedded with sensors and actuators and linked through wired and wireless networks, often using the same Internet Protocol (IP) that connects the internet. These objects (or Things) have the ability to communicate, and to connect people and machines anywhere and anytime.

2. A boundary object is a sociological concept describing objects that are flexible enough to adapt to a local context (with constraints), yet robust enough to maintain a shared understanding of its meaning.

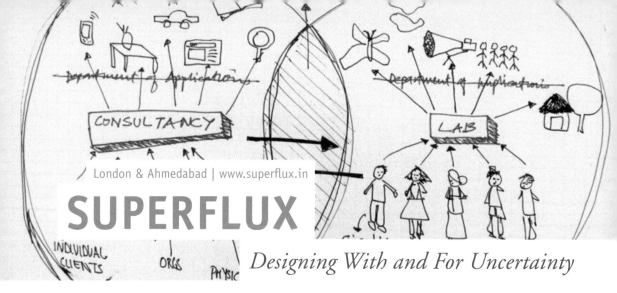

London & Ahmedabad | www.superflux.in

SUPERFLUX

Designing With and For Uncertainty

Anab Jain and Jon Ardern are Directors of Superflux, located in London (UK) and Ahmedabad (India). Here they share insights into their practices, and views on the current drivers of change in design. The vision for Superflux is to develop a new kind of design practice, that is responsive to the challenges and opportunities of the 21st century.

Tell us about Superflux, and what drives you in your work

Superflux is an Anglo-Indian design practice: based in London, but with roots and contacts in the Gujarati city of Ahmedabad. We work closely with clients and collaborators on projects that acknowledge the reality of our rapidly changing times, designing with and for uncertainty instead of resisting it.

We are particularly interested in the ways that emerging technologies interface with the environment and everyday life, and with our proven experience in design, strategy and foresight, Superflux is in a unique position to explore the implications of these new interactions. Ultimately we strive to embed these explorations in the here and now, using rapid prototyping and media sketches to turn them into stimulating concepts, experiences, products and services.

Our business has two parts. The consultancy is client-facing and offers bespoke services, while the Lab is a research space where we develop and test out new ideas. Though these two parts function independently we've come to rely on their contrasting rhythms for team sanity, the 'sweet spot' of unexpected synergies, and a steady stream of new ideas and provocations.

What do you think are the current drivers of change in Superflux's design practices?

Many of our drivers of change were captured in a 2011 blogpost (www.superflux.in/blog/design-futurescaping-value) which focused on Design Futurescaping. Here we talk about some of the key areas of influence on our practice, including building alternative possibilities, identifying 'new normals' and envisioning the future while working with the present and the 'game mind' of long-term thinking and visioning. Design Futurescaping brings these influences together, allowing us to work with clients and collaborators to inform their future products and services.

Whilst the focus of our work is design at the intersection of people and emerging technologies, we work with clients to explore their 'unknown unknowns' and examine spaces for new or alternative products, hybrids of products and services, and entirely new modes of business activity. This is possible because, through our Lab projects, we are always looking to push the boundaries of where emerging design practice sits: at the juxtaposition of technology, shifting economic conditions, climate change and culture.

What excites you about design at the moment?
The opportunity to be part of the space where a new kind of design practice is being created – a practice where the designer is not necessarily a star or hero creating 'iconic products', but rather someone who is involved with collaborators and the wider community to design new models of living for the 21st century. A designer who is, in effect, helping to widen perspectives.

What do you think the future of design practice will look like, and why?
Design practice will become a strange mutation of the present: networked, collaborative and multidisciplinary. We are already seeing design studios that have Associates rather than staff, projects that are undertaken collaboratively between two or more practices, and designers who prefer to remain independent and work with more then one 'studio'. We are also beginning to see people from other fields becoming part of the design team, and vice versa: designers becoming part of teams that would not

Superflux at work

previously have involved them. This may be seen in the obvious and already apparent designer-technologist-scientist collaboration, or the not-yet-visible designer-economist-policymaker-teacher collaboration. At Superflux we do not believe in design by committee and are very aware of our own skills, which have been obtained through rigorous training and experience. But the projects we will be tackling in the future are likely to be more complex, and to require more cross-disciplinary connection than before. This is because we are no longer being asked to simply design an interface in isolation. From the invention phase, where we are involved in helping shape a technology before it becomes 'product', to the design of strategy and systems, which then lead to tools and interfaces – our practice now engages at varying levels, which will require new and dynamic frameworks.
-end-

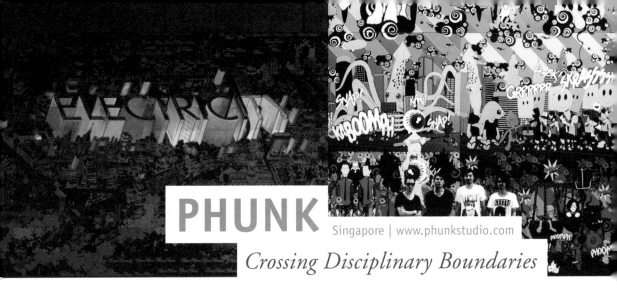

PHUNK

Singapore | www.phunkstudio.com

Crossing Disciplinary Boundaries

PHUNK is an art and design collective based in Singapore, whose members are Jackson Tan, Melvin Chee, Alvin Tan and William Chan. PHUNK's work crosses many disciplinary boundaries such as design, art, film, music, publishing and fashion. Here Jackson shares the changes PHUNK has been through since it began in 1994, as well as his own views on the current Singaporean design scene.

Tell us about PHUNK, and what drives you in your work

The four of us met in Lasalle College of Art in Singapore, where we completed a Foundation in Fine Arts and majored in Graphic Design. Due to our love of Hong Kong pop and music culture, we started a band called PHUNK. But we soon realized that our musical talents were somewhat limited, and so we used PHUNK as an excuse to create and experiment together. At the time desktop computers were just coming into their own, which made it easier for us to experiment digitally by creating graphics, interactive games, typeface and posters for rock bands. At the beginning we had no clients or money, but we had fun experimenting. It was the start of the 1990s, when designers like David Carson and Neville Brody were bringing their more personal and experimental voices into graphic design, and we were also influenced by London-based collective Tomato and the way they worked. Our first client was MTV Asia, and they have since become a long-term client and collaborator. For the first 10 years we were working on a

lot of commercial work – although we always had personal projects running alongside that, because there is always a personal voice in what PHUNK does. In the last few years we have started to receive more invitations to show our work in galleries and, as a result, have begun to focus more on the personal works.

The driver behind what we do is that we enjoy working together. For this to be sustainable, we recognized that it was important for us to be commercially successful and influential. After 10 years of working with multi-national companies like MTV and Nike, we began to question where we would go next. So we started to create more personal works in the form of paintings, prints and installations. At the moment, you could describe us as a cross between an artist group and a design group.

What is the Singapore art and design scene like today?

It is difficult to describe Singaporean design, as it is still emerging. Certainly you can see that designers here are very much influenced by

Western designers, but increasingly you see a lot more of the context, content and concepts emerging from a Singaporean identity. Previously it was more about the designer's own personal voice, and not necessarily a Singaporean one, but now you see more and more Singaporean humour in the work. What is interesting about the Singapore scene is that it has grown rapidly in the last 10 to 15 years, linked to the growth of globalization and its status as an emerging city. When we first started there were hardly any design practices here, because it was mainly dominated by advertising companies. The local design companies present at that time were doing mostly corporate work, which tended to lack any personal voice. Towards the late 1990s and early 2000s a new generation of Singaporean designers began to emerge, with more personal aspirations and voices. They work differently; they can be more niche because the scene here has evolved to allow for multi-disciplinary collaborations. At the same time, designers are crossing over to other mediums and disciplines as well. PHUNK, for example, has crossed over to the arts scene.

The Singapore design industry is now at a maturing stage, but it will always be playing catch up with the more mature industries found in Europe, the United States and Japan. However new possibilities are emerging, and I have never seen a model like ours working in the United States. We have taken existing models and made them work for our local context.

How has PHUNK changed over the last 15 years?
What has not changed is PHUNK being the four of us continuing to work together. But the context, and the work we do within it, has changed organically since we first started out. Experimentation is always there but the medium has changed quite a bit. When we

first started out we used our graphic design practice to express our art, but now we have transitioned to the point where we are creating art that is informed by our graphic design skills.

Another transition is our business model and revenue streams. In the beginning we focused on commissioned work, but now the balance between our studio work and personal work is different. Previously, it was about how we would fit the creation of 10 paintings in-between our paid work, but now it is about how we fit paid work around our art practice. We now have various revenue streams: commissioned work is one, commercial licensing of our work through merchandising is another, and licensing our art works for promotional purposes is yet another.

What are the current drivers of change in your practice?
One driver would be technology. The second, more obvious, driver is the economy. Affluence is important because as our culture and economy have become wealthier, people can travel more and the world becomes smaller. Clients can afford to pay more for designers, or collectors can pay more for artwork.

What excites you about design at the moment?
I am excited that design has gone beyond aesthetics. When we first started out, design was very much about form. Then it became form and function, and then it became form, function and content. Now it is about form, function, content and desire as well as the process of thinking – and this means that design can go beyond the designers. Designers are much more willing to challenge a brief, and clients are much more open-minded due to our more informed and affluent society and culture. *-end-*

FJORD

London | www.fjordnet.com

Moving from Digital to Service Design

Fjord's Transitions

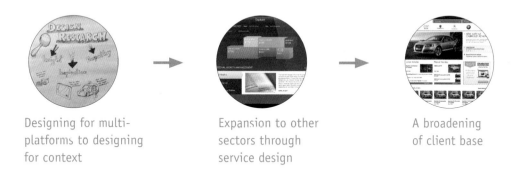

Designing for multi-platforms to designing for context

Expansion to other sectors through service design

A broadening of client base

Fjord is a leading service design consultancy with headquarters in London and offices around the world. They work with companies to design breakthrough experiences that make complex systems simple and elegant. As a practice Fjord has benefited from an early focus on mobile technologies, which have now become the dominant platform for content. Mobile technologies have also been a driving force for Fjord's key transitions as a company. Abbie Walsh, Fjord's Service Design Director in London, articulates the transitions experienced at Fjord and the key learnings that have emerged from them.

Fjord's background

Fjord was founded by Mike Beeston, Olof Schybergson and Mark Curtis in 2001 as a result of the original dot-com bubble burst. Mike and Mark had previously founded CHBi, one of the first web design companies, which was acquired by pioneering interactive agency Razorfish in the mid 1990s. Fjord has managed to maintain an innovative and pioneering approach, due in part to the fact that it is still run by its founders. Fjord specialized in mobile technologies from very early on, choosing this as their differentiating platform. This early focus helped us to develop particular expertise in designing for the limited abilities of mobile devices – and as the majority of content today is driven by mobile platforms such as smartphones and tablets, this has enabled Fjord to remained consistently ahead of the curve. We are headquartered in London and have offices in Helsinki, Berlin, Stockholm, and Madrid as well as smaller offices in Istanbul and Paris. Fjord has also expanded into the North American market, establishing successful offices in San Francisco and New York. We currently employ over 220 people around the world.

Fjord's philosophy

Fjord designs for longevity. We believe in designing for the heart and strive to design digital services that form an emotional bond with the people who use them, becoming an essential part of daily life. We help our clients' businesses by making products and services that really matter, creating valuable services that reach out to users. We are not a marketing agency, nor an advertising agency; but we understand the importance of reaching out and so everything we do comes from a service consideration, rather than creating 'pixels' for the sake of it.

Fjord's London practice

There are 40 people working in our London office. We have a design team of 20, and the rest of the office is made up of business development, project management, financial and administrative staff. My department specializes in service design, which – as a subject and practice – is evolving and changing all the time. This means that my role as the Service Design Director at Fjord is also changing and evolving, which is fantastic and very exciting. Generally my role is about mentoring, team management and growth. I look after the whole design team in London, and I am responsible for ensuring that we are attracting and hiring the right talent. The skills development of the team is another important component of my job. I have to ensure that our expertise is constantly being deepened in the right ways, and also that we are growing into new areas in a responsive way. My role also encompasses quality assurance, meaning that I take on a client and an external perspective to ensure that what we are producing is of the highest quality.

The Service Design Team consists of interactive designers and motion specialists in prototyping, as well as researchers. Research skills are really interesting to us because they are crucial to the way we think and design but, at the same time, we have to consider how they evolve within our team. I have a senior team of design consultants with a lot of industry experience, and they are now using design to help our clients rethink their business models, products and services rather than just designing products. I also project manage the implementation of digital products, because design and programming cannot be separated.

Our core offering at the London office is what we call 'Breakthrough UX'. This is also

Fjord designs for longevity. We believe in designing for the heart and strive to design digital services that form an emotional bond with the people who use them, becoming an essential part of daily life.

on offer at the other Fjord offices, but it was pioneered in London – as many of our more innovative practices are – because there is a very competitive and fast-moving market here. As a result we need to innovate all the time, and so we provide 'Breakthrough UX' services by supporting our clients in a start-up model. This means that we take them from a business idea through to concept and prototyping, as well as understanding their business modeling and potential business impact. Once we achieve agreement within the client organization to develop a product for market, we then work with either our own or our client's technological partners to achieve the best possible product or service. This type of approach has been described as 'Lean Consulting', as it uses lean philosophies but has business understanding and design principles at its core.

It is a really important mantra for us that products and services need to go live, and be placed in the hands of the users. A few years ago we may have been more renowned for producing visionary and conceptual pieces, but that has changed. The nature of the whole industry has altered, and is now increasingly about realizing the potential of digital. As a result we now need our designers to be highly conceptual thinkers, but also capable of delivering designs that work. We draw on Lean User Experience philosophy, which enables us to constantly experiment, iterate, validate and user test to ensure that the product or service

that we are launching is going to be viable. By adopting this approach we have seen our project durations dramatically shorten, and we are now beginning to prototype very early on – as early as the concept phase, in fact. This means that we are focused on trying things out rather than imagining them, which can mean actually building a working and coded digital prototype.

From designing for multi-platforms, to designing for context

You can track our development as an agency by tracking the development of the mobile platform. The mobile device has shifted from being a peripheral platform, becoming the primary platform for content and, indeed, our daily lives. A few years ago it was all about designing for multi-platforms, but now it is about designing for context. By getting a clear understanding of user context – such as the situations, physical conditions and emotional states people are in when they use a service – we become better at selecting the right device platform for delivery.

Obviously we need to understand technology, and the limitations and opportunities of different platforms and devices – but the most important thing to understand is the context of use, and the factors which inform the intent of the user in that situation. Devices and screen sizes will change, but the context of use is always going to be about real-life application. Part of this transition involves

Transforming digital banking on the tablet for Citibank

designing and working in the realm of both the physical and the digital, rather than solely on digital platforms.

Expansion to other sectors through service design

Another major transition for us has been the move from working mainly with mobile companies and handset manufacturers, to working with much larger clients in the banking, financial service, retail, travel, health and wellbeing, and government sectors. This shift has been enabled by the emergence of a broader understanding of service design; because although we may not be experts in retail, we are experts in the design of services in the digital world and therefore have a significant contribution to make to the retail industry's evolution in the digital age.

Companies across many sectors are beginning to realize that they are not set up for a digital way of doing things, and need to rethink how they are set up as a business. I believe that a paradigm shift occurred when the iPhone was released, and this disrupted the way we think about products and services. Companies are recognizing the impact the iPhone has had on their industry, seeing how established companies have struggled, and realizing how difficult it is to work out their unique offering and brand value. From a user experience perspective this led to huge fragmentation, from the existing interaction paradigm to one

that is more visual and user-led. The banking sector is already going through this transition, and the same is beginning to happen in the other sectors. Despite all this fragmentation, I think we've now reached a point where digital can offer a consistent service-driven approach – and this is what Fjord as a company are championing.

A broadening of client base

In the past the majority of our work took the form of research-driven, visionary projects with handset manufacturers and electronics companies like Samsung and Nokia. For example, we worked on an interesting project for Samsung Galaxy about a year ago, which focused on re-imagining the user interface in collaboration with artists.

The shift we are now experiencing means that a growing number of our projects are with smaller start-up companies, who approach us to help them define, develop and prototype a product idea. This enables companies to achieve their next round of funding through a proof of concept prototype, which in turn allows them to come back and work with us to design, build and deliver the idea to market. Our aim is to get the client to a position where they know there is a market for their idea and, if possible, to help them deliver the product. For example, we have worked very closely with Citibank in the United States to create the Citibank for iPad app. This product achieved international acclaim and recognition, and is widely considered a game-changer in terms of how personal banking is delivered.

Our visionary concepts re-imagined Citibank's personal banking service for tablets, using data wherever possible in order to provide visibility beyond the customer's own banking service. This enabled customers to visually compare their own data against averages, or other interesting statistics around banking. Through this facility customers are able to change their banking strategy completely, and channel their funds in particular directions. We are now working on a complete platform strategy for customers, and have released the live service on the iPhone App Store.

Fjord has also designed and developed a live service called *Sunday Times Driving* for News International. In this piece of work, we helped News International transform their classified advertising for high-end second-hand cars into an intuitive, engaging and shareable site at www.driving.co.uk. The experience of the site matches the high-quality editorial of The Sunday Times newspaper itself, while making it easy for users to browse for premium vehicles. This work is significant as it shows how an international publishing group is moving away from delivering pure news, and into the provision of added-value services for their readers. In addition to the core design work Fjord also helped News International with the branding for the new site, which is something we are increasingly becoming involved in. Crucially, this isn't about us repurposing the brand – it's more about defining that brand and reimagining it for a new service. Projects like these exemplify how our work has transitioned away from the delivery of visionary projects, and into helping companies deliver their products and services to market.

More recently we've started working with large retailers who are looking to understand how they can reinvent themselves for the digital era. In these instances we are working collaboratively to define new service offerings, and help these businesses uncover new opportunities to engage with their customers.

Another interesting development is that we are seeing shifts in the geographical spread of our new business. While the majority of our clients are based in the UK (with the exception of large multi-nationals like Samsung) more and more of them are coming to us from further afield, including the Middle East, Africa and India. With this change in geography we have also noticed that the work we're being asked to do is slightly different. Most recently we have been working with a client to reimagine their whole business through their products.

Working with News International to put service design at the heart of *The Sunday Times* www.driving.co.uk platform

It's an incredibly exciting time for us, and particularly pleasing for me to see the research we did two years ago to reposition our services starting to bear fruit. As Fjord's design leader it's never been so important for me to make sure the whole design team is learning new skills, so our thinking remains on the digital edge.

Adapting to rapid change

At the start of 2013 we launched our Skills Wheel. This is a spider diagram that documents the results of a detailed questionnaire that each member of our team filled in, ranking themselves based on their current competencies and the competencies they want to have in 12 months' time. This helps us to organized our internal training, ensuring that each person's career development is carefully managed. The most interesting thing here is that where people want to be at the end of the year is often quite different from where we are now. For example, technology is now a core part of our offering – even though when we first launched Fjord people weren't that interested in it. Today everyone has embraced technology, and everyone is designing by prototyping and working closely with developers.

Dealing with change has also meant carving out new relationships, and this is especially true with developers. You cannot design a digital service in isolation – after all, we are designing a living, breathing entity and the code is as much a part of the design as the design itself.

Change has also manifested itself in the way our team has adapted to not just design conceptually, but to deliver designs that are market-ready. To achieve this we have to understand how to translate business requirements into a design. I have been extremely impressed with how our people have embraced this change and developed specific new skills – for example, implementing user journeys in order to gather the right requirements from our clients.

Another new aspect for us is working in an agile manner, which we have been doing confidently since the start of 2013. In practice this has led to us working with our clients on site, face-to-face, developing as we design, working within natural sprints (the basic unit of development in agile methodology), sprint planning and working through many rounds of retrospectives. We're also learning the importance of copy. Traditionally the language used in a design has been secondary to the design itself, however this is now shifting. As a result, we are now working even harder to make sure the words we use to describe things in the design process ultimately form a part of the marketing messages our clients use when they launch a service.

The way we design for visual and interaction has also changed massively, and the two strands are becoming increasingly intertwined. Of course there are times when you need absolute specialists in visual design and interaction but, generally speaking, I expect all of our designers to be sketching, and to be interested in structure and information architecture as well as visual design. Our team are eager to upskill, and they have already developed relevant new skills – such as the ability to understand and explore brand value – and are now able to translate that insight into corporate identity work.

We have targeted the industry's top talent in order to grow and develop our team, bringing in new expertise with the expectation that it

Team building exercises   Fjord's Service Design Academy's skills wheel

will start filtering outwards. We have hired consultants and experts from outside the design industry, and this has had a massive impact. We now have a business consultant, who is also an ex-Creative Director, as our Managing Director. Once we bring new people into the team, others naturally become interested in their fields of knowledge, gaining exposure to new terms and concepts and are starting to ask different kinds of questions. Of course, not everyone in the team will want to become a consultant. For me, having an open dialogues with my team is key to developing an understanding of how they each want to grow. We expect everyone to respect the client and their needs, behave professionally and be curious; because we are not just designing for ourselves, we are designing for the client and – ultimately – that client's users.

Where next for Fjord?

We will be consolidating what we have achieved so far, rather than trying to focus on another leap forward. We have identified some opportunities, and have the chance to grow and develop our service branding competencies. This will allow us to develop services as extensions of a brand, rather than add-ons. There is also a huge opportunity right now to determine how services are

communicated and delivered to users and to clients through marketing strategies.

Looking to the future, we would love to work with more start-up companies – because we have found that both parties can learn a lot from these collaborations. In terms of the market, the financial services industry is already redesigning its services and the retail sector is also beginning to do this. The next sector looking to make this transition will probably be the health and wellbeing industry, and we are already thinking about how to work with those companies. For example, we are convinced there is a need to evaluate service delivery in the pharmaceutical industry and so are actively investigating opportunities in this space.

I am also excited about the development of our team strategy for next year. I am running design meetings to help my team get inspired and share skills, and I plan to take these sessions to the next level by empowering team members and giving them accountability in helping Fjord to grow as a business. This is not going to be a top-down structure, but instead will be based on a matrix structure of sharing skills while being accountable for our own learning. *–end–*

São Paulo | www.liveworkstudio.com.br

LIVE|WORK
BRAZIL

*Creating a Service Design
Market in an Emerging Market*

live|work in Brazil's Transitions

Forming a partnership
with live|work

The conception of a new
service design market

Shifting from Design
Thinking to service
design and innovation

live|work in Brazil was founded by Luis Alt and Tennyson Pinheiro at the end
of 2009, as a partnership with live|work in the UK that anticipated the demand
for service design practice to meet the growing needs of the consumer culture
in Brazil's emerging economy. When live|work began in London in 2001 they
were the first service design and service innovation company in the world, and
experienced similar challenges to those faced by the Brazilian studio in trying to
create a service design market. In our interview, Luis Alt shares the story of how
they created that new market in Brazil, and what was learnt in the process.

Forming a partnership with live|work

Before we came together as live|work Brazil Tennyson and I both had our own companies. Mine was Push Service Design, located in the south of Brazil, and Tennyson's was Design Loyalty based in São Paulo. Due to our different geographical locations, and the fact that we were two of only a very few designers working in service design at that time, we found ourselves sharing approaches and tools in order to help our respective regions. We both felt a good synergy between our practices, and foresaw a huge potential market in Brazil – and, as the only ones working in the area at the time, we started to talk about how we could do that work together. We were interested in working with an already-established service design company, as this would give us the support of a strong team, great business cases and the recommendation of an existing client base. We started talking to Ben Reason and Lavrans Løvlie, the founders of the UK's first service design agency live|work, about how we might collaborate. They were very interested in bringing their practices into an emerging market like Brazil, and we made it clear from the beginning that we did not want to be a franchise but rather a full part of the live|work group. After three months of conversations we reached an agreement, and in 2010 we opened live|work Brazil in São Paulo.

The conception of a new service design market

In the beginning we had two major aims: to educate about, and raise awareness of, service design. To achieve the first aim, our strategy was to teach on service design and design thinking courses, and also to create the first Latin American program on Design Thinking at Escola Superior de Propaganda e Marketing (ESPM), a renowned business school. To achieve our second aim, we opened up our studio to the public and delivered workshops to a range of Brazilian businesses. Innovation managers from the executive teams at top Brazilian brands started coming along to these workshops, because they recognized a need to develop better relationships with their customers. At the same time we were constantly writing articles and blogs to build our reputation, establish our credentials, and get ourselves noticed in the market.

Although we felt confident in what we had to offer, we could see there was still some uncertainty out there about how service design would work in Brazil. Some people felt things were too different here; that Brazil did not have a very mature service mindset, and there were still a lot of basic infrastructure issues to resolve before we could even start to think about creating great user experiences. What these people did not realize was that a human-centred approach could actually help them to resolve a lot of those issues. We also heard people say that the user-centred, collaborative and experimentation-focused approaches we were proposing had never been proven in Brazil, and it seemed that many of them were not willing to take a leap in order to try them out.

So, to begin with we conducted small projects inside companies, or ran small workshops that were part of bigger projects. This allowed decision-makers inside those companies to see for themselves the value that we could bring to their businesses. As these clients became more confident in our way of working, we started to get commissions to work on larger projects. During this time we were also developing our own views on service thinking; such as our belief that 'everything is a service', and the importance of understanding where value lies in order to build meaningful solutions that work for everyone.

For us Design Thinking is an approach that has three main pillars: empathy...collaboration... and experimentation...

For us Design Thinking is an approach that has three main pillars: empathy (understanding everyone involved in the project, from users to people within our client's organization), collaboration (getting those people to work closely with us in order to tackle challenges more effectively), and experimentation (trying things out as soon as possible, giving time to improve scenarios and situations before they are launched). Our combination of service thinking and Design Thinking has helped us to become more empathetic, collaborative and experimental. We wrote a book about our approach called *Design Thinking Brasil*, which sold more than 5,000 copies in less than a year.

Shifting from Design Thinking to service design and innovation

In the early days, our business strategy was focused more around Design Thinking than service design. People in Brazil did not really understand what design was about, and many still associated it purely with aesthetics. They didn't see it as a process to create useful, desirable and meaningful solutions – and so, for them, service design did not really mean anything. However Design Thinking was becoming a buzzword, and many people wanted to know more about it and how it could be used. For us the Design Thinking approach was always the power behind our service design projects, and so we took the decision to use that term in our communications with clients – at least until they were ready to be introduced to the idea of

service design. We were actually doing service design projects, creating new services and improving existing ones, but we were talking about Design Thinking.

One big challenge that we faced in the beginning was finding designers with the capability and experience to work on these kinds of projects. It wasn't easy, because the service design market was non-existent at that time, and so we had to start from scratch and teach the capabilities we needed. Our existing education initiatives with ESPM, along with our workshop formats, helped us to achieve this.

Even though we talk about Design Thinking, and have even written a book about it, our clients understand our three core offerings as service design and innovation, structuring of internal innovation areas, and service training. Our main offers are still the creation of new services, and bringing a more user-centred perspective to existing services. For example, we are currently helping the Brazilian state oil company Petrobras to rethink the way people are serviced when they fill up their fuel tanks at gas stations. We have also worked with telecom company Vivo, to explore the opportunities that might arise from technologies they already own, as well as helping them to make sense of those technologies from a user's perspective. We're working on projects for the financial industry, helping companies to develop their customer experiences, and we've also been

Co-creation workshop with teenagers

working really hard to revitalize the innovation structures, tools and processes behind a lot of our client companies.

Most recently we have applied this approach to the innovation departments of two banks: Bradesco (Brazil's most popular bank) and Itaú (the largest Latin American bank). One of these projects empowered business leaders and decision-makers by giving them new knowledge, and another resulted in us training over 150 executives on service design. While implementing a new human-centred innovation culture at Itaú, we unexpectedly created an abbreviated version of a training session that has now become part of their Human Resources welcome programme. This training will now be part of every single new employee's experience at the bank in the coming years. We have also been helping Whirlpool (an international home appliance manufacturer) to rethink their innovation methodology. We tend to work inside companies like Itaú and Whirlpool, in order to help them define the capabilities, skills

and tools they will need in order for service innovation to happen.

To this day, we still give talks, run workshops and teach in business schools all over the country. By continuing to do this, we are able to connect with new people and develop relationships that lead to different kinds of projects. Tennyson and myself are partners in Escola de Inovação em Serviços (EISE), the world's first service innovation school, where we deliver a one-year journey through service design methods, theory and practices for our 'explorers' (the term we use to describe our EISE students). This programme has been running for six months now, and it's proven to be very successful. We have explorers from a wide range of backgrounds and businesses, all working to develop the way we think about innovation in the service sector. We also continue to teach our ESPM program on Design Thinking, and this year we will be teaching in New York – which will hopefully enable us to connect with new people and markets.

Where next for live|work in Brazil?

You'll find new and different challenges every day in Brazil and, for us, that is the joy of our work. We don't have a specific topic or set of opportunities that we wish to explore. We can tackle almost any challenge that a company presents to us, and that is what we have been doing – helping industries to rethink their products and services. We're going to continue doing that, in order to create a better country for ourselves and for our next generation.

One area that we would like to explore is behavioural and cultural shifts, such as collaborative consuming and the enabling of 'game-changing' technologies such as new payment models and different methods of accessing information. The way people deal with the world today is very different to the way they dealt with it a decade ago, and that world itself is changing faster and faster. As we speak, new technologies are emerging that might change the way we interact with one specific service provider, or with the government as a whole – and here at live|work Brazil we are very interested in being at the forefront of these opportunities, so that we can continue to bring new and incredible experiences to life.

What really excites me is that we live in a world of possibilities. Design is going to diversify in many directions. As more and more designers start to work collaboratively with their users, two kinds of design world emerge: the artistic, and the collaborative. We are going to have design professionals who concentrate on creating beautiful, fun and (sometimes) useful things. But I can also see more and more people with a designerly mindset getting together and working collaboratively to deal with the world's largest problems. Both these forms of design need to exist, and they will continue to do so. But out of everything that could happen within design in the future, what strikes me as the most interesting prospect is the emergence of design entrepreneurs who can develop and sell their own products and services. *-end-*

Detail of the project for the School of Service Innovation (EISE)

USER STUDIO

Pioneering Service Design in France

User Studio in Paris is France's first service design and innovation company. Here, Founding Partner Matthew Marino tells us about User Studio's practices in bringing design to new territories, working in multi-disciplinary ways and helping organizations define innovative new services.

Tell us about User Studio, and what drives you in your work

When we started User Studio in 2009, service design was virtually unheard of in France. The three founding partners (Denis Pellerin, Matthieu Savary and myself) shared a common vision that design could be a key ingredient in helping organizations to create compelling services with outstanding customer experiences. Today an increasing number of French organizations recognize design as a strategic means of transforming their service offerings, and a small but growing local service design community has emerged.

Our company is also growing, and we are working on a broad range of international projects ranging across banking, local government, energy, telecommunications, healthcare, culture, media and urban development. We specialize mainly in innovation projects, where we integrate a large variety of disciplines in order to generate original results. We also work on R&D projects to develop new tools and skills, and

to sharpen our creative edge. Although we approach most projects in a cross-disciplinary way, we realize that many service delivery channels are now digital. This has encouraged us to develop a strong digital culture involving user experience, data visualization and information design expertise. These skills allow us to work efficiently all the way to the final stage of a design project.

We are committed to design that is not just accessible and useful, but also desirable. Although this seems like an obvious goal it is not as simple as it sounds. Service Design is still in its infancy, and in the past it often focused on making existing service architectures more useful and accessible. We strongly believe that Service Design can reach a new level by also concentrating on the creation of beautifully crafted service environments. From a business perspective, this translates into creating services that really stand out, attracting new customers while ensuring that the faithful stay onboard. But Service Design can also be used to reach broader social goals, such as encouraging people to change their behaviour. For example, a service environment that appeals to people on a visceral level might be more successful at getting them to adopt sustainable energy consumption habits.

What are the current drivers of change in User Studio's design practices?
More and more organizations and sectors are expressing interest in design's ability to help them innovate. This has motivated us to set up R&D, marketing and training initiatives that work in tandem to introduce design cultures to these organizations.

Most of our projects involve our team, the client's team and, wherever possible, end users. We have been exploring how to better facilitate collaboration between these groups; such as by developing software to help us conduct creative workshops, or teaming up with a professional facilitator who makes sure that all participants' voices can be heard.

Increasingly companies come to us with a general business goal, but no specific idea on how to reach it. We help define the service as well as designing the way it works, feels and looks. We specialize in designing services composed of multiple mediums such as websites, newsletters and physical spaces. This requires (and encourages) our team members to become very versatile designers.

What excites you about design at the moment?
I find the explosion of data exciting – big data, open data, personal data. As the production of digital data becomes increasingly accessible, designers have an essential role to play in making data meaningful to the public, as well as in helping organizations become more transparent to their customers. A new user-supplier relationship needs to be invented! To illustrate this idea we have prototyped

several concept projects – notably *Refact*, an independent service to help users transform data-heavy phone bills into easily understood infographics. We like to speak about the shift from data visualization (from a purely communications perspective) towards data use (tools created from a service perspective that allow you to use your data in useful ways).

What do you think the future of design practice will look like, and why?
Design entrepreneurs: We are seeing more and more design practices developing and marketing their own products. A great example of this is *iA Writer*, a word processing app for the iPad developed by Information Architects, a Tokyo-based design firm. This trend will challenge designers to find the right balance between their creative consulting activities and their product and service development activities.

Networks of independent players working together: More and more design teams seem to be composed of freelance designers, social scientists, developers and business consultants teaming up on a regular basis. It seems this trend will develop as designers work with an increasingly diverse range of industries, which in turn require diverse skillsets and expertise.

Client-designer partnerships: Designers and clients are increasingly seeking a highly collaborative relationship. This can manifest itself in many ways, such as sharing strategic research, seeking government-funded R&D financing together, or just working as a team all the way through a project – rather than interacting only at key project validation meetings. Our own experience has shown that this approach is much more enjoyable, and produces much better results. *-end-*

Nuremberg | www.workplayexperience.com

WORKPLAYEXPERIENCE

Bringing Drama to Service Design

Adam StJohn Lawrence describes himself as a customer experience and service design consultant, a professional comedian und an actor. Together with service innovator Markus Edgar Hormeß, and working under the name of WorkPlayExperience, they use unique theatrical tools to help companies turn good services into memorable service experiences.

Tell us about WorkPlayExperience, and what drives you in your work
We are known for being the theatrical ones. We are a global two-man company, with Associates whom we use when we need them. Marcus has a background in science and process consulting, and my own background is in psychology, marketing and theatre. We met on stage – Marcus is also a musician and we were doing a musical together.

What we do in service design is based on a theatrical toolset. Theatre is not only a presentation form, it is also an investigative tool. So we use techniques from theatre like rehearsal, where we try to find out how something might be by rehearsing it.

We also talk about dramatic arcs. What is the emotional journey of a service? Theatre is really the only way of modelling human behaviour that can deal with emotion. We use theatrical language so that we don't need to explain anything to anybody. If you go in with normal

service design tools, you will find yourself explaining customer journeys, touchpoints, value networks – which are all very useful. However it is much easier to talk about a scene, a prop, an actor, a character. It is much quicker to get discussions started using concepts that people already know. It saves half a day and allows for a neutral language. It is also fun and full-bodied. We do not have chairs, we are up and moving around all the time. Using your whole body also gives you a much more direct channel to emotions. Rather than talking about what something might feel like, you are actually feeling it.

Drama and design: where do you see it going, and what excites you about it?
I am really enjoying how people are getting more hands-on about things. People are getting much more co-creative, building and breaking, 'doing not talking'. The idea of the prophet designer, the wizard in his high tower who gets a lightning flash of inspiration and proclaims 'This is what you need!' is becoming

a joke now (although Apple makes a lot of money with it). In most of the world people have moved beyond that, and I find that exciting. I hope that design will move into other parts of life like politics and government too.

Could you tell us about the Global Service Jams?
A Service Jam is where people who are interested in services, and using a design-based approach to problem solving and creativity, meet up at various locations around the world. Each Jam is hosted by an interested individual or group in a spirit of experimentation, co-operation and friendly competition, and teams have 48 hours over a weekend to develop brand new services inspired by a shared theme. On Sunday at 3pm, the teams publish their services to the rest of the world. We have three annual Global Jams now: Service Jam, Sustainability Jam and GovJam. We had 59 locations for our first Service Jam. We had planned for three, so the success of it really surprised us. Two years later, the 2013 Jams had 126 locations and over 3,000 people participated. The Jams have a budget of nothing, and a staff of zero. The whole idea of the Jams is the doing, not the talking and it is amazing how much you can get done when you find other ways than just talking. Most Jammers do not label themselves as any kind of designer. People come along because they are curious or interested, and the majority have their first experience with Service Design at a Jam.

Could you talk us through how you might work with clients?
We typically work with a smallish team of mostly frontline people – although sometimes we get in friendly users or customers. Our first job is to establish a 'safe space', which is an environment where it is safe to fail.

This is a theatrical concept that I am used to, but people in corporate environments are unfamiliar with. We spend a good part of our first design session developing that safe space, which might take half a day but is massively valuable. If you have a safe space people start experimenting and get honest.

We then try and work on real stories, drawing on the experiences available to us and rehearsing those stories. We re-enact them – bodystorming, if you like. People start to think 'What if we did this?', 'What if we did that?' and so, very early on in the process, we find ourselves making prototypes. These prototypes get more and more solid, or they get abandoned, until we find ourselves rehearsing the final design into the delivery stage. The later rehearsals become about discovering people's freedom to be themselves. That is another big thing that we push – and which is often misunderstood about theatre. It is not about following scripts and replicating what others are doing. Compare Zeffirelli's *Romeo and Juliet* with Baz Luhrmann's South American, semi-automatic guns and sportscars version. The films are based on the same text, but they found the freedom within the process.

When we play, and when we use our full bodies, different things happen in our brains. We are measurably more creative, efficient and productive. That should be a goal in every work situation. You can be extremely playful and very serious. They are not opposites. If you are serious about your business? You should be trying to get more playful. *~end~*

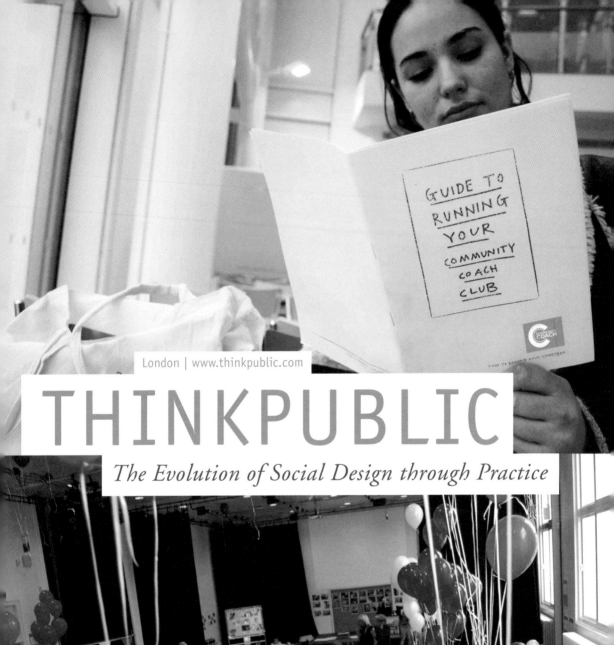

London | www.thinkpublic.com

THINKPUBLIC

The Evolution of Social Design through Practice

thinkpublic's Transitions

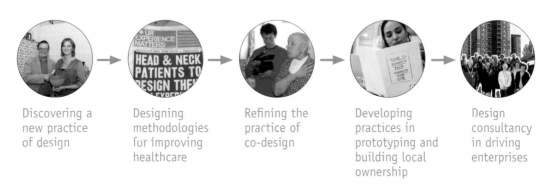

Discovering a new practice of design

Designing methodologies for improving healthcare

Refining the practice of co-design

Developing practices in prototyping and building local ownership

Design consultancy in driving enterprises

The UK design industry is a leader in the field of social design, spurred on by a number of economic and political conditions that included investment in innovative design practices, and the use of design to respond to government policy. thinkpublic is a London-based social design agency, and they have been using design to tackle big social challenges in the UK since 2003. thinkpublic is best known for their extensive work with the National Health Service (NHS) and particularly the development of Experience Based Design (EBD), an approach that uses design to bring staff, patients and other stakeholders together to improve the patient experience in healthcare services. EBD has been employed by hundreds of hospitals around the UK, improving healthcare and transforming one of the world's largest organizations.

thinkpublic was founded by Deborah Szebeko, who has won a range of awards including the prestigious British Council's 2008 UK Young Design Entrepreneur Award for her dedication to social innovation. Over ten years thinkpublic has progressed through many transitions, and each has deepened and developed the company's practice in line with their methodology of using design to create positive changes in society.

Discovering a new practice of design

I always questioned the purpose of what I was designing. For me, there has always been an element of design for a social purpose. I studied graphic design and advertising and always felt frustrated because I knew it could do so much more. It looked nice, but actually it could have a much bigger impact. I did not want to graduate with just another portfolio, I wanted some practical experience and so I volunteered at Great Ormond Street Children's NHS Hospital as a Project Manager, overseeing the design of a touchscreen information system. Whilst I was there I saw how small pieces of design could help improve the patient experience, environment and communication, and so I started to recruit other volunteers and ran small design projects. I was at the hospital for nine months, at the end of my volunteering I asked for a job and they said to me 'We don't employ designers'. That was a shame but, in hindsight, it was better for me because when I graduated from my MA in 2003, I applied to the first Nesta (National Endowment for Science, Technology and the Arts) Creative Pioneers Programme. This was based around giving creative people the confidence to start a business, along with a cash injection. I was successful in my application and used the money I received to start thinkpublic.

When I started thinkpublic, I realized that I could not have made the impact I wanted as a traditional graphic designer. I could only ever have reached a few people that way, and for real change to happen you have to change mindsets and behaviours, and involve people in solving some of these problems for themselves. In the hospital there were so many issues that could be resolved if only design was used, or if staff had access to a designer's tool kit. I was really keen to explore how we might give people those kinds of tools and skills. But there was no way designers were going to be able to achieve this in their traditional roles – and no way the hospital would be able to afford them.

At the beginning, the aim of thinkpublic was to help improve patient communications and experiences in the health sector, and so we were very health-focused. The first eighteen months was me trying to figure out how to sell this idea, and what words I could use to help people understand what I was trying to make happen. I met lots of people, did small design research projects for universities and gradually built my network. Initially I found myself doing lots of little graphic design jobs, and getting frustrated because I was not earning much money, reaching many people or making much of an impact. So I started to think about training programmes, and created a range of ideas about what I could train people in. I held a few mini-training sessions for healthcare professionals, and that was the first time that I applied my design skills meaningfully in a health context.

One of my first big projects was around designing patient experience tools for the NHS. These have been really successful, and are now being used across the world, but at the time I had no set process for doing this type of work – just a mindset about opening up the design process to others, rather than working in a closed way (which is how most traditional designers work). The NHS wanted to look at how Design Thinking and its methodologies could be brought into their organization to make service improvements. We were asked to think about how we might work with them to involve patients and staff in improving the overall experience of healthcare, and how creativity could be used as a different

Experience Based Design Project

approach. The NHS had looked at many different areas – like manufacturing and social movements – and design was another area for them to explore.

Early on, I hired a graphic designer and an anthropologist-filmmaker. It was just the three of us, and we got busier and busier doing these types of social projects. We got to a point where we realized that what we were doing with design was not just about healthcare – it could be applied to other areas as well. This was people based co-design. Everything we were doing was around involving people. The buzz around co-design started to grow, along with the recognition that engaging people was an important thing to do when designing, developing and implementing great services. In the early days we did lots of work on engaging people, as well as ethnographic research for councils, charities, and the NHS. As a result, thinkpublic kept growing. We had the opportunity to work on some very high profile projects, and created services that are now running across the country. Throughout all this, we never really committed to calling ourselves service designers. It has always just been about co-designing with people, and having the right tools and platforms to do that.

Designing methodologies for improving healthcare

We worked with the NHS Institute for Innovation and Improvement and a range of NHS hospital trusts to develop the Experienced Based Design (EBD) approach. We all came up with the name of the project together, which we thought was an important step in order to get patients and staff excited. Next we held a launch event to tell them about it, and asked patients and staff to come forward and share their stories. This was how our EBD process was created. As we were doing it, we were reflecting on what we were doing – and so a methodology began to emerge. It made sense to work with the people that used and delivered the service to better understand what worked and what did not, and involving them gave them ownership and belief. We ran the first co-design sessions, which went really well, and then each co-design group started to lead on their own and we were offering support and design skills to help them. We got to the stage where we had developed a rough methodology, and this went through several iterations based on testing at different sites across the NHS. The results of this eventually became the toolkit, which continues to be used in healthcare settings across the world today. We have also adapted it for use in different contexts – for example, we have recently adapted the toolkit for use in care homes.

Refining the practice of co-design

In 2007 we were part of the Design Council's Dott 07 (Designs of the Time) programme. We led a project called *Alzheimer100* which dealt with the challenges of dementia. At the start of Dott we did not want to do another EBD project, because we had been doing that for quite a while. But we knew that we had a methodology in EBD that we could make use of, and wanted to move it forward. The Dott project was a good way of experimenting with that.

In *Alzheimer100* we had a leadership role, which meant not only helping to shape ideas, but also giving people confidence in design. We were keen to open up the design process, and so we tried to create a process that would let the public be the designers as much as possible. Our role as facilitators started to become quite important here. At that point we were quite purist in our co-design stance, and we were not going to push our own concepts. Instead we would take the role of 'opportunity spotter' by supporting people's ideas and

Alzheimer100 co-design day

making them happen. This made *Alzheimer100* a transition project for us, because we were gradually stepping further away from our position as designers who shaped final ideas. However, our stance changed with the end of the *Alzheimer100* project in 2008. We were still the opportunity spotters, but we began to move away from the purist approach. This was because so much of our work was research-led and we realized that, while the public may have some great ideas, they are not always natural innovators. Designers are. As a designer you can see in your head how a thing works, and walk through the journeys of the people using it. The EBD and *Alzheimer100* projects were great for involving people and getting them feeling excited about their ideas, but the final ideas were not (in my opinion) innovative. A purist co-design approach is great if you want to make improvements, but to radically innovate the designer needs to play more of a leadership role.

Developing practices in prototyping and building local ownership

Our practice had started to evolve in line with the UK political and economical context, with the need for more locally-based solutions that could be delivered quickly and cheaply. It was a time of change for our approach. We knew we had certain tools and methodologies that were strong, but our main focus was on how decisions are made in a co-design process. We started to think about how this could be improved, and how we could drive sustainable solutions independent of public money.

With the *Community Coach* project, we had the opportunity to take ownership of the solution. This project was a great opportunity to explore how we could develop a service that was run by people and communities, rather than by a council. *Community Coach* is

Community Coach project

A purist co-design approach is a great if you want to make improvements, but to radically innovate the designer needs to play more of a leadership role.

a community-led life coaching service. Barnet Council had conducted extensive research around families, and life coaching was an idea that was suggested as being potentially beneficial for families with complex needs. Although the idea looked good on paper, when we got down to the practicalities of designing a truly engaging service it became very challenging. And so we took a step back in order to figure out if people really understood what was on offer, how they could participate, and how they might be involved in its delivery. We weren't going to just draw a nice process map here, we had to make sure it would work in reality and so it was important for us to engage people early on by asking 'Will you be part of our prototype?' in order to really bring it to life. There was also an urgency to make things happen quicker, and to speed up the design process. In past projects we had spent a lot of time doing ethnographic research and co-design. However, this client wanted us to move into the prototyping and delivery phases extremely fast. As a result we refined the idea quickly, and then had to engage our demographic in the prototyping phase by designing tools and training them in setting up their own prototypes. Today *Community Coach* is a successful service being delivered

across a number of different communities in the London borough of Barnet.

Design consultancy in driving enterprises
Toward the end of 2011 big changes came to thinkpublic. The continuing public spending cuts and government changes presented lots of exciting opportunities – such as designing services not for organizations, but for communities to own before they move into designing their own services. There have been a lot of changes in our practice since then. One of the things that we have been doing is thinking about how we might bring the private sector in to financially support and rapidly scale social projects. We have done a few small projects in this area, and are just about to secure a big project with a large company that will bring new learning for us. The thing that intrigues me about working with commercial companies is that their focus is very different to the public sector, and also their brands are very different. A big challenge that we have faced (particularly in our work around ageing) is the misconception of what charities and public services have to offer, and to whom. A lot of the Baby Boomer generation do not want to access these services, because they perceive them as services for 'old people'.

There is a real opportunity for us to present these services in a different way, that actually makes them desirable.

At thinkpublic we have also come to realize that we can design a service for an organization, or we can design an enterprise – which gives us more freedom and control over the final service. We are exploring how we can start up some of our own enterprises, and many of our enterprise ideas come from the research and insight work that we do. We are focusing on areas such as ageing and social isolation, because there are lots of really exciting things to be done there and we have lots of experience in those subjects.

It is difficult to start an enterprise with a social focus, and make it sustainable enough to keep going. The process of creating new businesses and raising funding around social issues is challenging, particularly in the current economic and political climate. However the biggest challenge of all is finding the right leaders, and getting those enterprises to scale – which is why we are interested in getting support from larger organizations who can drive scale and bring ideas to market quicker.

One of our own enterprise projects is the *After Work Club*. This is a social network for retired men to meet up and be inspired to redefine their retirement. It is basically an online platform that brings people together with organized events around particular social interests. Another enterprise we have started is the *Relative Friends* service. This is designed to help people in cities build family-like relationships in their local area. It is based on work that we have been doing on issues such as isolation and loneliness. *Relative Friends* is about recreating the kinds of support you might typically receive from family members, but in the local area. It involves both young professionals and older people, and it is different from a social network, which is about meeting like-minded people, in that it is about meeting people who are very different to you but can offer support. There is a website where people can find events, meet up, socialize and get introduced to each other. They can follow up their friendships online, and decide if they want to be friends. It is very much like online dating, and the service recently won an award a 2012 Design Week Award even though it is still at an early stage.

In our most recent project we have been doing something a bit different, working with British model and actress Lily Cole to raise awareness of the peer-to-peer gift economy. We have been helping to test and develop Lily's

Relative Friends project

This is less about us owning the solutions, and more about us changing organizational culture to embed new ways of thinking.

social business and network *Impossible.com*, through prototyping and testing of its different elements. The service is due to be launched in late spring 2013, and it will be interesting to see if working with a celebrity figure can reach different audiences, and encourage them to get involved in helping their local communities.

The future of social design

Social design is a young discipline. I think it still has to prove itself, and will go through a tougher period where it needs to be more clear about what it is by generating more case studies to illustrate its achievements. Ultimately, social design is going in the right direction and has the potential to be huge – but a lot of work needs to be done to make that happen. Maybe we will start to see more changes in five to 10 years time but there is already an amazing amount of energy around this space, which is a blend of wanting to do good but also a frustration at not yet making the impact that is needed. Social design is growing in so many different areas, which opens design up to more spaces than it is probably used to connecting with. Design can be very inward looking, but social design is going to be key to not just the design industry but many other industries in the future. In 2010 I was at an NHS event, and I was having conversations with people who understood what thinkpublic was doing very well. That was the first time since starting the company that I had thought: 'People get this'. A lot of our work has been a process of educating organizations in how to create real change in the public sector. This is less about us owning the solutions, and more about us changing organizational culture to embed new ways of thinking. We spend so much of the journey trying to educate and change cultures that by the time we get to the end, it feels like we have just started. We have been working with some of our clients for a number of years, and it is a lot easier to drive change in an organization that we are familiar with. It took seven years for a public sector organization like the NHS to reach a deep understanding of what we try to do. Now it is time to concentrate on the commercial sector, and the understanding will take time to grow there too.

Designers are more proactive now, whereas before they would wait for someone to approach them for a project. People are also aware that young people are running businesses like thinkpublic, Uscreates (see their story on page 72), live|work and Engine. Even though I had not worked in this industry for long, I was able to start my own business at the age of 23. In the past young designers would not even have considered social design as an area of practice. A lot of people go down the traditional route of looking for a job, but there is a lot more activism in design now and people are looking to different places for inspiration. We need future shapers, who can imagine better futures and help to shape the businesses and services that will bring those dreams to life. *-end-*

London | www.wearefuturegov.com

FUTUREGOV

Transforming How Government Innovates through Design and Entrepreneurship

FutureGov's Transitions

Setting up a 'DO' Company

Understanding communities and service delivery pressures

Delivering products and change at scale

Building an accelerator for start-ups and entrepreneurship

In 2008 Dominic Campbell and Carrie Bishop founded FutureGov UK to help shape the future of government. Dominic and Donagh Hargan, a FutureGov Design Strategist, share their insights into the company's transition from working on community projects with local government, to producing the future generation of public sector entrepreneurs.

Setting up a 'DO' company

At the start we had a practice that was focused on advisory activities rather than implementation, largely because we started with very little money and even fewer resources. So we were advising councils on how to use social media, but then we shifted our focus towards advising public services on the use of web technology for social innovation and change – a subtle but important difference that meant moving from communications as an end, to communications as a means to an end. We had a background in design and change through the digital, and this has always been where our interest lies. We also recognized the need to be involved in the implementation of innovation and, as a result, FutureGov was set up as a 'DO' consultancy in social innovation – as opposed to being just a 'thinking' consultancy. We began to focus in more detail on the design process, as well as building our own technology and working with partners to implement tools on the ground.

Design is core to our offer. Design is the vehicle that allows change to happen, while technology is the cog – acting as the facilitator and helping to make it stick. Our intention is to use a design skillset that is common across different areas of design, such as the ability to provide a creative response to ethnographic research using intuition and experience. Co-design – doing 'with' not 'for' – is central to the way we work. We gain deep insight into the problems we are trying to solve; partly through our own experience of working in local government, and partly through a design process that involves people throughout. Involving people is also important for making change happen, and stick. One of the main roles of the designer is to be a translator between all the parties involved in innovating

services in a social government setting – to bridge the different disciplinary languages and find the common ground within discussions.

An interesting thing about our organization is that we are largely based in London, but have people located all around the country. We meet up as a team 1 or 2 days a week, but we are communicating all of the time. Everything we do is in the cloud. We have at least one Skype conversation per day with a colleague. This way of working is a mixture of co-location and remote location. We work in a collaborative workspace where we have opportunities to not only co-work, but also work with other people. We think that, in the future, design practices are going to be a lot more fluid. It is going to be much more collaborative and more cloud based. People are doing one day a week with John here, and then one day a week with Mary over there.

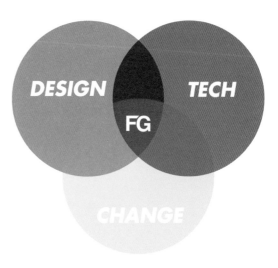

FutureGov works at the intersection of Design, Technology and Change

Design is core to our offer. Design is the vehicle that allows change to happen, while technology is the cog — acting as the facilitator and helping to make it stick.

Understanding communities and service delivery pressures

We began by putting on events, hack days and 'unconferences' to bring people from public service together around certain themes. At this point we were fairly consistent with our message, which was about the need to engage staff and citizens in designing and implementing projects, the importance of co-design, and the way that digital could be used to solve big problems.

This led to us gaining small low-risk projects, which started to bear fruit and required an expansion of our team from the initial five to today's total of 20 people. At this point we

started to work with local authorities to better understand their communities, doing ethnographic research, digital work, mapping online communities and trying to help the authorities to understand how to manage both online and offline relationships. Some of our initial projects were around community engagement through online and offline channels. However this project was rather unsatisfying for us as it was too narrow in scope, and what really interested us was being part of a wider change project. We took that learning and managed to seek out projects that would expand the scope and depth of what we do.

Left: Attendees at FutureGov's *Interactivism* event

Top: Discussing ideas at FutureGov's *Interactivism* event

Delivering products and change at scale

Our experiences of working with local government led to the development of the *Patchwork* project. This was a response to the 'Baby Peter' incident, in which a 17-month old boy died in London after suffering more than 50 injuries – despite having repeated contact with social services over an eight-month period. This tragedy highlighted serious failings in the UK's child protection services, and those failings indicated a lack of coordinated thinking across agencies working with children. As a result, FutureGov put out an open call for support from a diverse group of practitioners, parents, technologists and researchers to find ways of improving the coordination and sharing of information. With support from Nesta (National Endowment for Science, Technology and the Arts), and others such as the Nominet Trust (a UK based organization set up to fund internet-based projects that make a positive difference to the lives of disadvantaged and vulnerable people) and further partners in Staffordshire, we worked on a technological solution to the problem of joining up the teams responsible for supporting families, in order to enable earlier interventions and better outcomes.

We began developing the *Patchwork* prototype in much the same way as you would a start-up business, although it was incubated within FutureGov in order to ensure stability and support. From the beginning we took a collaborative approach, with our team working alongside external designers and technologists to help turn our vision into reality. This project tapped into current policy agenda, which led to the local council being enthusiastic about the work, which in turn meant that we got the funding to scale.

At this point we took the opportunity to bring skills in-house and build on the prototype design. This enabled us to develop technology and design teams, for this and other projects. We have been working on *Patchwork* for three years now, bringing together technology, design and – importantly – change management in order to help embed the changes we want to see. During the initial design work with Lichfield District Council, we conducted around 40 design interventions with practitioners, members of the public and clients. Over the last 18 months we have continue to iterate and build a fully secure web application. This has now been rolled out across both Staffordshire and Brighton, with the app becoming bigger and better to the point where it is almost unrecognizable when compared to what we started with. This has enabled us to prove ourselves to the market, and gain the trust of partners both old and new. This project, and others like it, have led us to stabilize as an organization, and we now have a cohesive group of 20 people who are doing consultancy, product design and technical development.

During this time we have had a couple of key challenges. We are not all full-time, but even so the team has grown a lot in the past year. We are very flexible in our response to projects,

We think our success lies in the fact that we are an optimistic bunch who really believe in our mission to transform public services in a very user-centred way.

and the team grows and contracts depending on what type of project we are working on. As you might imagine, when working with public sector clients there can be delays in getting contracts and being paid. We often have to start a project when a contract has not been signed, as the project might not be done in time if we waited. This is pretty much the norm. Next it is about finding the right skills, which can be challenging. There is always a balance to be found between specialist designers, and those whose design skills are more generic but who also have more experience. We need people that can interact with the public sector, and who have entrepreneurial skills. We need a core team of people we can really trust, who can be flexible, and who are willing to work hard during difficult times – because the work will always run ahead of resourcing, and so there will always be a lot of pressure on the team.

It has been important for us to know how the government operates, in order to know our market. From our experience we understand how the public sector operates and can position ourselves well in order to connect with organizations, and get the right ones on board. We also build evidence through our work to help others understand the value of what we do. We think our success lies in the fact that we are an optimistic bunch who really

believe in our mission to transform public services in a very user-centred way. This is not trivial; there are companies that focus on digital, who are design specialists or change management consultancies, but we bring all three of these aspects together. In the last year we have brought all the right skills in-house, so that we can deliver to a high standard and with no compromise on quality. This allows us to really focus on finding the solutions to problems that really matter.

Another key observation during this time has been the way our developers, designers and change managers work together. There has been a learning curve every time they engage. Often designers and technologists see change managers as an unnecessary addition to a project – they have designed a beautiful object based on user insights, and see no reason why it should not be realized. However, over time they come to understand that change managers have this rare skill of resilience and persistence, and are willing to engage in what could seem to be pointless conversations around the nuances and details of a project. This is something that designers and technologists tend not to have the desire to be involved in. Change managers also deal with stakeholder meetings and planning implementation, which some designers do not enjoy.

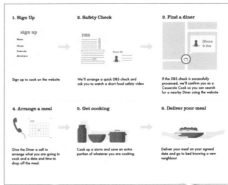

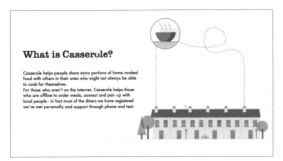

The *Casserole Club* project is aimed at reducing social isolation and improving meals on wheels services by coupling the willingness of regular people to cook an extra portion of dinner, with the needs of local community members who struggle to cook for themselves

Clockwise from top left: The home page of CasseroleClub, com, How Casserole Club works, What is Casserole Club?

We have also come to realize that we need to do a lot of learning together with our clients, we cannot just take a 'cut and paste' approach in project delivery. We want to help each of our clients to innovate on their own, using their own capabilities and not being dependent on consultancy. For example, if we are building a bespoke technology we have started to get our technical team to pair up with the client's technologists, so they can fully understand what and how the technology is being developed – meaning they can eventually replicate it for themselves. There is some role shadowing at the start of this process, and then we take on a mentoring role during the delivery of the new products and services.

Another current driver that is shaping our practice at FutureGov is the adoption of agile processes, which originated from software development and has now moved into our change and design processes as well. An example of our process involves going through rapid iterations at low cost, exploring how to collaborate better and facilitate different conversations across different agencies. The current financial context confirms what FutureGov believes: that the public sector is capable of being more resourceful, and that the way the government is currently using their resources is not effective. What we want to know is, how can we learn from other fields – and especially from technology and software development processes – in order to devise better approaches?

Building an accelerator of start-ups and entrepreneurship

As an organization, we have recently rebooted the company in order to 'up our game' and ensure that our standards are as high as possible. The market now trusts us to deliver. We have a team of high performing people with a passion to create only the best work, ensuring the delivery of high-impact projects that are capable of transforming local public services at scale. We recently flipped our business model away from change consultancy and towards a wholehearted commitment to using consultancy to generate ideas for products that can transform the sector at scale. We believe products (supported by strong change management services) are the key to truly disruptive change in local public services.

Based on all of our learning from the past five years, and our aim of supporting others in meeting their aspirations, in 2013 we are beginning to run more formal accelerator programmes to share our expertise in creating products and selling to government. In the past we have been involved in creating new products, where partners have asked us to pitch jointly in order to access a pot of money. We are now formalizing this approach by offering accelerator programmes that enable people through sharing our knowledge and experiences of making products and services work in the long term.

We believe products (supported by strong change management services) are the key to truly disruptive change in local public services.

Where next for FutureGov?

As we now have a strong foothold in the market, we want to ensure that we're the best we can possibly be. We have always focused on showing what is possible, and driving people in the sector to pushing boundaries and use digital technology as creatively as possible in order to transform public services. During 2013 we want to take our own projects to new levels of impact and scale, keep innovating new ideas, and help other people to do the same. *-end-*

WE ARE WHAT WE DO

Designing Tools to Facilitate Behaviour Change

We Are What We Do is a not-for-profit behaviour change company. They were behind the creation of the 'I'm not a plastic bag' carrier bag, and in 2004 they published the book 'Change the World for a Fiver' which sold more than 1.5 million copies worldwide. Tori Flower, We Are What We Do's Creative Director, speaks here about how the company designs products, tools and services that apply the 'Incidental Effect' to achieve positive behaviour change on a mass scale.

Tell us about We Are What We Do, and what drives you in your work

We Are What We Do originally started in 2004, and has been on quite an interesting journey since its inception. It initially started as a social movement, a campaign to encourage people to do small, positive things everyday in order to tackle major social and environmental issues. Through that work we produced the book *Change the World for a Fiver,* which became a top ten bestseller and was published in seven countries. The movement attracted a lot of attention. It was endorsed by Number 10 (the Prime Minister's department) in the UK, received a huge amount of international media coverage and spawned exhibitions, colleague engagement schemes, school projects, a Eurovision Song Contest entry and a series of follow-up publications. The focus of our work at that point was on creating beautifully designed, cleverly written materials that encouraged the public to do positive things.

Over the last five years there has been quite a noticeable shift in our approach to behaviour change. We have moved from being a messaging-based organization, to one that creates products, tools and services that facilitate behaviour change. This shift was a result of two things. Firstly, research into the effectiveness of our early work revealed that, whilst there was a high recall of our messages, this was not actually translating into tangible behaviour change. And secondly, learnings from research on decision making by social psychologists such as Daniel Kahneman, Dan Ariely, Richard Thaler and Cass Sunstein suggest that people are irrational when it comes to doing the 'right' thing, and place higher importance on their present satisfaction than the solving of future problems. People are also affected by what their peers are doing, and the context in which they make decisions.

By creating products, tools and services we are no longer relying on people to read a message and decide to change their behaviour. Instead we are providing tools that physically facilitate positive behaviours, making it much easier and also (crucially) much more enjoyable for them.

This approach to behaviour change is what we call the *Incidental Effect*: when products, tools or services are designed, created and marketed to have mainstream appeal due to their usefulness and/or desirability, but their use also helps tackle major social and environmental issues 'incidentally'. This approach means that we can reach a much larger audience, beyond those who respond positively to environmental and social messaging – what we call the '1% audience'. The incidental approach is described in more detail by our CEO Nick Stanhope, in a paper which is available on our website (www.wearewhatwedo.org/about/the-incidental-effect/).

Tell us how you work with the Incidental Effect
We start by researching a specific social or environmental issue. We look at all the everyday human behaviours related to that issue, defining the things we do that have a positive and negative effect, and then think about how we can make behaviours related to positive effects become easier, cooler, more interesting or fun. These behaviours inform the development phase of our work, which involves the creation of a physical or digital product, consumer service or live experience that can facilitate behaviour change amongst a large mainstream audience.

A tangible example of this is the *I'm not a plastic bag* shopping bag, which we designed in 2007. We created it in partnership with the fashion accessories designer Anya Hindmarch and Sainsbury's supermarkets, and it all started from our research into the issue of plastic bag usage. We found that we needed to create something practical that negated the need to get more bags with every trip to the supermarket, and that would also change the perception of reusable shopping bags – which at that point were considered 'alternative'.

So instead of a poster that said 'Don't use plastic bags', we created a tool that people could use – a real thing in the world that would facilitate the positive action. The bag was specifically designed to be desirable. By getting Anya on board, the bag was featured in every fashion magazine from Vogue to Grazia, as well as in newspapers and on TV shows, and was seen on the arms of many celebrities. We were able to re-position reusable bags as something desirable and mainstream, changing the way the whole issue was viewed. Importantly, it was not eco-warriors adopting the bag but ordinary people, who could now tackle an environmental issue without even thinking about it. This was an early example of the *Incidental Effect*.

What kind of projects do you work on?
We either identify social issues internally through research and consultation, or clients and partners from different sectors will come to us with issues they want to work on. Our detailed research into these issues then provides the brief for a project. For example, *Historypin* (an online communal archive of the history of our neighbourhoods and communities) was born out of our self-initiated research into the intergenerational divide that is damaging communities. But we have also been sent behaviour change briefs by a variety of organizations including Sainsbury's, Bestival, Sky, Liberty Global and WRAP (a UK organization set up to create a market for recycled materials). Working in partnership with companies and organizations enables us to reach larger audiences. More than anything, it is our approach that characterizes our agency, the problems we take on and the way we tackle them. *~end~*

SNOOK

Glasgow | www.wearesnook.com

Transforming Public Service in Scotland through Design

Snook is a social innovation design practice based in Glasgow, UK with a determined ambition to change the lives of the people of Scotland. Founding Partner Lauren Currie shares her insights into Snook's practices, and the current drivers of change in public service design in Scotland.

Tell us about Snook, and what drives you in your work

Snook consists of Scottish service designers making social change happen in public sector organizations, from the police force to universities. We work with frontline staff to embed service design in organizations and make experiences better. Since Snook's formation in 2009 we have been leading the provision of service design projects in Scotland. With our core team of eight, and a pool of networked Associates, we deliver work for clients such as STV (Scottish Television network), Barnardo's, Edinburgh Festivals and the Permanent Secretary of the Scottish Government. We also deliver our own service, *MyPolice:* an online feedback tool that gives the public a new way to talk to their local police force. We have piloted this service with a force in Scotland, and will roll it out across the UK in 2012.

Snook's particular passion is for public service design. We love working with people to improve services that determine quality of life,

like education, health, welfare and social care. We also love giving people the opportunity to take more control over services, or – at the very least – ensuring that services are suited to the needs and reality of their lives.

We use design to make things better. We believe in developing a point of view, and we value the way that service design brings to the surface the points of view of people who do not normally have a voice. Society is realising how important it is to involve people in decisions that affect them. We use a non-logical process to make this happen. It is fairly difficult to express in words, but very easy to express in action.

Snook's motto is 'transforming people'. This means giving them responsibility and empowering them in new ways. Co-design and co-production are important relationships between designers and the public. This form of design involves every single stakeholder in the design process. If you asked us to design a local bakery to strengthen neighbourhood relationships, we would involve the bakers, the cake-eaters, the delivery boy, the shop owner. Everybody joins in and it's good fun.

Snook transforms the way public services are delivered in four ways:
1. Embedding design in the public sector
2. Educating service providers and students in service design
3. Co-creating solutions
4. Doing it in Scotland

What are the current drivers of change in Snook's design practices?
Snook is driven by a desire to make design happen inside organizations. As opposed to design happening from the outside-in, embedding design enables organizations to truly innovate the way they do things. At Snook we like to think of this as design becoming part of an organization's DNA. It's about moving away from design being applied to specific issues and problems, and moving towards designers seeing an organization and its complexities holistically. Snook's design practice is also driven by our ambition to

The launch event of *The Matter* pilot in Edinburgh. *The Matter* is a way for young people to tell governments and grown-ups their opinions and ideas on problems that matter to them. It supports young people by helping them develop the right skills to secure employment (www.thisisthematter.com)

create a DIY Scottish Re-enlightenment. The Scottish Enlightenment was a period in the eighteenth century, characterized by an optimistic belief in the ability of humanity to effect changes for the better in society and nature, guided only by reason. We want to recreate this, but in a way that enables the people of Scotland to do it themselves – creating a country where citizens can find the solutions to their problems in each other, transforming the way public services are designed and delivered.

What do you think the future practices of design will look like, and why?
Service design is not about incremental change, but about systems change and transformation. At Snook we know from experience that the transformation of services and communities cannot and will not happen without engagement, participation and a shift in outlook from the people that inhabit, serve and use them. Alongside our work in services and systems, we are also investing in developing a learning platform – a place where cultural change and a new mindset can be hosted, informed, practiced and inspired. *–end–*

Snook worked with Edinburgh Festivals Innovation Lab to design a set of practical tools to help festivals improve the experiences they produce. The toolkit can be downloaded from: http://design.festivalslab.com

USCREATES

London | www.uscreates.com

Innovating Design Methodologies in Social Spaces

Uscreates is a social change agency located in London, UK. Founded in 2005 by Mary Rose Cook and Zoe Stanton, Uscreates helps organizations to understand, manage and maximize their positive social impact. Joanna Choukeir, Design and Communication Director at Uscreates, speaks about the three key drivers of change in their practice: co-partnerships, sustainability, and local collaboration.

Tell us about Uscreates, and what drives you in your work

Our key aim at Uscreates is to help organizations achieve social impact. Our design practices involve working innovatively and collaboratively with people and organizations to ensure ownership, sustainability and meaningful outcomes. We call this Co-creation, a process which starts with a Co-scope phase where we engage with local communities and organizations to get buy-in and develop a comprehensive understanding of the people and issues at the heart of the problem. We then move on to Co-develop, where we share insights with everyone involved and work together to develop, prototype and test ideas and solutions to the challenges identified. At the Co-implement stage we harness community assets and co-production by supporting and empowering local organizations and individuals to deliver new interventions, programmes, campaigns, and services. Finally, we continuously Co-evaluate the work we are doing to ensure that social impact is measured, and that

learning from the work contributies to the improvement of our practices. Over the past six years our work has demonstrated positive impact on social issues such as early detection of cancer, sexual health, alcohol consumption, community cohesion and wellbeing.

What are the current drivers of change in Uscreates's design practices?

Design has always been at the forefront of change. It foresees future requirements and addresses them early on. We believe that design practices need to be in constant flux in order to be prepared to respond to tomorrow's needs. We can identify three key drivers of change in today's design practices: co-partnerships, sustainability, and local collaboration.

Co-partnerships

It is usually expected that the public sector will consult with the public, and co-create solutions for social change. Today the public sector is becoming more interested in demonstrating that their products and services achieve a positive social impact.

There is potential in this area for design agencies to partner with private organizations using engagement, co-research and co-creation approaches to harness their skills, assets and resources towards positive social change.

Sustainability

Ecological, sociological and economical sustainability are topping global priorities. This is creating a transition from commissioning to building capacities and capabilities, and from one-off products and campaigns to 360 degree services and programmes. This is driving design agencies to show organizations how the work is done, rather than doing that work on their behalf – thus enabling the client to replicate the process for themselves in future projects.

Local collaboration

The spirit of global self-centred individualism which has been predominant in the last two decades is quickly making way for local collectivism. Many are realizing that local collaboration is essential to the building of communities that are more resilient to the challenges of the 21st century. Organizations, whether public or private, are shifting their focus away from scaling up to reach a standard global mass, and towards tailoring for local communities' needs and assets.

What excites you about design at the moment?
The most exciting thing about design at the moment is that is it regaining its original position, as a way of thinking which can be applied to any discipline, organization or context. Design today is more about innovative problem-solving, and less about creating a range of physical outputs.

What do you think the future practices of design will look like and why?
Over the past ten years the separation between design producer and design receiver has become more and more blurred. This is leading to a culture of participation, where stakeholders and interdisciplinary experts join up their efforts to design ideas and solutions. Designers are no longer autonomous authors. Instead they are becoming facilitators of collaboration and innovation. We envisage that, in the future, practices of design will involve creating open systems and processes that empower and support communities and organizations to 'do-it-themselves'. This will ensure that design aligns to, and keeps up with, those three key drivers of change: co-partnerships, sustainability, and local collectivism. *-end-*

Community Fun Day to increase awareness of lung cancer symptoms among older men

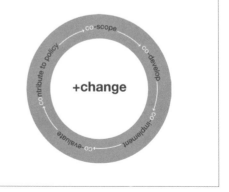

Collaborative process diagram used by Uscreates

STBY

London, Amsterdam | www.stby.eu

The Emergence of Global Design Research

STBY's Transitions

Co-developing
practice

Collaborating
with practices

Transitioning to
global design
research (REACH)

Coaching design
research

STBY specialize in design research and service innovation. Founded in 2003, they have offices in London and Amsterdam and are a networked company connected with eleven partners around the world to form the global design research network, REACH. REACH undertakes international projects at scale while retaining the agility and flexibility of small independent design companies embedded in a local context. Geke van Dijk, Co-founder and Strategy Director of STBY, shares the story of how the company came to found the REACH network and co-develop the specialist field of design research, which is increasingly seen by business and government as a key driver for innovation and strategy.

The STBY story

We support our clients to innovate their service offering, based on our deep empathic understanding of the experiences and perspectives of the people who use those services. We use a 'creative ethnographic' approach to design research and service innovation, generating insights into people's everyday practices and motivations which in turn inspire and guide our concept development processes. We build on the methods and techniques that have been established in the field of ethnography over the past century, such as observation, in-depth interviews and diary studies. We describe our approach as 'creative ethnography' because we also incorporate more designerly methods and techniques, such as probe studies, design documentaries and co-creation workshops. Designing the research is key to every stage of our projects. We design the research materials, we design the research process, and we design the research outputs.

The founding of STBY represented a transition point for myself and Bas Raijmakers (STBY Co-founder). We came from a background of human-centred design and user experience research; we were both researchers in the internet industry, working as part of a design team in a company we had co-founded in 1995, in the early days of the dot com boom. We did not use the phrase 'design research' at that time, as 'user experience research' was more common, and our methodologies were mostly focused on the digital delivery channel. Our company grew steadily with the expansion of the internet industry, and by 2000 we had a team of 25 people and decided to merge with one of the largest digital design and IT companies, Lost Boys (now LBi). We sold our shares and stayed on as managers of the Content & Usability unit within the new company. By 2002 we noticed that our

clients interests – and also the lives of the research participants we were interviewing – were changing rapidly, and becoming more and more about integrated multi-channel experiences. We realized that to explore this new territory, and seek out new opportunities for multi-channel design research, we needed to start a new company. So we left LBi, and used the money we earned selling our previous company to start a new and ambitious adventure: STBY.

On the academic side, I also wanted to deepen my knowledge about the strategic element of research and so I started a PhD that bridged service marketing at the business school, and human centred design at the computing school. Bas recognized that he wanted to develop richer visual outputs, because at that stage user experience research was mostly lab-based and not ethnographic in terms of going out into the field. These were the trigger points that prompted Bas and I to start the new company, and dive into the development of new methodologies fit for the current timeframe through our PhDs at the RCA (Royal College of Art) and Open University. We wanted to work much closer with both design teams and strategy teams, and also to integrate video at an earlier stage in the concept development process – because usability research typically happens later, and usability evaluation at a point where the solution is already going in a certain direction. If you really want to contribute to the design and innovation of anew solution, you need to be involved at an early stage. We wanted to get out of the usability lab, use richer materials and be engaged and involved at an earlier stage. This became the catalyst for STBY.

I can say now that, over the years, we have really achieved what we set out to do. Our transition was not a break into a completely different direction, rather it was driven by a feeling that something needed to be changed. A lot of our tools are based in the methodologies of ethnography, so they are not completely new. But we intuitively felt that we needed to add more ingredients into the mix, and so we decided to just head off in the direction of our vision and explore what these ingredients might be.

When we started our first company more than 15 years ago earlier, it was based in user experience research. Design research was not an established field at that point. Interestingly, in the first years of STBY we started to encounter other people around the world who were making the same transition as us – moving toward design research and service design at the same time. We did not have the proper words to describe it at that point, but we were co-developing the same thing from very different fields. We had in fact been heading in that direction intuitively, through trying to respond to what our participants were telling us, and what our clients and design teams needed.

Co-developing practice
Since starting STBY we have seen shifts from the client side, with more and more of them becoming comfortable with the methodologies we are using. A few years ago these methodologies were quite experimental. Now many clients confidently request in their briefs that they want ethnographic interviews, and talk explicitly about their need for design research. This demonstrates that the momentum in the field has been building, and is matched by our clients' vision and intuition to advocate changes in the way they conduct research. If you really want to innovate, you need to do much more early stage exploratory research. Some senior managers were not comfortable with this, and so initially we did a lot of research through pilot projects in order to prove our methodologies. There are people within our clients' organizations who are curious to explore, and want to change things. They have the confidence to start walking, even when they do not know exactly where they might end up. They are the pioneers, and we constantly have our antennae out so we can find and hook up with them. Then we go through a lot of collaborative trial and error work, to develop a showcase that will convince others within the client organization to give us the freedom to carry out our work. This is what we call 'co-developing practice', which is not just about us suggesting ways of working, but also involves earning our client's trust and being offered a space to keep experimenting. Whatever client we work with, we try to not simply repeat what we have done before. If you work for a client over a period of time they become more and more willing to give you the extra space that might result in something unexpected. We work for a wide range of clients. We are not specialists in a specific

We describe our approach as 'creative ethnography' because we also incorporate more designerly methods and techniques, such as probe studies, design documentaries and co-creation workshops.

sector, rather our clients appreciate that we are specialists in an approach, a methodology and a way of working.

Most of our direct client contacts understand the principles of design research, so they are generally part of the project team. They are not responsible for conducting interviews or analyzing the data, but they tend to follow our research process closely. They often have a lot of expertise in their field, which we do not, so having lots of conversations throughout the project is very useful to us. This is one of the main differences between our approach and the way research is usually conducted in user experience studies. Traditional large-scale marketing companies mostly use what our clients call a 'black box' approach. First there is the brief, then a lot of negotiation and pitching, and from the moment the project is won the client loses control. They do not know exactly what is going on, but suspect that it involves a lot of improvisation, and in the end the company delivers a certain result. Of course, a lot of these companies produce good work and deliver useful outcomes – but the process is very fussy and, as a client, you are not very involved and you do not get much out of the process itself. In our experience, the clients who want the black box approach are the ones who do not have, or do not want, to invest time in the process themselves. Their role is usually to commission the research, receive it and then spread it around their organization. But there are other clients who do really want to be involved because they realize they will have a better understanding of, contribution to and ownership of the project results. This means that as an agency we need to be comfortable with sharing that space. We have to reflect on how we work and open up, to ensure that it fits with the client's company culture and offers a high level of transparency and participation.

Reed Elsevier Project

Collaborating with practices

One of the projects that helped us make a major transition in our practice was for Reed Elsevier. They are the largest academic publisher in the world, and one of their main offices is based in Amsterdam. When we started the project in 2008, Elsevier's challenge was to keep up with the internet's open source capability – as demonstrated by Google Scholar and the Creative Commons movement. Many of these services were challenging the traditional publishing model, so Elsevier approached us to help them respond to that challenge by exploring new opportunities that would add value for their clients. Elsevier allowed us to team up with Radarstation, who are a strategic design consultancy in London. Even though we had no strong track record of working together at that time, Elsevier trusted us to work strategically on the project. We agreed that STBY would be responsible for the research while Radarstation handled the design, but that we would collaborate closely throughout the project as an interdisciplinary design research team. This project was about service innovation with an open innovation approach. After we conducted the preliminary research we facilitated a three day workshop with a 10 person client team. Back then, it was still fairly uncommon to have such intensive workshops. We developed a strong partnership with Radarstation throughout the project, and really pushed the boundaries in terms of design research. This strengthened our vision of creative partnerships and collaborations between small independent agencies, and co-creating project outcomes with our clients. Working in a highly collaborative way with the client team for three days meant that we pushed the results further than we ever could have by working on our own, or just sitting with Radarstation and trying to move it up a strategic pyramid. This was a really catalyzing project for us, and it put us on the road to creating the REACH network. In 2008 nobody used design research as a core profile. Now it is much more accepted, but we really had to legitimize it back then.

Transitioning to global design research (REACH)

A big change happened in STBY three years ago, when we began doing a lot of international work. Before that we were mainly working in the UK and the Netherlands, Many of our clients were interested in finding a balance between a general global service offering, and bespoke customized offerings for specific contexts. Today we are able to offer truly global design research through the REACH Network (www.globaldesignresearch.com). All partners in the network are small, agile independent businesses with highly experienced teams of designers and researchers. STBY was initiator and co-founder of the REACH Network, and our partners are based in many countries around the world. We have eleven partners at the moment located in China, Japan, Singapore, India, Brazil, the USA, Spain, France, Germany, Denmark and Hungary. We feel very strongly connected to those partners, and being in London really helps because many of our network members had worked in London before moving back to their home countries or moving to another country. For each project, a relevant selection of partners is involved. To work together you have to share trust and a

Some of the REACH Network members

strong perspective. Between all our partners, there is a generous culture of sharing ideas, experiences and materials. Over the years we have built and nurtured an open and flexible style of collaboration that has proven very effective. It ensures that each design researcher can contribute to the best of their abilities, without being micro-managed. It goes without saying that, on a more formal level, we also have all the necessary paper work in place, such as mutual NDAs, project contracts, project admin, secure shared online server space and a set of online collaboration tools. Being experienced professionals working for large-scale corporate clients, these things are part and parcel of our daily routines. The REACH Network allows us to handle complex and large scale international design research projects without compromising our agile approach, flexibility and sensitivity to local nuances in consumer understanding.

For us this was a new challenge: an ambition to fulfill our liking for newness and complexity. It felt like we were pioneering a new approach to consumer research. At the time, international consumer research was very established. The big international marketing research companies were like huge tankers with their 'black box' ways of working. We knew that we could offer a similar kind of service but make it more transparent, more agile, cheaper and more effective. Many clients need

to conduct studies in a number of contexts, so we had a hunch that setting up a network was the answer.

The international network is based around remote teams, but projects are managed centrally. For instance, if a project starts in London then STBY is the main contractor and our partners in the network are sub-contracted – but remain quite independent in the way they conduct their field work and analysis. We built a strong shared methodology for projects, and we coordinate so some of the materials are prepared by us and then used in slightly different ways to suit the local context. We make sure that with all the teams we focus and structure the data so it is easy to synthesize. Clients always want results fast and on a limited budget, so we share knowledge with our partners because we know how important it is not to waste time on endlessly discussing things or experimenting. We share our materials and we also Skype a lot, which only really became possible five years ago.

Because of the REACH network, our projects are now on a completely different scale. International projects are much more complex, and what used to be a single project in the Netherlands or the UK is now six connected projects in six different countries. The amount of data we handle has changed, and so have our teams, but fundamentally the questions

What are people dreaming about? What are they struggling with? What do they like? What do they dislike? Ethnographic research is a stepping stone to the generation of new ideas that can improve things.

ZuidZorg Project

we ask are still the same: What are people dreaming about? What are they struggling with? What do they like? What do they dislike? Ethnographic research is a stepping stone to the generation of new ideas that can improve things.

Coaching design research

Another STBY transition project has seen us acting less as external research consultants, and more as coaches who guide an organization towards absorbing and adopting the research process for themselves. For two years we have been working with a primary care healthcare organization in the South of the Netherlands near Eindhoven, called ZuidZorg. Originally they came to us with a design research project for innovation, and we partnered with Dutch design agency De Waag. The project was about older people, specifically seventy-five years old and above, who were living at home independently. We conducted ethnographic research, made the initial analysis, and also held workshops with the client to create

personas and developed concepts for service innovation. Since that first project we have continued to work with ZuidZorg every few months. When we first started they did not know anything about service design or design research, but they took the opportunity to learn more and ultimately really embraced it. Now they are transforming their organization to be able to research and innovate their own services internally. We are no longer the external consultants doing the research for them – rather we are doing it with them. They have appointed people internally to form a service design team, and we are providing them with coaching and guidance. They are more or less repeating our methodologies, and every once in a while we throw in something new for them and tweak the methodology. It is really nice to have a long term relationship with a client, because sometimes you can go from one project to the next without knowing what really happened in the organization. This project was a transition for us because we started to realize how much of a partner we could be to our clients. We do not just work on a brief and do repeat business, instead we go to the next step together and then help them absorb that into the organization. We are now constantly on the look out for more of these kinds of relationships. ZuidZorg are even thinking about becoming a consultancy themselves, having teamed up with the local library and city council to provide services to communities. While learning from us, they have seen other organizations struggling with the type of challenges they have successfully overcome, and as a result they are becoming the consultants.

The future of design research and networked collaborations

The design research approach to investigating complicated issues and generating ideas for radical innovation evolves around a curious and optimistic attitude. This is not primarily about efficiency and validation, but is more about experimenting, prototyping, trial and success. It is important to stress that this doesn't mean there is no process or structure, because there is. Clients are increasingly recognising the strategic value of this process, in addition to their traditional internal R&D and business analysis.

I have an inkling that in 10 years time, we will have developed our international work even further. We are convinced that networked collaborations are the way to go, and that they need to be trust-based and make sense to each business involved. There will always be a delicate balance in maintaining any collaboration but, if you can make it work, it will be a joyful experience for all involved. We get many requests from companies wanting to join REACH, but this wasn't about setting up a service design network to get as many members as possible. That model would be

an association, whereas REACH is a business network that needs to grow organically, and only with good reason. For example, we may find that we need a partner with a specific type of expertise, or we come across an agency that we really like or that immediately sparks new opportunities. We are careful to avoid competition within the network, and we need personal commitment because we invest quite a lot in our members. Often when a request for a project comes in, the proposal needs to be submitted within five days; so you need quick no-nonsense work with a tight focus. I am sure that we could handle much more work than we have right now, but our strategy is not to grow too fast. Networked collaborations are of course not unique to us; many businesses are experimenting with this, so it is fairly timely. For us the drive also comes from our experience of businesses growing in the traditional 'pyramid' way. You need to have certain layers in your team: you have your seniors along with lots of assistants, and when you reach fifteen people you also need project managers. I've been there, and I learned a lot, but it is not my ambition to develop this company in that way. We want to work with really good people, and those really good people tend not to want a fixed job. It takes many different types of specialized design expertise to develop innovative new services. You cannot have all of these in-house, unless you are a large-scale full service agency. To stay agile and flexible you need to be able to team up with the right consortium of experts for each project, with each contributing a specific added value or deep expertise. If we are all generalists, the end result is way too shallow. This exchange usually leads to a mutual added benefit in the REACH network. We aim to be inspired by what the other experts can teach us, and to contribute to their discipline, thereby making sure to add value.

The design research approach to investigating complicated issues and generating ideas for radical innovation evolves around a curious and optimistic attitude. This is not primarily about efficiency and validation, but is more about experimenting, prototyping, trial and success.

I generally support change, but do not expect that our work will change drastically any time soon. I think we have built some good foundations, and we will of course keep tweaking and changing things. But there is no reason to make a big splash right now. Our transition is about doing different things at a small scale, while improving understanding on a deeper level. Knowing Bas and myself, in a few years time we will definitely be doing something else – but it will not be a clear break from what we are doing right now. More likely it will be a continuation of the path we are on already, but focused on the next thing that needs pioneers who are willing to experiment. And this will surely be something that, in the end, contributes to the ever-changing course of design research. *~end~*

Tokyo | www.hakuhodo.jp

HAKUHODO INNOVATION LAB

Catalyst for Innovation

Hakuhodo Innovation Lab's Transitions

Fostering an
innovation ecosystem

Fostering innovation
for the public sector

Nurturing
innovators

Initiating research

Established in Tokyo in April 2008, Hakuhodo Innovation Lab is part of
Hakuhodo, Japan's second largest and one of its most established advertising
agencies. The Innovation Lab offers two core services of foresight and ethnographic
research, working with a range of commercial, educational and governmental
organizations. We spoke with Fumiko Ichikawa, a Design Researcher at the Lab.
Fumiko explains why Hakuhodo Innovation Lab's human-centred approach is
unique in Japan, and shares how they are working to become Japan's catalyst
for innovation.

Hakuhodo's background

Hakuhodo is Japan's second largest advertising agency, and is ranked amongst the top ten agencies in the world in terms of turnover. It has a very long-established reputation, having been set up in 1895. Hakuhodo is well known for coining the term 生活者発想 (Sei-katsu-sha Hasso) as early as 1981. It is used as a definition to describe the kinds of people that they communicate with – loosely translated, it means 'People with everyday lives'. This concept is perhaps best understood in opposition to the concept of 'Sho-hi-sha', which refers to people as consumers. Sei-katsu-sha is a broader concept that goes beyond consumers, and views a person as a whole. While conventional marketing refers to 'consumers' or 'users', depending on the industry, Hakuhodo has been suggesting that a person's act of consuming or using is merely a tool to reach their real goal: of fulfilling their lives or accomplishing their happiness. The Sei-katsu-sha insight is the cornerstone of Hakuhodo's philosophy and work. This is one of the reasons why phrases such as user or customer-centred design have never really been used in Hakuhodo, as we had an implicit human-centred focused from the very beginning.

Historically Hakuhodo provided a range of advertising, branding and strategy services, and we continue to offer these today. We added to these services in 2003 with the launch of Hakuhodo Foresight, and ten years ago ethnography came onto our radar, becoming another official part of our offer in 2006. These two pillars of service were brought together under the name of Hakuhodo Innovation Lab in 2008. The Lab consists of a very small team of ten innovation consultants. Around half of that team are researchers, with the other half coming from creative and business backgrounds.

Foresight and ethnographic research practices

Hakuhodo Innovation Lab's two core offerings are foresight, and ethnographic research.

Foresight is quite a powerful approach that offers our clients the opportunity to foresee what society will be like in ten to fifteen years time, and to understand how that will affect their business. We use three specific methodologies in our foresight work: Future Dynamics™, Scenario Generation and Diffusion Dynamics™. Future Dynamics™ is a method that we have developed with great support from Business Futures Network (www.businessfutures.com). This helps us to generate many ideas, and usually involves an intensive two day workshop where participants scan through a large amount of material to identify all the possible changes that could occur, in order to foresee multiple futures. Scenario Generation is another method for predicting the future, where participants map out topics in order of likelihood to generate an emerging picture of a future scenario. Diffusion Dynamics™ is another of the Lab's proprietary research methods, which is used to uncover the mechanism of how innovation propagates from early adopters to late followers.

When it comes to the future, many of us see it as just an extension of how things are today. This approach has a limit, since (a) the future we envision will be limited to what we know of today, and (b) that future becomes less accurate the further ahead you try to see. This is what we call 'forecast' – and, as with the weather, it is based on how things would change as a linear extension of today. It is not difficult to imagine that such forecasts cannot take us very far. For example, let's look at how we lived in the past. Fifteen years ago in Japan mobile phone penetration was still growing, the job market looked very different, and many

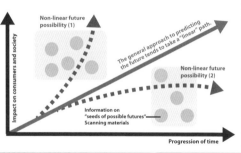

Foresight workshop

Foresight graph illustrating the nonlinear future forecasting possibilities

people assumed they would be with a single company until the moment of retirement. People felt quite safe about what they are, and they bought cars as a sign of adulthood and success. Today in Japan, none of this is true. Penetration of mobile phones has maxed out at nearly 100 per cent, and more than 30 per cent of university graduates have not found a steady job, resulting in over 600,000 so-called NEETs (Not in Education, Employment or Training). From bird flu to mad cow disease, food safety is constantly in question and, for young adults under 30, buying a car is beyond imagination – as a 24 year old man told us during an interview, it is in fact 'a disgusting idea'. It is almost impossible to imagine an industry that has not been affected by the scale and diversity of these changes over the last fifteen years.

While it is important you attempt to envision the upcoming technologies and trends within your core business, the chances are that in ten years none of them will matter. If people stop buying cars, will making them faster have any impact? An incremental advancement within the company's existing business is what we call *Inside-Out* thinking. Instead of focusing on how to make *Inside-Out* visions more accurate, we offer *Outside-In* visions. By offering up some of the weak signals we periodically collect, our clients start to see

that there are external societal, environmental, and political factors that could result in a substantial deviation from their core business. In our foresight workshops we use methods that intentionally clash the client's *Inside-Out* perspective with these *Outside-In* materials. As these can also change dynamically in response to societal trends, the ideas and scenarios generated through these methods are different every time we run the workshop.

Our second core offering of ethnographic research has been a service of the Innovation Lab for the past ten years, but Japan has been relatively late tapping into this area. We started offering this service at a time when the internet brought about digitalization, and the ability to offer people content and a longer engagement with services. For many established Japanese firms, this change meant that their product-centred business model was no longer effective. Until that point manufacturers had been creating products to maximize the joy of ownership at the point of purchase. The excitement and satisfaction of owning a product was, without exception, meant to diminish over time. But once those products could be connected to the internet to download updates and new features, their actual value and lifespan could not determined as simply as before. It was obvious that what companies really required was a

Ethnography workshop and consultation session

better understanding of their users, in order to provide them with a better quality of user experience.

As an advertising agency with a long history of partnering with these companies, we understood that we needed to offer them more than just market research. Our role was not only to deliver insights, but also to take our clients along with us in a journey through ethnography. While this process took time and effort it was often very rewarding for both the client and ourselves, and resulted in genuinely innovative ideas. We also offer training for practitioners, and over the five years we've been running these courses we have taught a broad range of participants from industries including pharmaceuticals, food and beverages, automobiles, telecommunications, home appliance manufacture, and even amusement parks. Our five day course is probably one of the most exhausting training programmes they will have ever encountered, but many of them have found it extremely intellectually rewarding.

One of the characteristics of our ethnographic research work is our emphasis on innovation. When we were approached by Kao Corporation, one of the biggest personal care companies in Japan, our mission was to reframe their anti-ageing product lines. Anti-ageing is a very interesting area, but it's also a fuzzy product domain with many companies positioning themselves somewhere between beauty and healthcare. Together with the client, we visited people who offered us new perspectives on ageing. We spoke to a businessman in his 30s whose physical condition had been assessed as being equivalent to someone in their 50s, as a result of the diabetes he had developed through his work-intensive lifestyle and unhealthy diet. We also met a young theatre actress in her 20s who often found herself playing the role of a much older woman. All of these people were in unique situations that made us reflect on what we considered ageing to be. Through our research we realized that people experience ageing at different points of their life, not just on their fortieth, fiftieth or sixtieth birthdays. We found that ageing was associated with identity crisis, which often takes place because of disease, marriage, or the birth of a child. In other words, anti-ageing should be relative and social, rather than absolute and personal. Once the team obtained this 'lens' on what it means to age, they produced a series of amazing ideas for the client.

Fostering an innovation ecosystem

Looking at the global landscape of innovation today, it is clear that no single corporation or institution will achieve a breakthrough on their own. For years we have had great relationships with Silicon Valley but, more recently, we have started to look towards other emerging innovative clusters. We had opportunities to get to know cities and countries such as Boulder in Colorado, Berlin, Finland, and Israel. These all vary in their size and financial impact, but what they share is an open and active network where government, industry, and educational institutions play a key role in supporting innovation. In other words, if someone wants to take a risk and be innovative, these regions will offer them a safety net. Writing in the Harvard Business Review[1], Art Markman describes this support as being similar to a coral reef structure, which protects the fish and provides food and safety. We call these structures 'innovation ecosystems', and we would like to be able to say that Japan has such platforms to support start-ups, entrepreneurs, and innovators within mature firms – but we believe this is unfortunately not the case. Japan has for some time been ranked as one of the lowest industrial nations in terms of entrepreneurship. This is the primary reason why, here at Hakuhodo Innovation Lab, we are taking a huge step to develop and foster an innovation ecosystem in Japan.

Fostering innovation from the public sector

For some time, the successfully fostering of innovation has been a key concern of both national and regional government in Japan. Innovation Lab members have been working with the national government for several years, and have been an administrative member of the committee formed by the Ministry of Economy, Trade and Industry. There are quite a few areas where public institutions could play a unique role, from creating an innovation index to supporting innovative practices. Based on these discussions the Innovation Lab, together with several other institutions and the Innovation Network Corporation of Japan, are now setting up a not-for-profit organization called Japan Innovation Network (JIN). This network intends to promote innovation and create a platform for both Japanese and global institutions to actively discuss the reinvention of corporate and social cultures of innovation, to encourage individuals to become the innovators of tomorrow.

Nurturing innovators

Innovation does not take place without innovators, and people working to support those innovators. This is why we are very active in educating both staff in corporations, and students in higher education. We have been involved in i.school, an innovation leadership programme at the University of Tokyo. Our research director Hiroshi Tamura is a founding director of i.school, and has supported the programme in becoming a leader in human-centred innovation. It is an intensive annual programme that includes five to seven workshops, with each workshop

Looking at the global landscape of innovation today, it is clear that no single corporation or institution will achieve a breakthrough on their own.

featuring facilitators from internationally renowned institutions. In 2011, a professor from Aalto University in Finland ran a workshop on designing a service based around the theme of gift giving. This summer, a professor from the UK's Royal College of Arts conducted fieldwork with students to identify new business ideas for Tōhoku, an area whose industries were devastated by the 2011 tsunami and earthquake. Ziba Design from the USA (see Ziba's story page 140) have also been generously offering annual workshops, where students have learnt their thinking patterns and even reinvented them. It is exciting to see how students change their way of thinking, with some even becoming social entrepreneurs. It is one of the most exciting and rewarding programmes we have been involved with to date.

Initiating research

The key to all our different practices is rigor in our research approach. Because of this, in the past two years we have changed our practices so that we initiate research projects prior to client requests. This is us practicing the *Outside-In* thinking approach that we use in our foresight work. Instead of looking at things from the perspective of one specific company or industry, we make people our starting point.

We identify their values and behaviours in order to identify problems that need solving. Our provocative themes and in-depth insights enable us to work across many divisions with commitment from the senior leadership of a company, rather than working in isolation within a specific division such as R&D or sales. *The Future of Ownership* was an example of this approach, initiated with our European partners Claro Partners based in Barcelona (see Claro Partners story pg 134). This project investigated the idea of ownership, what it is and how it might change in the future, and involved research across China, Japan, India, Brazil, the United States, Denmark and Spain.

Where next for Hakuhodo Innovation Lab?

We have talked about the transitions that we have been through in the industry, however the biggest transition right now is taking place within society itself, and particularly in Japan which experienced the devastating earthquake and tsunami in 2011. The word 'design' has shifted its meaning away from the aesthetics and functionality of a product, and there is an increasing acknowledgement that design can play a role in mediating change. This shift has substantially influenced the way we work at the Innovation Lab. We often ask ourselves now if our effort on a project should cater for a

i.school workshops

Ethnographic research in different countries as part of *The Future of Ownership* project

single company, or if there is the potential for a wider audience to benefit from our work. Our clients have also changed, and we now have more public work coming from government. In the future we expect to collaborate with not just national, but also regional and local government. Our innovation education effort will also expand from professional and higher education training, to education for all ages.

We feel that our work will become increasingly systemic. Through diversifying our practices and projects, we are redefining our ideas about the role of design. Ideas within design have often been judged on their competitiveness or uniqueness, but when it comes to innovation today, these qualities are less important than looking into social realities and identifying genuine problems that exist in society. If you are trying to overcome these problems, then all design ideas are valid. We have come to realize that if there are already values and beliefs that exist in the world, our ideas should be derived from observing them. This is a more retrospective than prospective approach, and this way of thinking has definitely changed our practice and helped us to recognize how fundamental ethnographic work is to the Lab. Japan lost its financial power many decades ago, but it is important to nurture our human resources and talents and ensure that innovative practices take hold; not only in the corporate world, but also in the social world of education and government. *-end-*

Notes

1. Article can be accessed at http://blogs.hbr.org/cs/2012/12/how_to_create_an_innovation_ec.html (last accessed 6th July 2013)

We have come to realize that if there are already values and beliefs that exist in the world, our ideas should be derived from observing them.

Aanmelding op seminar over missie	Aanmelding & bevestiging (EMP)	Intake voor match- making	Deelnemers bijeenkomst	Op reis	Evaluatie

Developing Relationships to Move into Strategic Design

DESIGNTHINKERS GROUP

Amsterdam | www.designthinkers.nl

DesignThinkers' Group Transitions

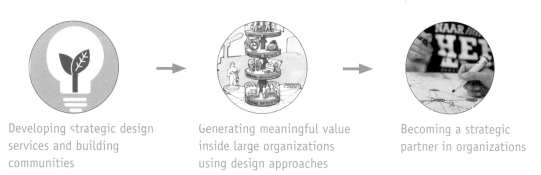

Developing strategic design
services and building
communities

Generating meaningful value
inside large organizations
using design approaches

Becoming a strategic
partner in organizations

Founded in 2007, DesignThinkers Group is a design driven innovation agency located in Amsterdam, The Netherlands. The Group helps organizations strengthen their capacity to innovate, and enables the co-creation of value with all stakeholders through the design of brands, products, service systems and cultures of trust. Their goal is to create a sustainable business based on a long term and human-centred vision. Arne Van Oosterom, co-founder of DesignThinkers Group, shares with us his insights into how the Group has grown over the years, from a traditional marketing communication company to an inter-connected group of design driven innovators located in the Netherlands, UK, Chile, Brazil, Israel, the USA, Singapore and China.

Developing strategic design services and building communities

At DesignThinkers Group we believe that design can be used more effectively at a strategic level in organizations. From the very beginning we wanted to offer more than just traditional design services, and so we developed a wide range of strategic design services. Our innovation offering includes the facilitation and design of brands, products, services and networks through the co-creation of value with stakeholders. At the start this range of services was hard to sell, and we sought forward thinking clients who could see the value of our design approach. To help us find such clients, we established a network of partners and associates from different backgrounds such as design, management and marketing.

Most of our early projects originated from our background as a marketing communication company, working with existing clients such as the Ministry of Economic Affairs and the Holland Brand. It was always our aim to work in the areas of innovation design and facilitation, taking on large organizational change projects and forming new collaborations through our design approaches. In the early days it was important for us to develop our client relationships in a way that would allow us to move into strategic design

Bringing people together and building communities is a key driver of our innovation facilitation...

spaces. We realized from our previous work that companies had a need for innovation facilitators, because they were struggling to collaborate internally. Organizations generally work in silos, and those silos are organized around market-driven efficiency. While this can sometimes be a successful approach, most companies have great visions and values that are not translated into their everyday key performance indicators (KPIs). Our innovation facilitators help organizations to create new collaborations, and translate values into meaningful services for all the people involved. As facilitators we bring in an outside viewpoint, reinventing collaborations internally to create a culture of trust. We get stakeholders involved in solving the problem, exchanging information, exploring and trying out new ways of working towards a solution. We see Design Thinking as the glue between all of the disciplines – we ask questions, aid conversations, and help people to see in new ways and develop ownership. Our goal is to make ourselves expendable by helping people to do all this for themselves. We are transparent in our processes and, as a result, we gain a lot of trust from our clients.

Bringing people together and building communities is a key driver of our innovation facilitation, and we do this in a number of ways through the DesignThinking network, DesignersDNA, StartUpLab and the DesignThinkers Academy. The DesignThinking network is an open network of professionals engaging with Design Thinking. DesignersDNA is a closed platform that we developed and now facilitate, to help our clients from large organizations build partnerships with each other and co-develop services. It includes members such as Phillips, Volkswagen AG, SAP, Radboud Hospital, DSM, Sara Lee, Schiphol Airport, Miele, Océ/Canon and Rabobank.

In order to strengthen our client's capabilities to innovate, we felt it was important to embed the required skills within their organizations. This is why we set up the DesignThinkers Academy, to offer and co-create training programmes for professionals and teams in corporate and governmental environments. Activities include team and individual coaching, study tours, masterclasses and summer schools. The results of all these network initiatives have led us into further partnerships with creative teams and associates from around the world.

Generating meaningful value inside organizations using design approaches

We began working with large organizations, using design approaches to help them innovate and discover value spaces. Organizations had to experience design in order to understand it and be persuaded of its value. This led to us putting on events such as the 'Customer Journey Lab' and Unconferences in New York, London and Milan, in order to share our service design approaches. Through running these events and talking to organizations,

we realized that in order to develop services of value we had to help those organizations internally; we had to find out why they do what they do, and help them translate their vision and values into services and KPIs, to provide meaningful value to their employees and customers.

To give you an example, we were invited to work with Nederlandse Spoorwegen (NS), the Dutch national railway. The railways in the Netherlands are actually comprised of two different organizations: NS and ProRail. They were previously one organization, but were split into two in 2003. NS is the passenger railway operator, and cooperates with ProRail, who are responsible for the Dutch rail infrastructure. At the time of the project, Utrecht Central Station was being renovated and we were initially asked to create the service experience for travellers passing through that station. However, we identified that the challenge was not so much about creating wonderful ideas for services – it was really about the fact that the railroads were run by two separate companies with

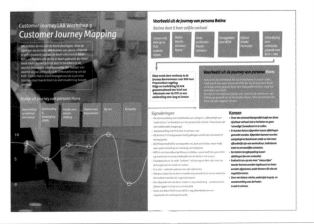

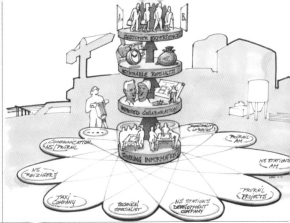

A customer journey mapping for the Ministry of Economic Affairs

This service process visualization was created for the project with the Dutch National Railways to illustrate the desired customer experience during the renovation of Utrecht Central Station

lots of departments that did not collaborate. This gave rise to many problems, including different understanding of the term 'customer experience', and a business model that was not human-centred. We realized that NS and Prorail did not work from a shared mindset, and so it made no sense for us to spend time creating a wonderful multi-channel experience. Instead we focused our attention on developing better collaboration between the two companies. We ran a series of workshops involving both organizations, focused around 'the customer plan'. This customer plan then became part of the bigger building plan that NS makes whenever a station building is renovated, and building activities are likely to influence the customer experience.

Another example of us working closely with an organization to help them innovate and discover new value spaces, is Dutch media company Telegraaf Media Nederland (TMG). DesignThinkers Group worked with TMG to develop the vision, brand, positioning and implementation of their first online brand, Dichtbij. Dichtbij is growing against the industry trends, and this community news and infomation platform already has more than 102,000 accounts registered.

From experience such as this, we know that organizations need to develop a design mindset. The design mindset is all about allowing yourself to ask questions, understand the context, see the bigger picture, be open to inspiration from unexpected areas, collaborate, be comfortable with chaos and make ideas visual so that people can share and talk around them. With such a mindset, people see new dynamics and start having different conversations. Our role is to enable the development of that design mindset within organizations, and part of doing that is creating the right environment where it is safe to experiment and fail. We create environments where people are able to explore new ways of doing, thinking and collaborating, and we hope this will encourage people to take more responsibility for what they are doing.

Reflecting back on these experiences, we have helped companies to put people first and to use design at a strategic level. To do this successfully we have had to work from inside those organizations, firstly to help them understand their own ecosystems before guiding them towards understanding their customers. We see the customer as an equal partner in the value network, along with all the other stakeholders involved in the delivery of the service. We talk about this being a people-centred approach – because ultimately it is about organizations creating value with people for people.

Becoming a strategic partner in organizations

Over the years our networks have crystallized, and new products and services have been built around the DesignThinkers Group brand. As we grow, we have expanded into different service areas such as healthcare, banking, mobility, telecoms, government and fashion. The DesignThinkers Group is now valued as a strategic partner in organizations. We have expanded our networks locally within the Netherlands, as well as partnering with international design innovation companies in Chile, UK, Germany, Brazil, Israel, US, Singapore and China. We now work together on international projects, sharing our learning and growing as a family – but this eco-system will change again over time, as we start to think about how we might create even greater value for our clients and for ourselves. In order to gain the most value from that ecosystem, we consider the people we work with as the key drivers of change. We aim to create an environment where people are creative, happy and have the freedom to explore and prototype all of the time, to come up with ideas and be proactive about them. If you have an idea,

Dichtbij Project. DesignThinkers Group worked with Telegraf Media Nederland (TMG) to develop a vision, brand, positioning and implementation for TMG's first online news platform

97

From Here to There project, commissioned by the Dutch Ministry of Infrastructure and the Environment. DesignThinkers Group developed a campaign called *The National Travel Request*. Through social media and co-creation sessions, passengers were challenged to come up with their own ideas for improvements and proceeded to design and implement the winning idea

we encourage you to go with it and see what happens. We also endeavour to sustain that feeling of family – supporting and helping each other, and being organized in such a way that we can deliver the best possible services to our clients.

Where next for DesignThinkers Group?

We have been growing the Design Thinking network in order to create more value for members. In the future, we want to have many creative teams in different parts of the world. You gain a lot of richness through sharing and diversity, and innovation happens where there is diversity and new ideas. We have created our own ecosystem where we can inspire each other continuously, see different viewpoints, challenge and help each other. It is our dream

to be able to swap with our international partners – for example, to work for a time in Brazil and for our Brazilian partners to then come and work with us in Amsterdam.

Our motto is to drive positive change on both an individual and organizational level. To achieve this we need to keep moving, because that is when serendipity happens. Luck and change have been a big part of our success. We are strong believers in serendipity, and we truly believe that if we keep moving, trying new things and exploring, then the DesignThinkers Group will keep moving along too. *-end-*

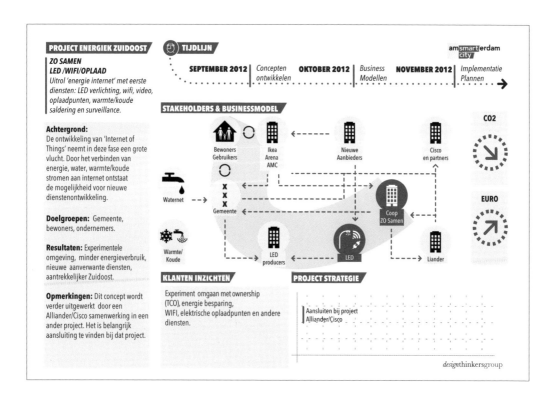

Smart Cities project in collaboration with GreenBizStartup. Commissioned by the City of Amsterdam, DesignThinkers Group and GreenBizStartup deployed service design to bring together companies, institutions and the general public. The project aim was to explore how stakeholders in the borough of Amsterdam-Zuidoost could work together to reduce their energy consumption

IDIOM

Bangalore | www.idiom.co.in

Redefining Design in India

Idiom's Transitions

From Esign and Tessarat to Idiom

Design as a catalyst for innovation

Shifting focus for needs to dreams

The value of design

Creating design leaders

Idiom is a design and consulting practice based in Bangalore, India. It is an integrated design consultancy, which 'incubates business ideas for societal transformation, and ideas on life and living'. Idiom designs business strategies, brands, experiences, communication and products for a variety of emerging sectors including retail, healthcare, education and hospitality. The practice has grown significantly since its foundation in 2006, from 30 employees to over 100. They have worked on a range of high profile projects such as the design and branding of the 19th Commonwealth Games in Delhi in 2010, and recently gained international attention for their high-profile open innovation project DREAM:IN, which has been named as one of six global Game Changers by Metropolis Magazine. Here Sonia Manchanda, Co-founder and Principal Designer at Idiom, shares the story of its evolution, its practice today and what the future of design at Idiom will look like.

From Esign and Tessarat to Idiom

The journey towards Idiom started with a brand, strategy and communication design company called Esign. Founded in 1995, Esign specialized in branding and radical business, design and communication strategies. The company evolved to meet the needs of its entrepreneurial clients, while keeping design thinking firmly at its core. "We were proud to be pushing the boundaries of design, and you would often find us in the Esign office wearing a hoodie that said 'Thinking Design'".

Esign was a small, warm and friendly place that was always aiming to do big things. The company was deeply engaged with one of India's first public-private partnership initiatives for the city of Bangalore, and created a movement called *Bangalore Forward, By Design*. 'Movement' comes up a lot in our work, and this is probably linked to the need to change the way things are done in India. For *Bangalore Forward*, Esign developed several design, branding, and communication initiatives. An old jail was reconditioned and returned to the city as a park – rechristened Freedom Park – through a contest designed to involve the city's design and architecture talent. Other design projects within Bangalore Forward included a road signage manual for the city of Bangalore and a clean-up initiative. In 1995 I was introduced to Kishore Biyani, an emerging retail entrepreneur and the CEO and Managing Director of Future Group, which runs runs several large retail formats. The introduction was made by Jacob Mathew, from the interior architecture and design firm Tessaract Design. A partnership between Mr. Biyani, Tessaract Design and Esign was formed and this collaboration led to India's most successful hypermarket brand, the *Big Bazaar*. The *Big Bazaar* is a combination of an informal bazaar and a hypermarket. It brought together a diverse range of people

from the community, mixing audiences from different economic backgrounds in a space that was accessible for all. It was familiar yet different. This was a place that had customers arriving on bicycles as well as in Mercedes cars! We wanted to have fun and create something new, gamechanging and innovative. Our success with the hypermarket means that it is now a 'movement', being replicated across India. While Tessaract was designing the store itself, Esign was brought in to design the brand, shape the shopping experience, create new retail formats and provide design input into the business. The partnership brought together business strategy, Design Thinking and experience design. While Esign and Tessarat offered 'form', we were also offering the 'thinking' part of the process. It was in this relationship that the seeds of Idiom were sown. Idiom was set up in 2005, with Mr. Biyani acting as mentor and investor to the practice. Mr. Biyani had seen firsthand how powerful Design Thinking could be in comparison to typical management approaches, and recognized the value of scaling the Design Thinking approach.

Our aim in setting up Idiom was to find and define the Indian 'Idiom of Design'. What is the Indian need for design? What is the Indian expression of design? What is the Indian thinking for design? At Idiom, we start from local insights in order to realize global strategies. We wanted to create a large, vibrant and young interdisciplinary design firm, committed to taking ideas from mind to market with skill, speed and imagination. Partnering with business leaders, and building relationships to demonstrate the difference design can make, became an integral part of our game-changing projects. We were and are interested in helping leaders realize their vision. As a leader, you cannot be caught up with business results from the last quarter.

Foodhall @1 MG ROAD

The *Foodhall* project

Instead you need to focus on the long term. You must imagine the new, and create systems within your organization that embrace this type of thinking.

The context of working in Bangalore, which is a hub for India's entrepreneurs, has been the major contributing factor to our success. Over the last 10 to 15 years Bangalore has seen vast growth, changing from a retirement town into a base for entrepreneurship and IT development, stimulated by individual and government investment. We have learnt a great deal from working with entrepreneurs, who challenge us by giving opportunities to explore new territories, create new systems and paradigms.

Design as a catalyst for innovation

What is the Indian need for design? What is the Indian expression of design? What is the Indian thinking for design?

As a country, India is recognized for leapfrogging many steps of development – and we want to demonstrate design's role as the

What is the Indian need for design? What is the Indian expression of design? What is the Indian thinking for design?

catalyst to achieving that. We aim to create ideas or directions that are many steps ahead of current thinking. An example of this can be seen in our project with a business group from the Andhra Pradesh region. The people from Andhra Pradesh are very enterprising, in fact there is a term for it: 'Andhrapreneurship'. We worked with two entrepreneurs in Andhra Pradesh who had started an International school, and needed help in scaling, branding and communicating their ideas. Our intervention went beyond design into a business plan that could be shared with potential investors. At the same time, we also worked with them to create a new business venture. This came from a small but important observation that there were 'no clean toilets' on Indian highways. This led to conversations that explored opportunities and possible solutions to this problem. Out of that conversation came the idea of developing a highway food court called *Seven*. Given that Andhra Pradesh has many successful entrepreneurs with a penchant for big cars, and is halfway between two destination cities, we thought these factors would encourage road travel. Our two Andhra Pradesh entrepreneurs purchased a large plot of land next to an existing highway, and we designed and built a landmark food court with clean toilets, where buses and cars could stop. This was an entirely new concept, as India does not have a highway culture. However *Seven* rapidly changed that culture, as new roads are now being built and more affluent Indians are able to afford cars. We were involved in business design, brand, architecture and service design of this roadside service. At a relatively modest cost, it is the first service of its kind in India, and has demonstrated spectacular results after only the first month.

In India we talk a lot about *jugaad*, which is a word used to describe frugal innovation. This type of innovation is well known in India, but has not yet been connected with Design Thinking. *Jugaad* is really an example of Design Thinking; it is more holistic, using design to help people create breakthrough ideas which are not incremental, but game-changing. We prototype fast, and we allow to fail fast, and through this have found that when we bring design to the front of the process, the chances of success grow phenomenally. In the projects that Idiom has been involved in, the success rate for new business ventures is very high. We have found that introducing design at the beginning of a project, along with venture capital support, has contributed to a radical increase in the chances of success. Design and funding is all that

enterprises really need as start-up fuel. *Foodhall* is a gourmet supermarket format that experienced Idiom's insights, ideas and implementation lens as part of the development of its second store in Bangalore, India. The key insight from our work was that, even though there are few thriving gourmet stores in value-conscious India, Indians do live to eat and are always happy to bring new ideas to their palate and to their plate. We wanted to bring out concepts such as 'the love of food', sharing a love of cooking, of experimenting, of new tastes, of getting it right and of entertaining. The Indian spirit of *seva*, which means selfless service, became the binding value around which we designed many unique service ideas. For example, customers are offered a choice of how their vegetables can be cut, in as many as six different styles, and free of charge. Customers can taste expensive cheeses and oils at uniquely-designed retail units, and they can even choose the flavours their nuts are tossed in. We call this 'food thought leadership', using good business and design sense. Besides living to eat, Indians also love to offer food as gifts. We modernized this tradition by offering a complete gifting, packaging and communication service. These new innovations have made *Foodhall* a successful and innovative business from year one.

Shifting focus from needs to dreams
India gained its freedom 60 years ago. However, there are some ways in which we are not free. We are a country with a lot of people, and we have to think about them in the right way. Typically, most industry leaders will talk about the 'pyramid'. A pyramid has a top and a bottom – but there is a fundamental problem with this idea. Most leaders will also talk about the 3 strands of society: India 1, India 2 and India 3. India 1 represents the leaders, the elite and the intellectual class. India 2 represents

DREAM:IN Project
Clockwise from top left:
DREAM:IN project logo,
methodology card, capturing
dreams, documenting dreams

We talk a lot about inclusivity, but not many leaders actually understand real inclusivity.

the service providers and aspirants, while India 3 represents the very bottom, the ones still striving to survive. As a nation, we know how to leapfrog stages of development in our pursuit of individual aspirations. But are we listening to, or even aware of, the aspirations of people from different classes?

We talk a lot about inclusivity, but not many leaders actually understand real inclusivity. Imagine if we could look at the world, or India, through an equal lens. Rather than peering down from the top, we should instead take an inside-out, optimistic approach to working *with* people at every level, rather than working *for* them. Can we think more intelligently and intuitively about systems, to understand the deepest aspirations of these people? To shift their focus from their needs to their dreams? That is the idea behind the DREAM:IN project: to wake up society, to give all people the equal right to dream, and to

understand individual aspirations by employing open innovation networks at a massive scale. The project aims to create new value and meaning through scale and impact, and create bottom-up development and sustainable progress in society, rather than just replicating models from the developed world (models that are crashing as we speak).

DREAM:IN, a radical innovation project
The DREAM:IN Project is an attempt to get people to think about sustainable ideas. We need to create new value and new meaning, but the two need to go together. We need to consider a more equitable world. The DREAM:IN Project is a radical innovation project using an 'inside-out' process to change the focus from needs to dreams. Our process uses collaborators, or Dreamcatchers, to connect with people and understand their dreams. We sift and analyze dreams, and shape them into collective 'dreamscapes'.

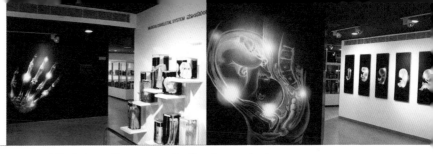

MAP: the Manipal Anatomy and Pathology Museum revitalisation project

The DREAM:IN project has morphed into an impact venture, whose vision is to empower people to imagine a better future for themselves and the world.

DREAM:IN Brazil

Interestingly, the country that has found a real affinity with the DREAM:IN approach is Brazil. Carlos Teixeira, a Professor at Parsons The New School for Design, is based in New York but has been deeply involved with the inception, creation and spread of DREAM:IN within Brazil. As a result, a Brazilian version was in development since January 2012, led by Carlos and The Institute of Vivarta. Professors from the design departments of six Brazilian universities have been trained to teach the DREAM:IN method, which emphasizes the role of innovation and Design Thinking in creating new value and meaning for the people of Brazil. These universities then created their own Dream Journeys and Conclaves, investing their own energy, time and resources. All the data and energy from those universities was then channelled into creating the DREAM:IN Conclave in São Paulo in August 2012.

DREAM:IN Next Gen

The most recent expansion of DREAM:IN is DREAM:IN Next Gen. This is a prototype to demonstrate the validity of the idea beyond data collection and synthesis. It is a plan, and a journey from dream to realization; an endeavor to transform young people from consumers of income and employment, into the creators of sustainable new value via new enterprises. We will travel 3,000 miles across an emerging and progressive South India to catch and collect 10,000 young people's dreams, and create 100 Next Gen enterprises. The dreams will be selected, shaped and shortlisted down to 500 sustainable ideas. These will then go before a panel of investors, who will identify the 100 ideas that will go to market. This process will be supported by the DREAM:IN mentorship and team.

The venture will be showcased at the DREAM:IN Conclave in the presence of eminent business people, policy leaders, thought leaders, creative thinkers, entrepreneurs and potential investors of national and international repute and standing. We are also developing www.dreamin.in; an open and safe place to dream, believe and realize, and a source of rich qualitative and quantitative human data. The purpose of this is to enable leaders to understand the aspirations of people everywhere and to foster deep connections, a progressive community, and an ecosystem to create fresh ideas.

DREAM:IN Next Gen is already underway and over 90 institutions have been in touch. The first group of Dreamcatchers are now being trained, and we have a physical space dedicated to this within Idiom. This space will serve as the super-incubator for Next Gen enterprises, bringing in the best mentors and subject matter experts to advise and shape the next generation of entrepreneurs. From this experience DREAM:IN will also create an

independent incubator in Bangalore –
the perfect setting for a design and innovation
incubation studio and workshop, as it is
considered to be the knowledge capital
of India.

There are future plans to create a 'Dream
Fund' that will nurture enterprises that
apply design, innovation and technology to
intrinsically local and sustainable ways of
doing things. We are also planning to create
a DREAM:IN Enterprise platform online
(www.dreaminenterprise.in) and have plans
to expand that platform globally.

The value of design

As Idiom matures and our relationships with
our partners evolve over the years, we find it
easier to demonstrate the value of a design
approach that is much more holistic, long-term
and sustainable. We see a greater engagement
from those who have gained from the design
process, and we believe that those engaging
with design fall into 3 categories. The first are
Initiators, who are testing the waters. For them,
design is a tool to enhance a particular aspect
of their enterprise or process. They hopefully
will go on to become *Reapers*, and start to
engage with design people and processes much
more, eventually learning to articulate process
for themselves and adopting the 'design way'.
At the final stage are the *Believers*, who begin
to design their own businesses, send their
children to design school and fund design-
related businesses. After all, with business
models you can only build from the past,
while design allows you to leap boldly into the
future. I personally believe that design is not a
set of tools, a means, or a behaviour – but an
end in and of itself. It is a change in mindset,
behaviour and lifestyle and it is important that
many more businesses and leaders make design
integral to their organizational behaviour, and
not be content with it being a pretty silo filled
with red sofas, whiteboards and people who
wear black t-shirts.

Creating design leaders

For design to go beyond a process and a system
to become a philosophy, practitioners need to
actively teach and share their knowledge and
reveal their process to others. Our initial goal
was to become an internationally recognized
and leading design firm, and now our next
challenge and opportunity will be to help
create a new generation of design leaders. At
Idiom, we are doing things that have not been
done before. Young people who work with
us now have to take the lead. We would like
to enable our younger designers to carry our
philosophy across their work. There is so much
work to be done that we cannot expect our
ideas and philosophies to spread overnight.
Instead they need to be spread in a lateral
manner by turning young people into leaders.
Idiom's vision is to encourage young people
to share their process, try new things, learn
from new contexts and experiences and, most
importantly, to take on big challenges knowing
that they are supported by strong mentors.
Independence, encouragement and a great
spirit of co-creation will go hand-in-hand with
a deep sense of ownership and responsibility
towards the firm. The 'wicked problems' that
Idiom is faced with on a daily basis are a great
learning experience for our next generation.
However, as a practice, our values, processes
and spirit all need to be strengthened in order
to prepare the next generation for the exciting
future ahead. *~end~*

INSITUM

São Paulo | www.insitum.com

Innovation Consulting in Emerging Economies

INSITUM's Transitions

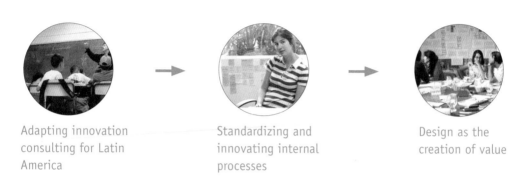

Adapting innovation consulting for Latin America

Standardizing and innovating internal processes

Design as the creation of value

INSITUM was founded in Mexico and Brazil in 2002, and is a global innovation consulting company with offices in Mexico, Colombia, Argentina, Brazil, and the USA, and partnerships with companies in India, China and Japan. INSITUM works with multinational companies, start-ups, governments and Non-Government Organizations (NGOs) to provide deep understanding of real user needs, solving complex problems through Design Thinking. INSITUM describe themselves as the leading innovation consulting firm in Latin America. We spoke with Luis Arnal, one of the founders and current Managing Partner, and Yoel Lenti, Director of the Brazilian office, about INSITUM's practices, and asked them to share their key transitions during the fostering of an emerging market for innovation consultancy.

Founding INSITUM

INSITUM was founded upon Luis' experiences in design, research and business. He trained as a designer at the IIT Institute of Design in Chicago, and his research focus comes from his experiences working at Doblin Group with Larry Keeley, and a two year stint at E-Lab in Chicago with Rick E. Robinson, John Cain and Mary Beth McCarthy. Luis considers E-Lab to be the ideal combination of research (Rick), design (John) and business (Mary Beth). E-Lab was one of the first companies to combine social sciences with design and business, and it was an inspiration because, for the first time, Luis was able to view the business benefits of design and the way it interacted – rather than conflicted – with other disciplines. Luis' business and strategy perspectives were polished during his time with management consulting companies IconMediaLab and DiamondCluster (formerly known as Cluster Consulting), where he was a management consultant working in Europe during the Internet boom.

INSITUM's global expansion

The vision when starting INSITUM was to form a global company. Its first incarnation was in Mexico and Brazil (the two largest economies in Latin America), together with our partner Charles Bezerra in Recife, Brazil. However, after a few months Charles moved to New Zealand to take up an academic post and he officially left the company in late 2003. At that point Roberto Holguin returned to Mexico after finishing his PhD studies in Chicago, and it was when he joined INSITUM that we really accelerated, and began to expand the company with new clients and projects.

Our US office started in 2006, and offered a good opportunity to target Hispanic market innovation in an already well-established market. Luis then moved to Brazil to invigorate and direct our office there, and we established a Colombian office in 2010 to work in that emerging economy. In 2011 we opened our Argentinian office. This was unplanned, but the opportunity arose because we had an Argentinian friend relocating back home and we suggested that he open an INSITUM office there – which he did.

Due to our quick expansion in the last three years, we now have a presence in all of these emerging economies, working on interesting projects for global companies. These companies also needed projects in other emerging economies such as China and India, and these opportunities led us to establish alliances with similar innovation companies in those countries by forming Innovation Union, an international alliance of innovation

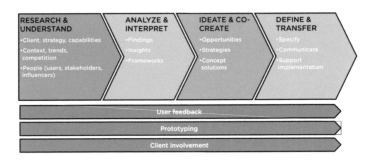

INSITUM's Process

consulting firms in China, India, Russia and Latin America.

INSITUM's philosophy

As INSITUM is involved in innovation consulting, we are constantly adapting our offer to the environment and the type of client that we have. We are always questioning and changing, because we believe innovation should start from the way we understand our client's needs and adapt solutions to meet those needs. We spend a lot of time thinking and reading about design, research and business, attending academic conferences, and thinking about ways to bring these disciplines closer together. We then take these theories and apply them in a professional context. In a given year, we will bring in new methodologies, techniques and ideas in order to create innovative offerings that will attract more projects.

However, as much as we enjoy our work, we always try to find a purpose in what we do. We believe our work needs to have a social impact, and leave a positive footprint on the world. At INSITUM we achieve this by influencing corporations, and making sure they spend money in appropriate ways that have an effect on people's lives. We could be content with what we're already doing – but if you want to multiply and grow, you have to invite other people to share your passion. Rather than contributing money, we believe that we should spend our time, energy and mental abilities helping other people through Design Thinking.

Our passion is for solving problems in a way that brings about a long-term positive impact on society. We believe that the most effective way to do this is through companies and organizations, because they have the resources

One of the design behaviours at INSITUM is having 'critique sessions', in which consultants who are unfamiliar with the project provide feedback to the team

and 'clout' in emerging countries to really change people's lives.

For INSITUM, innovation consulting is the ability to help companies create solutions that are novel to the world, relevant to the user, and coherent with the company strategy. In order to do this, we start by understanding three key contexts: world trends, users and company capabilities. Innovation starts with research, and with learning. You cannot innovate in a vacuum, and research provides good inspiration. That's why our motto is: Innovation through Research.

INSITUM's culture

At the heart of everything we do, we are very persistent about our values and beliefs. For example, we do not take on any work from tobacco companies, casinos, or other businesses that we do not feel a deep appreciation for. We also understand the need to create the right type of environment for innovation. Our employees would not thrive in a closed system or a non-design environment. They lose their

Co-creation is at the core of most of our projects. In this example, a group of users are helping to ideate mobility apps for smartphones

Observation is a skill that allows you to discover insights that are less obvious and more relevant for innovation, but many people are not used to trusting their instinct. This is the room of a Hispanic immigrant to the US and it gives us a sense of his new life

value if placed outside of the environment that we have carefully cultivated for them. This is an environment where they can interact with people who are different from them (such as designers, sociologists, anthropologists and journalists) and work on a diverse range of projects; from researching the high income segment, to redefining the private banking experience, to understanding how to sell cosmetics to the largest but poorest socio-economic group, the 'Base of the Pyramid'.

We build teams to work on projects. Each project has its own dedicated room that we come together and work in. We try not to work with the same group of people for too long, to prevent us from falling in love with a solution. We keep changing, building new things and working with people from different backgrounds. We can be talking about the design language of vehicles in the morning, discussing women's sanitary pad preferences in the afternoon, and working with a copper mining company in the evening.

Herbert Simon once said, 'A designer's work is about changing an existing situation into a preferred one'. However designers can suffer

from having too many ideas too quickly, and the market is not quite ready for this type of intuitive thinking. We have to manage our designers, and their creative process – it is not always about the idea. You need to develop how designers analyze and think at a strategic level, because they can sometimes lack an overall vision and be too focused on the material things around a solution. To help overcome this, we have to give our designers a lot of feedback and equip them with the tools to reflect on the bigger picture. We evaluate whether we have fully covered what was in the original project proposal, and avoid concentrating on micro issues. This is always a big challenge for our employees, and it is our operational department that ensures we always keep that focus on the wider picture.

Adapting innovation consulting for Latin America

The business context in Latin America is heterogeneous; some countries have greater innovation maturity, which means that leading companies in those countries are more likely to demand innovation consulting services than others. Today in 2012, Brazil is ahead of Mexico, and Colombia and Argentina are in joint third place. Countries like Peru and Venezuela are way behind, with only a handful of companies there investing in this type of work. However all governments lag behind even the Peruvian and Venezuelan companies! For this reason, INSITUM has had to adapt our offer to different clients' needs – but we always have three main overlapping elements: research, innovation and strategy. The key is to design an offer based on this menu, but tailored to the client's specific needs. If we are working with a start-up them there will be an initial need to refine their business model and improve their website interface. These are two different things, so we normally start with the interface and then the business model will emerge and change. Most of the time we start with a small project, and work our way towards larger and more strategic projects. We may start a small brand positioning project for a product category, but after six months we could be working on that company's future product pipeline – and after a year we might be helping them to define a new business model around distribution. With some of our more well-versed clients, we work on a retainer model. For example, when we started working for a leading microprocessor manufacturing company six years ago, we

began with exploratory work around their education ecosystem, which then lead to work on informing the features and, most recently, defining the design language of the product.

In emerging markets we have to carry out a lot of educational activities with our clients. Companies are used to market research, but they are not familiar with innovation consulting. As we work with them, we help to develop their teams and make them more sensitive to innovation and Design Thinking approaches. But we always take a long-term view on client relationships; we know that if we do not establish good relationships from the outset, it will be difficult for them to trust us with future projects. However, it can be tough to sell innovation at the beginning. We have learnt many lessons since we first started INSITUM. In the past our main focus was on selling our methods of ethnography and ideation, because that was what fascinated us. What we've since realized is that clients are not concerned with how we do it, as long as they get results. That's why we are now focused on selling the output, rather than the process. We have to adapt to our environment, otherwise no one will listen to us – or even worse, they may think we are crazy!

Working with a leading microprocessor manufacturing company around education ecosystems, in order to inform new product features and design language

We have evolved the way we build relationships with our clients in order to take on more complex, interesting and strategic projects. It is only through these kinds of projects that you get to interact with decision makers at the highest levels of organizations.

Standardising and innovating internal processes

Another key learning for INSITUM has been related to our internal processes. We have had to standardize and innovate these in order to adjust to the competitive context and changing client requirements, and to be able to swiftly meet the demands of larger and more strategic projects. It is crucial to constantly question whether we can improve the way we do things, and so we are always experimenting with new ideas to evolve our practice. These could be new ways of presenting a project, a new methodology, or changing the sequence of our processes. 'Trying to do better everyday' (like Toyota's idea of constant improvement) is a big part of what we do, and we always push our staff to think about the way they are working

It is crucial to constantly question whether we can improve the way we do things, and so we are always experimenting with new ideas to evolve our practice.

and find new ways to improve.

It's good to use your experience to achieve the same result using a faster method, but when you are growing as a company you need to experiment with different methodologies and processes. Designers have this need to try out new approaches, and sometimes they fail and learn in the process. This attitude is really important, because we fail a lot in strategic projects and we need to be transparent about those failures with our clients: if you don't fail, you don't grow.

The challenge on global projects is trying to manage teams that are located in different countries. For example, when we need to conduct deep analysis it is difficult to reach a common understanding. We have tried to conduct analysis between different countries, but have so far failed. As a solution, we now come together in the same country to analyse as a team. In order to conduct deep analysis and achieve insight, we have to be emotionally and physically connected to one another – which is impossible to achieve remotely.

Design as the creation of value

Ten years ago, design was just a 'nice to have' option. But it has slowly gained more and more visibility, and we are now learning from companies that historically had design at the core of their business – like Dyson, Bang & Olufsen and Apple. Today people see design in a different way, and they want to use it for reasons other than its aesthetic value. We would not have been in this position without companies like Apple or the work of Steve Jobs, who was the quintessential design thinker. However there is a risk that our type of work is still not recognized as design. Design skills are now seen to be adding value to businesses but, even though this is growing, it's still a niche market. We believe

Teams from different offices coming together to develop a common understanding on global projects

that clients will have to incorporate design into their businesses, regardless of whether they are a manufacturing or a service company. They need this kind of thinking in order to grow and be more adaptive. As a result we will see an explosion of consulting firms, but also of clients who are looking for design and innovation services and skills.

There is still a long way to go before design can have any deep impact, but we are starting with large corporations and then moving on to government, start-ups and NGOs. There is a German political party called the Pirate Party, and they are applying innovation and Design Thinking approaches by posting ideas to an open web platform, asking the public to vote for the policies they prefer, and then refining them before presenting them to the government. They are gaining a lot of trust because of the transparency of this process. This is really innovative, and it is a model that should be adapted for NGOs, corporations and governments because of that transparency, and the user-centred control and decision making it offers to citizens.

Where next for INSITUM?

We will continue to evolve on a yearly basis, and will strive never to repeat the same offering as the year before. We will keep expanding the types of projects we do, and in the next ten years we aim to be the leading innovation consulting firm in the emerging economies. We have been thinking about how to change our business model, and we are now more knowledgeable about who we hire. Five hundred years ago there were no medical specialists, and so a doctor had to be able to treat every type of illness. As medicine improved, specialists emerged to provide more dedicated health care. We believe that, in a similar way, we are going to see more service design companies beginning to focus on particular sectors, such as the financial service or healthcare. It will take longer for this type of practice to get established in the emerging markets, because the market there is not as receptive as it is in other regions like the USA and Europe. However there is a growing market of companies requiring design, and the need for Design Thinking will increase as the needs of those companies change. *-end-*

Wellington, Auckland, Sydney | www.optimalexperience.com

OPTIMAL USABILITY

Three Horizons of a Transitioning Company

Optimal Usability's Transitions

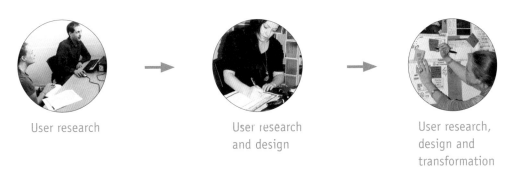

User research → User research and design → User research, design and transformation

Optimal Usability began in New Zealand in 2002, as a user research consultancy founded by Trent Mankelow and Sam Ng. Since then they have travelled across several horizons as a business and in practice. As a business they have evolved from being a local New Zealand-based consultancy to having a presence in Australia, and today they are globally recognized through their spin-out company, Optimal Workshop. In practice, Optimal Usability has transitioned from research to design, and from design to strategy, while maintaining a clear focus on their roots in user research. Trent Mankelow is Co-founder of Optimal Usability, and here he articulates the company's story and its vision to transform companies into providers of world-class customer experiences.

Optimal Usability in the beginning

My co-founder Sam and I met when we were both working for a giant IT services company called Unisys. They would spend a lot of money on developing cutting-edge telephony applications, but nothing on making sure that those applications actually worked for people. I remember once, one of the developers put together a test website that he had designed over a weekend, and that ended up being the final version we went live with. I could not believe that there were companies creating products without considering the goals, characteristics and context of the people they were designing for. These experiences really catalyzed Sam and I into starting a company with a focus on user research. When we founded Optimal Usability in 2002 we did not consider ourselves to be designers, but our clients kept asking us to help them with interaction design projects. In response we started hiring designers and, given our roots, it's perhaps no surprise that today our design practice is very much user-centred, and with a particular focus on co-design. We only take on projects that will involve users, and our philosophy is that everyone can help define and solve design problems. In co-design workshops we take the role of facilitators, to pull designs from our clients' heads.

Three business Horizons[1]

We describe our progress, and our transitions over the past ten years, as moving us across different horizons. Horizon One was starting Optimal Usability in late 2002, as a user experience company based in New Zealand. Most of what we did then was observational research. Optimal Usability is still the engine of the company today, with over two hundred clients in New Zealand and 20 staff members.

Horizon Two was opening our Sydney, Australia office called Optimal Experience, in early 2008. By virtue of its market size, Australia was the obvious next horizon for us – Australia's population is 22 million people, while New Zealand's is 4 million.

Horizon Three was our products company, Optimal Workshop. This started with a card sorting tool that we created for a client in 2004. We built our own online tool because we had to do a specific piece of research, and the existing tools did not give us what we wanted. So we built Optimal Sort, and then one thing led to another until, in 2007, we made the decision to create a separate spin out product company. Andrew Mayfield is the current CEO at Optimal Workshop, which has tens of thousands of users and a truly

Optimal Usability team

Part of the Optimal Usability team working with users and researchers

global customer base. The kinds of customers we have for Optimal Workshop include Bank of America, BBC and Nokia. In 2007 Sam transferred to Optimal Workshop and no longer did consulting work for Optimal Usability. This made it easier for him to focus on building a great suite of usability tools, without the pressure of billable consulting work. It would be really hard for a consulting company to build tools, unless it had a separate company like this.

It is nice to step back now and think about how our journey seems to have been all planned out – but at the beginning it most certainly was not. We've crossed horizons as a business, but we have also evolved internally as a practice across the horizons of user research, design and transformation.

Practice Horizon One: User research
At Optimal Usability we started out doing expert reviews and usability testing as our 'bread and butter'. We have moved on a lot since the early days of user testing, which involved carrying LCD monitors around with us while we recorded user interaction using digital video cameras. Our first big break came in 2003, when we worked with sportswear company Canterbury Clothing. We decided to do an $8,000 usability review and only charge them $2,000, but with an agreement that we had the rights to use them as a case study in the future. This case study became a key document for us because Canterbury Clothing was a very well-known brand, especially in rugby-mad New Zealand.

At Horizon One the research space was core, and it was what we had been doing from the very start. User testing will always involve representative users doing representative tasks while you watch and listen and look for patterns, but the kind of user testing we do has since broadened. In 2008 Air New Zealand came to us with an interesting problem. IDEO had been engaged to develop a new long-haul flying experience, and the concepts that came out of that project needed to be taken to the next level. Air New Zealand came to us and said, 'We have these five different seat design concepts, and we want you to help us figure out which one to go with.' That was a great demonstration of their faith in us, because up to that point our work with them had been mainly focused on user research for websites. Now we increasingly work on product-related projects, because we have more people from a greater variety of backgrounds – and because we are good problem solvers.

What a great design team needs is a multi-disciplinary approach. We have designers, but we also have people from the social sciences and even the 'hard' sciences – one of our staff was trained as a physicist. We have people with different ethnic backgrounds and different nationalities such as Germans, Canadians, Americans and Brits. We have been fairly deliberate about achieving this level of diversity. If we hire someone from England who has experience of working in that country, then they can share their experiences of what does and doesn't work there.

What we do not have in our team is a diversity of values. We are very clear about our values, and often describe ourselves as being like mountain guides. We help our clients to climb the right mountains, addressing the size of those mountains and planning for the expeditions. It would be difficult for someone to work in our culture without agreeing with our values.

Practice Horizon Two: User research and design

In March 2005 our clients started asking us to not only critique designs, but also to create interfaces based on our understanding of and research into how people work. For quite a long time, we were not involved in the delivery of visual designs. We generally stopped at the interaction design stage, where we might be presenting a clickable prototype or a series of Visio screens. However, we found that this approach was letting our clients down because they would then have to go on and manage the design of the visual layer. For us, there was always a reason why a button was labelled in a specific way or positioned in a particular space, and the entire interface was always considered as a whole. In order to be sure that we were delivering our original vision to the clients, we began hiring people who had the visual design skills to ensure that nothing was being lost in the development of that visual layer. We care about world-class customer experience, and we were losing that by stopping short in our process. We do not do software development but we do clearly articulate the interface, to better equip the developers to implement it. In our experience developers are less interested in design, and more interested in writing elegant code. From a design point of view the fidelity of the deliverables is key, and so we have moved from wireframes to high-fidelity visuals (when appropriate). This shift was the first change on this Horizon. The second change came in the way we approach design problems. For the most part, we try and recruit clients onto the design team to co-design with us and work towards a solution. However there are limits to this approach; it can result in very offbeat and disparate ideas, but then it is down to the skills of the designer to take the core of those ideas and mould them into workable solutions.

State Insurance is New Zealand's largest personal insurance company. They came to us for the design of an online quotation and purchasing tool for personal motor vehicle insurance. They wanted a design that was based on user research, and that had been validated with real users. We started out with a discovery phase, interviewing key stakeholders in order to understand the business needs that

Moving from wireframes to high-fidelity visuals to test concepts and ideas

would affect the design direction. Following on from this, we interviewed customers to inform personas that would be used throughout the project to inform design decisions. In the next phase we used those personas, along with the insights from the previous phase of work, to inform a conceptual sketching workshop with key stakeholders. The resulting concept sketches were refined and two key concepts were taken into usability testing. The usability test findings were then used to refine the two concepts into a single design, and this design was developed into a set of wireframes that were prototyped for another round of usability testing. The visual design was completed by another agency, and we reviewed it prior to one final round of usability testing. The positive user experience in the final round of testing was a testament to our user-centred design methodology.

One thing we did differently in the *State* project was to visually map the design concepts against the client's strategic goals and the goals of the personas, in order to prioritize the concepts. To better develop these visualization techniques, we will often practice them internally. For example, we run a monthly 'Beers with the Boss' session where we talk about the business performance, and we have recently created a one-page visualization

of where Optimal Usability is currently positioned within the market.

We use the same process within our service design practice. Sam's last act as an Optimal Usability employee was a three month project using the company itself as a case study. We asked the question, 'How do we improve the Optimal Usability client experience?' and I asked Sam to run the project as someone outside of the day-to-day business, and to

What a great design team needs is a multi-disciplinary approach. We have designers, but we also have people from the social sciences and even the 'hard' sciences – one of our staff was trained as a physicist.

speak directly with our clients. One of the findings that came out of this exercise was a realization that, when clients meet us for the first time, they sometimes find it quite hard to understand what we do. As a result we decided to create an introductory document for our clients and prospective clients: a 'Hello' booklet that contains descriptions of what we do, and a range of portfolio examples.

Practice Horizon Three: User research, design and transformation

Today we have significantly broadened the range of domains we work in, which leads us to our Horizon Three. We are very driven by transformation, and a vision to transform our clients into providers of world-class customer experiences. The bit we understand well is the 'world-class customer experience', but the real work is in transforming these large organizations.

In 2010 we began working with Metlink, the organization responsible for Wellington's public transport network, to develop an experience strategy for the way their users accessed transport information through multiple channels, at home or on the move. We guided Metlink through a process of mapping different user needs and the different parts of the customer journey. It quickly became clear that there was an entire part of that customer journey they had no control over. Operators are hired to run the trains and buses, so as soon as a customer boards a bus or train Metlink loses control of their customer experience. The things they could control were the planning, pre-departure and waiting aspects of a bus or train journey, and some of these aspects were more important to particular user groups. For 'regulars' the focus was mainly on pre-departure and waiting, while for less frequent users the planning aspect was the most vital. Based on initial

feedback, we researched commuter needs and the types of communication channels they preferred to use. It was very clear that the focus was on communication via mobile phones, giving commuters public transport knowledge while they were on the move. The mobile solution that we created had a fantastic uptake. It went from 0 per cent of their overall web traffic to 25 per cent, in the space of just three months. The key thing that we did here was to explore the issues through workshops, and it was the client who decided on the important issues. We often conduct user research and stakeholder interviews to seed our workshops; otherwise you can just end up with lots of different opinions around a table. It is about the designer acting as facilitator, rather then prescribing a strategy. It would be presumptuous of us to go into a well-known New Zealand company and decide on their strategy for them.

Not everyone in our team will do this third horizon stuff, because not everyone is wired that way. You need to have presence; you need to have 'mana', which is a phrase we use here in New Zealand. It is about presence and respect. We often talk about our clients needing 'mana' too, because they are the ones who will ultimately become the project champion, owning the outcomes and driving the work forward.

The future of design according to Optimal Usability

Something we have been talking about for a while is the end-to-end customer experience. Our vision is for world-class customer experience, and that has to be cross-channel – but if it is cross-channel then our clients need to change. There are a range of things that organizations need to fix before they can truly deliver world-class customer experience. For a start, they need to look at organizational structure and incentives for staff. And at Optimal Usability we have got to get better at change management. In order to turn around huge ships like telecoms companies or government agencies, we are going to need the ability to influence organizational cultures. That is the struggle within service design internationally. There are very few Chief Experience Officers in the world who own all of the customer-facing channels. If you look at a government it becomes even more complex, because there it's not about interactions across different times or channels; these are interactions across completely different agencies and Non-Governmental Organizations. In our most recent research we have discovered that people do not actually know where the edges of government are.

There is a lot of complexity here. To achieve our vision we have to be bold, maintaining the core of our business while extending ourselves in the way we do research. To do this we are adopting new remote research techniques and building on our quantitative research skills. On the design side of things, we have to focus on keeping up with the constant changes in multi-channel and multi-screen media. User research is core to our practice. We started out as researchers, and we still stress to our clients that we do not do design without that element of user research.

I probably can't tell you anything new about the future of design. My caveat is that I am not a trained designer, but I still think we have much more to do on the basics. So many $10 million or $100 million projects are commissioned without having a designer on the team. Why is this the case? I worry about a government agency replacing their core IT system at a cost of $NZ1 billion; that's a lot of money for this small country. I worry about how they are going to do the design. I worry that it is going to be an afterthought, even though they have a service design team.

My hope for the future of design is that we see more designers working inside organizations. In software engineering today, you would never roll out a $10 million system without conducting independent software testing. I would like to think that we will get to a point where a system would never be released without some kind of usability testing, where you would never think to start an IT project without getting a designer on board. If people are really serious about taking on customer experience, then design has to become a core internal skill. There is an attitude that needs to change – we need to value not just design, but the designerly way of thinking. A lot of people on the ground already understand what design and customer experience is about, but there are also a lot of people who don't. Part of our role is to educate those people, and to continue driving our vision of helping companies become providers of world-class customer experiences. *-end-*

Notes

1. The three horizons of growth describes how companies pursue opportunities for growth. This framework first appeared in *The Alchemy of Growth* by Mehrdad Baghai, Stephen Coley, and David White (1999, New York: Perseus Publishing) and is widely discussed by McKinsey (McKinsey Quarterly, 2009)

Shanghai | www.frogdesign.com

FROG

Meeting the Needs of Asia's Open and Experimental Market

frog Asia's Transitions

frog launches
in Asia

Building global-
local teams

Adapting practices
for China to build
design capabilities

Collaborating
with start-ups

Founded in Germany in 1969 by Hartmut Esslinger, frog is a global product strategy and design firm that helps create and bring to market meaningful services and experiences. In 2007 frog opened its studio in Shanghai in response to China's growing domestic economy. Today it serves as the company's Asia-Pacific headquarters, servicing clients in markets including China, Singapore, Japan, South Korea and Thailand. Here the studio's co-founders, Executive Creative Director Brandon Edwards and Executive Strategy Director Ravi Chhatpar, share the transitions the company has experienced in order to meet the wide-ranging needs of the Asia-Pacific market.

frog launches in Asia

In 2007 frog opened our studio in Shanghai, initially to help one of our most prominent clients to understand the Chinese market. The client was a primary sponsor of the 2008 Beijing Olympic Games, and the Shanghai studio was set up in advance of the Games to help that client figure out how to approach different markets across a wide range of business units. This was not our first project in Asia as, since the inception of frog in 1969, we have consulted and worked with multiple clients in Asia, including Sony, Samsung and Acer. By opening the Shanghai studio, we have further strengthened our presence in Asia and enabled frog to extend its footprint and capacity across multiple Asia-Pacific markets.

Prior to this point frog was best known for designing the iconic Apple II computer – but apart from this brief moment in the spotlight, our reputation was almost non-existent in China. Some Chinese consumers and technology firms knew a bit about our history, but there was very little awareness of frog's practices and how our services had evolved over the past 44 years. When we first started out in Shanghai our team worked diligently on developing frog's brand presence, communicating our service offering and helping clients to understand the value of design services. Much of our activity in the early days involved lecturing and running workshops at universities in Beijing, Shanghai, Hong Kong and Tokyo, teaching the students about the tremendous impact you can make by combining business with design.

One of our core competencies in the Shanghai studio is design research, and we use this to help our clients understand the market. For the first couple of years, a third of our clients were Chinese companies looking to innovate domestically or expand globally with their products and services. The other third were Western multinationals looking to innovate for China, and the remaining third were a mix of multinationals and Asian companies designing for markets such as Japan, Korea, Taiwan and Singapore. Our portfolio has now expanded significantly, and our projects range from designing intelligent water filtration solutions for rural India, to mobile banking in Southeast Asia and affordable smartphones for Tier 4–7 cities in China.

Our team has had to learn a lot about the Chinese market, which is often misunderstood and misrepresented. Chinese companies are sometimes unfairly labelled as copycats, but they are not the only companies who have been accused of this practice. You could argue that the first Canon camera was a copy of the Leica camera, until Canon introduced a microprocessor. Once they introduced this new type of camera it opened up a new world for them in terms of what they could produce for the market. We see it as a question of what you can offer an emerging market as the consumer sector grows. In our research we have found that while consumers may not be able to afford high-end designs right away, they still aspire to have the same kind of experience. We believe the Chinese adapt more rapidly to new technology compared to the West. They have higher expectations than Americans, and a willingness to adopt technology even if it is new or experimental. We also recognize that each region, province and city in China has its own historical background, culture, food and language, which means that some brands and products may be more popular in the north than the south. It is critical for us to be aware of these differences in the Chinese domestic market, especially as purchasing power increases.

One of our core competencies in the Shanghai studio is design research, and we use this to help our clients understand the market.

We have observed a change in consumer expectations since Apple entered the Chinese market four or five years ago. Today's consumers want design excellence from their products and services. They are demanding more from the brands and companies they interact with, and they are expressing those demands vocally through Sina Weibo, WeChat and other social media platforms. In a recent study conducted by frog on Chinese youth, we found that consumers feel it is their moral obligation to share their experiences of companies with others, given the lack of trust in formal institutions and traditional media. Many are aware that they are not getting the same experience as consumers in other markets, and so they either complain very loudly or stop purchasing – or both.

Building global-local teams

Today in 2013, our Shanghai studio has grown to over 50 people representing 15 different nationalities. This kind of diversity has become a key characteristic of the studio, informing change in our process over the years and contributing to our ability to work faster, leaner and smarter. When we first started the Shanghai studio it was not our explicit aim to have a diverse range of staff. But as we began responding to the needs of businesses in Asia, we had to ensure that we had the right cultural expertise to serve our clients appropriately. This meant getting the right balance of Chinese employees working in the office, which has involved developing our creative teams.

frog has been good at evolving the way we resource our staff, to build teams up across and within studios. One way we do this is by sending staff from Shanghai to other studios to work on projects, and vice versa. We have staff from the Ukraine, India, San Francisco and Austin studios all working side

frog's research in the field

Building a multi-disciplinary global-local team. Left to right: frog and client synthesizing the results after conducting field research

by side with our Shanghai teams. Five years ago that would never have happened, and it is a testament to the way the company has become more global. It also means that, if we do not have the right people in Shanghai for a project, we can draw on our range of talented people from other studios to create the perfect team. We were fortunate to have Jan Chipchase join our Shanghai team two years ago as Executive Creative Director of Global Insights. Jan is a well-known researcher and consultant who specializes in understanding how technology works across different cultures. His appointment has further strengthened our research capabilities.

Expanding our studios has allowed us to tackle larger problems. Over the years we have shown that frog is capable of thinking and delivering systemically across multiple touchpoints, services and business reorganizations. This has allowed us to build trust with our clients, which has in turn leads to us being trusted with even bigger challenges. Our Shanghai studio is not so very different from our other studios, and while each studio has its own personality we are pretty consistent across the globe. In the past two years we have been doing research and strategy all the way through to detailed implementation and execution for clients such as Huawei, Lenovo, Standard Chartered Bank, Tencent, Visa and others.

Adapting practices for China to build design capabilities

We have learnt that it is important to work closely with our Chinese and Asian clients, because some of the affordances and intuition around design are simply different here. For example, if you are a foreign designer unable to communicate in the local language, the design rationalization you provide to the client often gets lost in translation. The closer you work with people, the more you are able to overcome those communication barriers.

We also have to respect the historical relationship between engineering and manufacturing activities in China. This relationship is unbelievably strong, and needs to be respected rather than criticized. It is one of the strengths of the market, and it is a strength that Chinese companies are learning to use hand in hand with design. In one of our projects we put together five engineers from the client's side with our designers and technologists during the prototyping stage. This is a very different practice to what we are used to with our US or European clients, who rely on us to do a lot more of the engineering work. The Chinese firms are a little different – they have the capability to do it in-house, and they want the challenge of innovating on their own.

We prefer to be working closely with our clients, not only to ensure that we are working from the same page but also because our clients like to roll up their sleeves and get their hands dirty. They want to learn how we do what we do, and in the past clients have asked if we can teach that to them. As we are not a university we do not teach them in the usual way; instead we transfer our knowledge by working with them, as in our view the best way to learn is through experience.

This type of collaboration enables the client to understand the materiality of a product better, and makes it quicker and easier for us to come up with a completely new idea. We have seen a smartphone that looks exactly like an iPhone created in nineteen days. If they can recreate a product like that in just nineteen days, what is going to happen when they start producing ideas on their own? The potential here to disrupt the entire global market is very high. We are not far away from the point when this will start to happen, and at frog we are very excited that we are going to be a part of that revolution.

China is a manufacturing powerhouse, and so consumers and businesses here have a much

We have learnt that it is important to work closely with our Chinese and Asian clients, because some of the affordances and intuition around design are simply different here.

deeper sense of materiality than in other parts of the world. The immense speed at which products reach the market has forced design companies like us to be much more nimble and flexible in our processes. Design practices are adapting to this changing context, which is increasingly becoming the norm across the world. Design firms can no longer afford to take a consulting posture, as the nature and definition of consulting is also drastically changing. Today it's not enough to meet your client once a week to provide status updates.

Collaboration and supporting start-ups. Left: Startup Weekend event. Right: frog partners with social incubator ECSEL to support young entrepreneurs in China

It is now critical to involve your clients as early as possible, and in all areas of the project; from research and ideation through to prototyping and implementation. Our clients will sometimes head into the field with us to conduct immersive research, and this is about building the relationship, creating meaning, discovering new ideas and being able to make those ideas real by working together.

Collaborating with start-ups

A lot of clients come to us when they need help understanding the Chinese market. We started working with start-up businesses because of our earlier work in market strategy, consumer research and business strategy. The majority of these companies are joint ventures, wanting to know how to start their business and develop a brand – not only for domestic markets, but internationally too. We have seen more and more of these types of organizations in the past two to three years. In the US many joint ventures and start-ups traditionally avoid working with consulting companies, in order to retain their talent and intellectual property (IP). However, start-ups in China are a little bit different. They have the talent and the IP, but they are so well-funded that they are willing to consider working with consulting firms to help them get ahead faster. As a result we do a lot of projects with start-ups, especially across the automotive and mobile telecom sectors. It is important that we acknowledge this fact, and that our role is to augment and strengthen start-up entrepreneurs rather than replace them, because they are talented people who are very close to the products they are creating.

What's next for frog in Asia?

Two years ago our Chief Creative Officer Mark Rolston was quoted in Forbes saying that 'within ten years the Shanghai studio will be frog's largest, passing its San Francisco headquarters'. In fact we would like frog's Shanghai studio to become the headquarters for the entire company, and this is probably not far from becoming a reality due to the shift of international focus towards the China and Asian markets. In terms of China specifically, we have been doing some amazing work with Tencent, one of the largest Internet companies in the world. We are helping them change their organization, and produce products that

Working with Tencent, one of the largest software companies in China on their organizational structure and product range. Left: Creating mood boards. Right: User validation session

Our clients will sometimes head into the field with us to conduct immersive research, and this is about building the relationship, creating meaning, discovering new ideas and being able to make those ideas real by working together.

can compete in the Chinese domestic market while also surpassing other products globally.

Capability-wise we are really impressed with the work that our teams are producing, but at the same time we are always trying to push our boundaries. As designers we are perfectionists, and so we have to keep growing our capacity to do great work, and fostering our creative talent. It is about giving our teams the right platform, and doing it in a scaleable way – not only in China but also in Asia Pacific.

A lot of the designers we hire in our studio are self-taught, but in the past two years we have started working with universities. We have seen significant changes in the quality of talent coming out of universities, and as a result we are now offering internships.

We are seeing our community change; not only in the local Chinese community, but also in the way that the foreign community is collaborating. We know we have competitors, but we're also seeing a more collaborative spirit between freelancers, agencies and independent artists. People who work at universities are coming together more frequently and in larger numbers, to try to solve social issues. They are also communicating with each other and building a network. We're not really sure why this is happening right now – it could

be due to the current generation of Chinese designers coming of age, or it could be due to a critical mass of foreign designers. Maybe it's a combination of both these things. Sometimes it just takes a couple of individuals in each city to spearhead and be really passionate about a movement to make it work. *-end-*

Shanghai | www.designaffairs.com

DESIGNAFFAIRS
SHANGHAI
Developing Strategies and Designs for an Emerging Market

Lidan Liu is the founder of XLPLUS, a design consultancy based in Shanghai. In 2011 XLPLUS merged with designaffairs, a leading European design agency in the fields of design, research, strategy, engineering and innovation, with headquarters in Germany and numerous offices around the world. Lidan shares her views on the current Chinese design scene, and the importance of offering a complete solution in an emerging market.

Tell us about designaffairs, and what drives you in your work

designaffairs became independent of the Siemens Design Centre in 2007. We now have three offices branches worldwide, with headquarters located in Munich, Erlangen and Shanghai. Our Shanghai office has 20 staff, and designaffairs group has 84 in total. Prior to setting up the Shanghai office, I had a design agency named XLPLUS. XLPLUS and designaffairs knew each other through various networks, and had worked together in previous projects. We found that we had the same working philosophy, in that we always strive to offer customized solutions that are user-centred and tailored to our clients' needs. During our time as XLPLUS we were looking at offering our clients a more complete solution to meet their needs – but we were limited in our ability to do this due to the size of our company. We started talking with designaffairs, and the merger was the final result of that discussion.

Globally, designaffairs offers four main types of service: Research, Strategy, Design and Engineering. Research includes market research, user needs, technology and trend research as well as finding out about our clients' needs.

Strategy includes brand, product, portfolio and service strategy. Design includes industrial design, user interface design, colour and material design and packaging design, and we also provide Engineering support which covers usability, mechanical, software and electronical.

The goal of the Shanghai office is to become designaffairs' Asian headquarters. Our office has a strong emphasis on the Research and Design offerings, while the German office has a more equal range of expertise in the four areas. We select the most appropriate mix of people for each project team, based on their specific expertise. We often host our German colleagues here in Shanghai during a project, and vice versa. Currently the designaffairs brand does not have a strong reputation in China, and we have to start building this.

What are the key differences between the Chinese and European market?

Our Chinese clients are still unfamiliar with the vocabulary and processes of design, and as a result we have had to do a lot of work in educating them. We have to make very clear what the outcomes from our research process will be, and then translate those outcomes into a format that clients will be able to make use of in the future. We are also aware that we cannot just adopt a German or European logic in China, and so we have had to adapt those methodologies to better suit the Chinese context.

How would you characterize the design industry in China at the moment?
The demand for design is growing. The Chinese government recognizes the role that design can play in helping companies move from a manufacturing industry to one based on innovation. Companies need better solutions, which means not just design solutions but better design strategy. Chinese customers are also becoming more exposed to design through globalization, and more aware of what it can do for them. One way to illustrate this change is to look at how XLPLUS changed. We started out in 2005 as an industrial design agency and now, following the merger with designaffairs, we can offer a more complete solution that covers research, strategy, design and engineering. Our clients are now much more willing to listen. Back in 2005, clients believed the only design service they needed was industrial design. Today they approach us for help with their product strategy, and are much more open to our suggestions. The length of projects has also become more reasonable. Before, clients were entirely focused on bringing their product to market as quickly as possible, rather than thinking long-term and considering the sustainability of their business.

There is currently a great deal of demand for user experience services in China, because the Chinese design industry has evolved around industrial design. Many industrial design companies are beginning to focus on user-centred design as a way of differentiating their product within the market. Design strategy is also becoming more important, due to the focus on brand value. Chinese companies are good at manufacturing cheaply and quickly, and the next obvious step for them is to use design to differentiate their product. Due to the educational model and the engineering focus behind most Chinese companies, creative thinking does not come so naturally. That's where we come in. Material design is also becoming interesting now as a lot of companies are looking for new material technologies and treatment as a way of innovating their products. The Chinese domestic market is still growing, and this provides real opportunity for companies to expand their market.

What has brought about this change in perception of design?
Companies have realized that good design leads to increased profits. The cost of human resource is increasing in China, and marketing is becoming less effective. This has forced companies to rethink their strategy in order to maintain profit and growth. There will still be a market for single-specialism design agencies. However, similar to ourselves, many companies are expanding their service range to include user experience and design strategy. I think that a lot of Chinese design agencies will start producing their own branded products and services. For instance, Mooma Design have their own brand of ceramics and furniture products.

What do you think Chinese design companies will look like in the next five to ten years?
Due to the increasing number of international companies moving into the Chinese market, the demand for design here is going to increase. This will drive up the quality of design services, and I also believe that different models of working will emerge. We are already seeing that today's younger designers now prefer to work on a freelance basis, and I believe that we'll see this trend continue. *~end~*

Barcelona | www.claropartners.com

CLARO PARTNERS

Creating Value for Society

Based in Barcelona, Claro Partners draws on approaches from social science, experience design and business strategy to create value for society through innovation projects. Claro Partners founders Aldo De Jong and Rich Radka share insights into the company's practices, explaining the drivers behind their business and what they think the future of design will look like.

Tell us about Claro Partners, and what drives you in your work

We are a business innovation firm, and we partner with clients to transform understanding into value. We seek to understand people by understanding their needs; to understand markets and uncover new opportunities; and to understand technology in order to enable new experiences. But first and foremost, we seek value for society. We hold the conviction that, if we create value for society, there has to be value for business. Where there is real value then people will be willing to pay for it. Once we are clear on a value proposition we play around with the different levers of a business model, to figure out what role our client can play in delivering on that proposition – and whether they have the capability to do so. While we start with an aim of creating value for society, the business side is incredibly important. However cool your idea is, you need to be able to frame it within a commercial context. Sometimes our solution is not to make something new, but to advise our clients that they need to acquire a new capability. We are not necessarily product,

object or even service orientated. We always ask: 'What is the most appropriate solution?' We transform understanding into value by bringing together capabilities, techniques and methodologies from the three key domains we believe to be essential for successful innovation: social science, experience design and business strategy.

We are not necessarily experts in each of those areas, but we are working at the crossroads between them by pulling together a team that comes from across these backgrounds. There are no domain labels at Claro, so people are no longer 'a designer' or 'an anthropologist' or 'a business analyst'. They become 'Claros' or 'Associates', and work on projects in mixed teams. This model of intersecting domains is fundamental to the way our practice works. Most innovation practices have a dominant domain within the company, to which all other practices are auxiliary. We strive to keep a balance between our three disciplines in all our projects, and look for people who can balance left and right brain thinking. Not being defined by skillsets means that our solutions are defined by what needs to happen, and we can have a small and responsive organization that is able to bring in teams and expertise on an ad hoc and impermanent basis.

Our projects are mainly focused at a strategic level, and their outcomes almost always require a transformation of our client's organization, their business model, or a combination of the two. We cannot avoid the idea of change management and leadership, and so we give our clients tools to allow them to manage their change. We must also generate excitement for moving the organization out of their comfort zone, and give them the confidence to enact the changes we recommend. Design is uniquely positioned to turn a set of boring bullet points into an interesting and compelling narrative that excites people.

What are the current drivers of change in your practice?
There are a lot of external factors that require us to keep adapting. For example, the way value is moving from products to service to experience. Value is no longer just monetary. It is not a one-on-one relationship any more, nor is it synchronous. This is a huge area for us to design solutions in. Another factor is that value is no longer created solely by organizations, but by the collective effort of individuals within a network. An example of this can be seen in the car-sharing service Zipcar (www. zipcar.com), which facilitates a network of people in sharing their vehicles. We need to help design services like this, defining how these networks are set up and how they work.

What excites you about design at the moment?
At the moment, what is exciting to us is the concept of rapid prototyping and lean methodologies to get things done quickly, using design for thinking through doing. Rather than theorizing, planning and then starting the design, we choose to prototype quickly. We get something out there fast in order to get feedback – similar to the early sharing of ideas in participatory design. This is about letting the right audiences play with an idea, and collectively collaborate to develop it further. In this situation it is our job to shepherd, orchestrate and bring as many people together to help shape the eventual solution.

What do you think the future of design will look like and why?
For every trend there is a counter-trend. We see a new focus on design as a philosophical approach to problem solving, and the other side of this is a greater need for new and different applications of designers' technical skills. With the huge data explosion we expect to see over the next 10 years, designers will need to be helping users to extract and understand information from within that data. Designers are going to be not just 'doers' but storytellers, who can look at a dataset, understand the story it reveals and then decide on the best way of telling that story. The ability to translate the needs and experiences of the end consumer will be part of the standard job description for designers in the future. The future of design also lies in the area of business design; not business model design, but being able to conceive a new business from the ground up by encompassing product, service, experience and network design.

This shifting landscape is changing the context in which designers design, and they will need to understand this change in order to be able to design for it. Designers have to ask themselves: How does this effect my practice, and how does it affect my route to market? It is a very confusing, but also empowering time for designers right now. *~end~*

ASILIA

Consultants to Design Entrepreneurs

Asilia is a multi-disciplinary creative agency based in London and Nairobi, Kenya that adopts a holistic approach to creative communications intervention to create positive change. Asilia's Creative Director Lulu Kitololo speaks about the company's entrepreneurial transformation, moving away from a consultancy model towards developing and owning their own products and services.

Tell us about Asilia, and what drives you in your work

We are strong advocates of passion at Asilia, and this informs all of our practices. We like to work with clients who are passionate people such as artists, activists, pioneers, visionaries, storytellers, rebels, explorers, tree-huggers and students of life. We work collaboratively with our clients, encouraging them to share their ideas and to co-create with us. This ensures that we receive feedback at every stage of the process, so there are no surprises. We like to think that, while we are the experts at what we do, the client is the expert in their own product or service offering. Because of this they are likely to have the better and more extensive knowledge of their audience, including important insights that will inform our creative process.

Our company has bases in the UK and in Kenya, and we currently have a remote working structure with most of the team working from home. The flexibility offered by this approach is of great benefit in terms of how each person manages their own time, and in terms of being adaptable for our clients. This model also forces our team to become better communicators, as we have limited face-to-face time. The internet has facilitated easier connection and collaboration between people all over the world – we've worked with clients from Somaliland to Switzerland and Egypt. But this means that good communication skills become even more important to ensuring successful outcomes from projects that run smoothly.

What are the current drivers of change in Asilia's design practices?

One thing we are concentrating on right now is reducing our dependence on client work. We want to diversify our income sources and develop more of the self-initiated projects that we love devoting time to, to a point where we can share them with the world. We want to give them the attention they need but, as a business, we have to be realistic about the financial aspect and so we need to ensure that a good proportion of these projects can be monetized. While a lot of our work involves creating materials that enable clients to communicate to their audiences, our internal projects need to be more directly commercial. We need to sell the outcomes as products or services. An example of one of our self-initiated project is *Afriapps*, an online platform inspired by the vision of a digital and connected Africa. The platform consists of a blog, app directory, jobs board, events calendar and associated resources. As we are effectively our own clients for projects like *Afriapps*, our design practices take on a different form. The stages become less rigid, and time constraints become less fixed. We may create a prototype of something, and then work on developing the visual aspect of it over time. This process may not be as linear, and the end point is less defined. We are in the beginning stages of really pushing this approach, but the current drivers of change in our design practice lie in our desire to be more self-sufficient; to give form to our many ideas and push the boundaries of what a design agency looks like.

What excites you about design at the moment?
Diversity is what excites me. I come from an African background and have worked with a lot of African organizations. People have observed that there is an African flavour to my own and Asilia's work. I am interested in challenging what that means. What does African design look like? How can our work represent the culture it is speaking to without resorting to the same old clichés?

What do you think the future practices of design will look like and why?
I see a continuing growth of independent designers and design innovation emerging from within this diversity and desire to do things differently. With a growing population of freelance designers, the variety of design practices will also grow as people create practices that work for them rather than conforming to practices that are imposed by an organization. Also, as it becomes harder for people to find jobs, an increasing number of designers will graduate and learn the ropes by trial and error rather than through internships, work experience and employment experience. Because of this, practices will be less rigid and more likely to evolve easily and often.

Considering current changes in technology, and the growth of interactivity and user-generated experiences, I think that design will increasingly become less about end products and more about experience. Users will become more involved in design, and so designers will need to shift away from having control over a process or an outcome, instead assuming a role that is more like that of a facilitator. *-end-*

ZILVER INNOVATION

Design Driven Innovation

Zilver Innovation is a creative consultancy based in Rotterdam, The Netherlands. The company was founded in 2006 by Erik Roscam Abbing, a strategic consultant, design thinker, teacher and business coach. Erik shares his views on how he applies Design Thinking to business, along with some key learnings from his practice.

Tell us about Zilver Innovation, and what drives you in your work

Zilver is a creative consultancy specialising in 'brand driven innovation': turning vision into value. Brand driven innovation is based on the understanding that, in order to innovate meaningfully and sustainably, organizations need a deeply-rooted shared vision. This vision helps us do all the things that are required for successful innovation: to take calculated risks, envision potential futures, work across silos, and understand what constitutes value to the customer and value to the company.

Our design background is very much at the core of what we do. By working in a visual, inspiring, and co-created way, we bring about tangible and compelling innovations using working methods, processes and tools that are based on design thinking approaches.

We have four key guiding principles at Zilver. Firstly, we treat our clients' challenges as 'ill defined problems'. Our job is to find not only the right answer, but also the right question. Helping our client discover the exact nature of the challenge they are facing or problem they are solving is an important part of the value we offer.

Secondly, our processes are iterative, non-linear and often improvised. We do not offer a 'one size fits all' solution, and we are not suggesting that there is an easy way out of complexity. But while our process may be organic and partly improvised, it also sits within a well-defined framework and involves the client through the use of carefully crafted tools and workshops.

Thirdly, we are optimistic prototypers. This means that we firmly and fundamentally believe that things can be better. It also means that we like to try things out, and are not afraid to fail. To us a prototype is a new way of asking the question, and not necessarily an answer to the original question – which sometime clients are not comfortable with.

And finally, our fourth guiding principle is that we understand people. As designers we have always worked *for* and *with* real human beings. 'Design empathy' brings tremendous value to our clients, and we help them get much closer to their customers by engaging them in design research, context mapping, diary studies and house visits. We also help our clients to create a much stronger internal bond, by bringing people from different backgrounds, divisions, functions and levels together to work around shared themes like customer understanding and vision.

Our brand-driven innovation process consists of four key stages. At Stage 1, we help companies build a shared vision by forming a deep understanding of themselves and their customers. At Stage 2, we help them turn this vision into a roadmap for growth. Then in Stage 3 we help them design the products and services that make this growth tangible. In the final stage we help companies orchestrate touchpoints and implement the products and services designed in the previous stage.

What are the current drivers of change in design practices at Zilver Innovation?
A very important discovery we have made, through working with our partner agency, Protopartners in Australia, is how tempting it is to think of designerly approaches to problem solving as being diametrically opposed to businesslike approaches. Qualitative versus quantitative research, visuals versus text, creativity versus control, synthesis versus analysis, right brain versus left brain. Actually, the two need each other and work fantastically well together. We have discovered ways to integrate all of these things into our research and design processes, and the results have been fantastic. We now combine qualitative research and design intuition, with very strictly-defined numeric performance indicators and solid business cases. This means we have a much more involved and committed management team on board during our work.

What excites you about design at the moment?
Slowly but steadily, design is growing out of its 'making things look prettier' stage and moving towards solving the more complex human challenges. Design, and especially Design Thinking, is finding its foothold in health, education, finance, mobility, politics, urbanism and sustainability.

What do you think the future practices of design will look like and why?
I believe in strong partnerships between design and business, design and the humanities, design and technology, design and entrepreneurship, design and economics. The onus is on designers to build bridges between the disciplines, and make them relevant. We have to stop moaning about being misunderstood, and reach out to make ourselves understood. I think designers have to stop thinking of themselves as a counterforce, protecting the pristine intrinsic qualities of whatever it is we are working on, in splendid isolation and without any relevance to others. We have to become part of the companies we work for, the projects we are involved in and the problems we solve. In the future, design will no longer be a department in a company but a quality you look for in everyone you hire. *-end-*

ZIBA

Portland | www.ziba.com

Continually Expanding the Scope of Design

Ziba is a global design and innovation consultancy based in Portland, Oregon in the USA, with offices in California, Munich and Tokyo. We spoke with Steve Lee, Senior Service Designer at Ziba, about the company's practices and what the expanding role of design and the designer means for business and governments in the UK and USA.

Tell us about Ziba, and what drives you in your work

Ziba exists to design beautiful experiences. We are an interdisciplinary studio which started out 28 years ago in the field of industrial design, and have subsequently expanded to work in design research and trends, communication design, UX, branding and service design. Put simply, we make things better for our clients and their users.

Many service designers have expressed the 'service designer's lament', complaining that they do not get involved in making stuff anymore. It is crucial that designers stay connected with how their thinking changes things. Ziba is a very exciting environment for a service designer to be working in. We are able to influence, and be influenced by, a lot more of the process and practices that turn our designs into reality.

What are the current drivers of change in Ziba's design practices?

Internally, there is a huge desire to do great work that crosses (and blurs) the boundaries between the traditional design departments. We realize no product lives in a vacuum, no communications are without context, and no two digital experiences are the same. There is an increasing drive to foster more collaborative techniques across Ziba. Honing our skills in this area allows us to better facilitate and embed this approach to innovation with our clients.

With each project we further our thinking on the role of design, but we have also witnessed a great deal of change in our clients and what they ask for. They are dealing with a complexity that they struggle to manage, and believe that design holds some important answers that cannot be found through operational re-shuffling, efficiencies or quantitative-based approaches. In fact, many companies are aware that doing so may look good on the books in the short term, but this can actually dilute and obstruct the service offer, affecting delivery and the resultant quality of experience for users.

Even though Europe has had a head start in the service design industry, since my arrival in the US I have found clients in the public and private sector to be just as, or even more, receptive to designers tackling large-scale and complex problems. These problems tend to relate to both external shifts in trends, behaviors, expectations and competition, and internal processes and principles that evolve the culture and practices of an organization to deliver better services more effectively.

What excites you about design at the moment?
In a short period of time we have seen the scope of the designer's role expand greatly, particularly in the field of service design. Design Thinking has emerged to return some common sense and consumer championing into the industry, putting aside the business-dominated decision-making that has eroded experiences and made some service sectors truly painful to interact with.

At the moment I am also fascinated by servitization and its ability to base a service on the outcome of a product, rather than ownership of the facilitating product, while making an environmental, economic and social impact. Portland (where Ziba's headquarters are based) is a city eager to embrace these new consumption behaviors, and servitization can be seen everywhere from car-sharing services to informal tool libraries.

What do you think the future practices of design will look like and why?
There will always be room for specialists and generalists, but the business sector's changing perception of design means that it is now being seen as a way to champion and represent users across channels, service offerings and systems. This has changed the game for those with a cross-discipline overview.

Great services are hard to design, and even harder to deliver. We are excited about continuing to explore how we support organizations to make the challenging shifts required to deliver exceptional services at every level – and most importantly, at delivery points, where design intent is often lost in the process of contending with the realities of interactions in dynamic environments and across multiple touchpoints. *-end-*

Ziba helped Umpqua Bank to re-imagine their banking experience in 2003, so that customers could enjoy spending time in their bank

Previous page, top right: *JumpSeat*, designed for a 175-seat auditorium in the Umpqua building

SECTION II

NEW TERRITORIES

Organizations looking to embed and apply design approaches

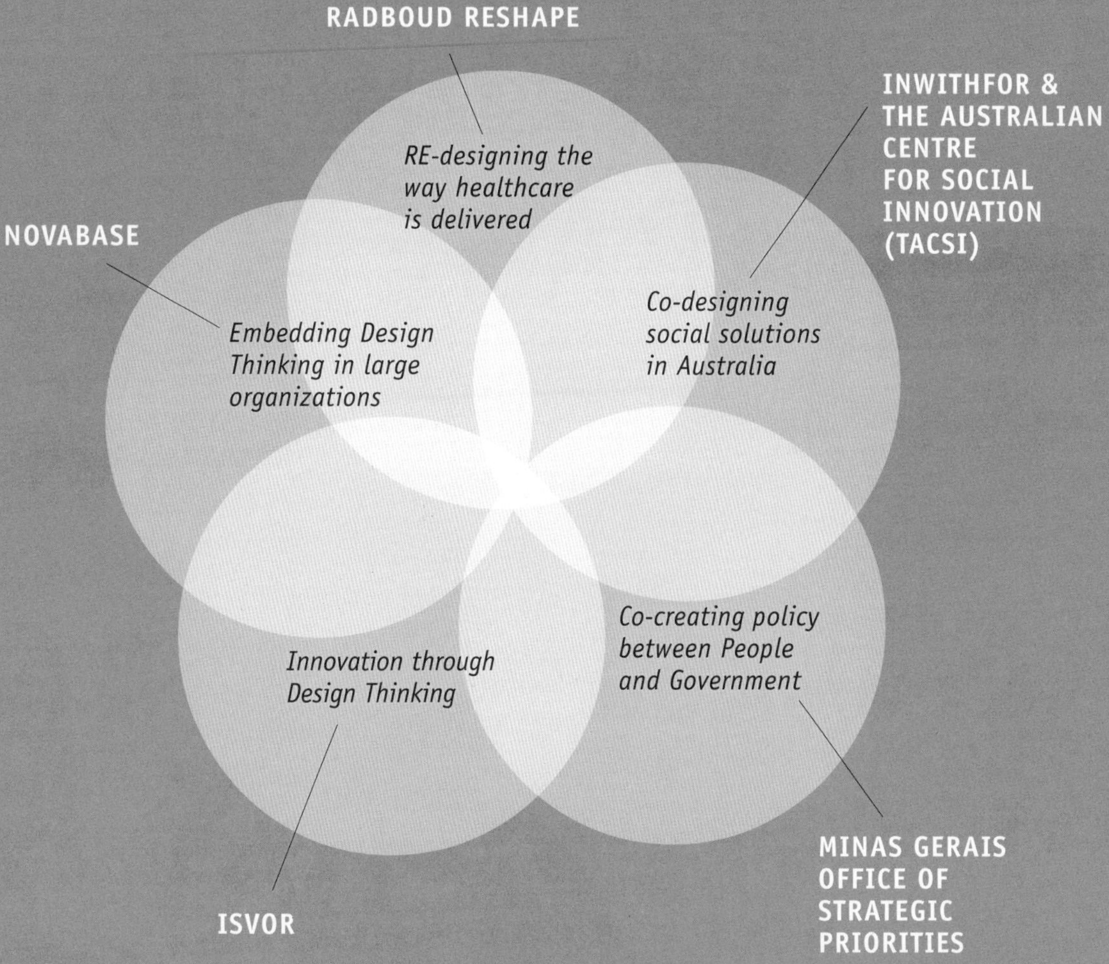

RADBOUD RESHAPE

RE-designing the way healthcare is delivered

INWITHFOR & THE AUSTRALIAN CENTRE FOR SOCIAL INNOVATION (TACSI)

Co-designing social solutions in Australia

NOVABASE

Embedding Design Thinking in large organizations

Co-creating policy between People and Government

Innovation through Design Thinking

MINAS GERAIS OFFICE OF STRATEGIC PRIORITIES

ISVOR

Lisbon | www.novabase.pt

NOVABASE

*Embedding Design Thinking
in Large Organizations*

012. THE DESIGN THINKING METHODOLOGY

Don't wait, do.

Novabase's Transitions

Reinventing the organization

Bringing Design Thinking into Novabase

Embedding Design Thinking at Novabase

Founded in 1989 at a research centre in Lisbon Technical University, Novabase's name translates as 'new database' and derives from the organization's initial core expertise in databases. Today Novabase has over 2,300 employees, an annual turnover of €230 million and offices in locations around the world including Spain, France, Germany, England, Mozambique and Dubai. Pedro Janeiro is Novabase's Head of Business Design, and has been involved in the process of embedding Design Thinking within the organization. Here, Pedro shares the story of Novabase's transition into a Design Thinking organization.

Reinventing the organization

Novabase is the largest IT company in Portugal, with an annual turnover of €230 million. The company has been through a series of dramatic changes since it was first established: growing to a team of 400 people within the first seven years, going public in 2000 during the internet boom, and then being restructured in response to the dot com bubble burst in 2002.

In 2009 Novabase decided to review the business structure again, and revise its positioning in response to market changes. This restructuring involved a review of the organization's culture, values and mission as well as the devising of a new brand. Prior to this the company's internal culture was quite competitive, with everyone competing over clients in order to increase their individual portfolio. Although this culture helped to grow the company, as a working culture it was not entirely people-focused. Novabase wanted to change this culture to become more collaborative. This new vision marked a significant shift, as previously the focus had been on becoming the largest IT company in Portugal. Now the company did not want to be focused solely on its European or global ranking; but rather to build a vision that was focused on people and collaboration.

It is our CEO's view that life is complex, and IT is even more complex – but it doesn't make sense for technology to make our lives more complicated. Our new mission statement represents this vision: 'We make life simpler and happier for people and businesses'. When the new vision was launched, many people in the organization were shocked by the change of direction and, for a while, some of our colleagues had a hard time understanding it. But we knew that, in order to achieve our vision, we needed to change from inside the organization.

When we worked on the brand redesign with a local communication design agency, they came up with an approach and method that they termed 'Design Thinking'. That was our first introduction to the concept. The branding project worked so well that our executive board thought Design Thinking would be the best method to bridge between the old and new incarnations of Novabase. As a result, the senior management team enrolled onto the executive course at Stanford University to learn more about Design Thinking. Our CEO wanted to know how Design Thinking could transform Novabase to be globally competitive, with a distinctive approach and a strong business differentiator. He didn't really know what to make of his experience on completing the course; he found it alien and disruptive compared to his own approaches. He also found it difficult to reconcile his engineering way of thinking, which is very logical and structured, with the more emotional focus of Design Thinking. It had a really strong impact on the way he thought about things, and as a result I was asked to attend the same Stanford course with two of Novabase's other top executives and our Head of Training. When we came back from the course, we reflected that a lot of what we had been doing at Novabase over the past year had involved the type of techniques introduced in the Stanford course – like shadowing users, focusing interviews on emotions, and using photography to capture products and services in a real environment. It was comforting and refreshing to know we had been on the right path.

Bringing Design Thinking into Novabase

When I joined Novabase in 2004, my initial role was to bring a business process

Example of visual prototyping and large scale posters used to visualize and explain project findings with clients

consultancy approach into a company that was largely IT-focused. My background is in management, and I worked as a financial auditor at Coopers and Lybrand and then at Deloitte in business process reengineering. As part of the restructuring exercise the CEO asked me to start a small team, which we called the 'Business Design team', to focus on understanding Design Thinking and testing it in every aspect of our work – from developing new products and services to the way we deliver projects. We took several training courses, but they were really hard to find in Europe, and conferences on the subject were also quite sparse. I placed members of the Business Design team inside small project teams, to make sure we were testing the concepts of Design Thinking in the field in order to really understand how it can be adapted to the world of IT consultancy.

We also did a lot of work with our company's User Experience team, which includes staff from a diverse range of backgrounds, from graphic designers to ergonomists. Those kinds of backgrounds are quite different to the rest of our staff, who mostly have degrees in software engineering. The diversity of experience and skills in these teams led to a successful layering of different disciplinary methods, such as software engineering, user experience and Design Thinking. Brought

together they represent a powerful and innovative approach, very unique to Novabase and highly appreciated by clients – a true competitive advantage.

The User Experience team and my Business Design team have been working together on embedding a user-centred approach within the organization. Clients who are exposed to this approach have been very excited about the outputs of their projects, because they feel refreshing and new. Instead of presenting a 200 page report on how a client's business processes have changed, we used a large 90cm x 280cm poster to visualize and explain our findings, offering the client a very quick overview of the proposed system. Most technical reports are far too complicated for a layperson to understand, and our clients simply do not have the time to read them. The reason a lot of IT projects fail is because companies create these massive and complicated reports that nobody understands. As a result, the final outcome of the project is often compromised and targets missed. That is why we have started producing different kinds of outputs, like large format posters to illustrate concepts and quick software mock-ups in the form of interactive websites to show our clients a rough version of how a system might look. They are able to respond better to these type of cues, and understand what is being proposed, so they can then work with

Examples of the the Do-It-Yourself manual and notebook

us to improve the system iteratively. This has made a huge difference at Novabase as we are now able to work collaboratively with the client at a much earlier stage, getting accurate feedback from the start and engaging in a constant dialogue. However, there is a small price to pay. Design Thinking methods have had to be watered down and adapted to make them more palatable to our staff. The sheer impact of full design approaches proved just too overwhelming, even alien, to our engineers.

Embedding Design Thinking at Novabase
Over time we have also had to work out how to embed Design Thinking into the Novabase culture. Every year we have a company kick-off meeting attended by everyone in a managerial position, about 300 staff in total. An executive who had attended the Stanford boot camp had a crazy idea. Instead of having a one day kick-off meeting, he suggested we run a two day boot camp to teach the top 300 people in our organization what Design Thinking is. It took six weeks for the organization to consider and agree to this. It was risky, as no one had attempted to use this method to train such a large group of people in Design Thinking before. Our boot camp would be four times bigger than anything Stanford had done. It was daunting, but with careful planning we managed to carry out the training successfully.

As a result most of the senior people at Novabase are now aware of Design Thinking. This is important, because it can be difficult to create real change in an organization as large as ours.

When I spoke with Claudia Kotchka, former head of Design Thinking at Procter and Gamble (P&G), she said it took seven years to create a Design Thinking culture there. Although Novabase is smaller, I think it will still probably take us around five years to achieve our ultimate goal. It is difficult because it involves a lot of change management, and changing ways of working. This is what we are finding challenging now, as the Business Design team is quite a small group. We get a few requests to help out internally on projects, business proposals and developing new offers,

The reason a lot of IT projects fail is because companies create these massive and complicated reports that nobody understands.

but we cannot work on three hundred projects at the same time. We can only reach three or four projects every quarter, which only amounts to about one or two percent of the current project workload. Seen in this context, we see that we will never make a wide impact in the company. Suddenly, trying to embed Design Thinking has turned into a change management issue.

We tested many ways of spreading Design Thinking across the organization. Today we understand the importance of ensuring that as many people as possible in the organization are using Design Thinking on a regular basis, because they know that it can make their lives simpler. A lot of what we did in the beginning failed. It was either too different from the company's previous practices, or required sophisticated skills – visual design, meeting facilitation and so on – that are not yet abundant within the organization. So we had to take smaller steps, conquering ground slowly but confidently. We ran a generic Design Thinking training programme across the organization, based on the Stanford bootcamp, and in six months we trained eight hundred people. We continue to run this training as an induction to Design Thinking, and in addition we have developed a 'Do-it-Yourself' manual so that people can see how Design Thinking can be applied, with details, photos and clear descriptions of the approaches. It is in a similar format to a cookbook, with step-by-step instructions accompanied by photos. We are approaching teams before they start working on a new project, to make sure that training will be immediately applied, on the job and in a live project. We are also establishing internal ambassadors for every business unit, people who are trained in using Design Thinking methods for IT. At the end of 2012 we had

probably 40 people who could deliver Design Thinking projects. We still need to train at least fifty more 'internal ambassadors', and this is a hard task. They need to do at least two projects to give them the confidence that these new methods based on Design Thinking are better, and also easy to replicate from project to project.

When we first started embedding Design Thinking in Novabase, one of our initial challenges was a lack of subject awareness in our clients. We had to educate them, and so we organize and run an event called N-Talks designed to introduce our clients to Design Thinking. In order for them to understand what this is, we get them to experience Design Thinking for themselves by going through a series of stages: Empathise, Define, Ideate, Prototype and Test. We invite speakers from diverse subject disciplines to come and share their experiences, and so far we've featured a scientist, a car maker and a paediatrician.

We know it will take time to really embed the culture of Design Thinking into Novabase. To overcome all of the challenges will require a lot more change management than design knowledge, and so we need to combine a lot of the well-proven techniques of change management with Design Thinking approaches. We started by raising awareness within the company, and then went on to create our own Novabase-specific methods. We then set about training and encouraging our staff in the use of those methods. Our next step will be to fully embed all of these approaches and methods into Novabase's working culture. *-end-*

ISVOR's Transitions

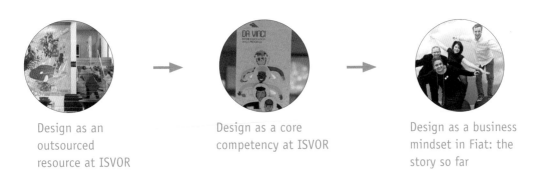

Design as an
outsourced
resource at ISVOR

Design as a core
competency at ISVOR

Design as a business
mindset in Fiat: the
story so far

ISVOR is one of Fiat do Brasil companies, responsible for Corporate Education.
It acts as a Corporate University for the Group in Latin America.

Fiat is an international auto group that designs, produces and sells vehicles for the
mass market under the Fiat, Alfa Romeo, Lancia, Abarth and Fiat Professional brands,
as well as luxury and performance cars under the Ferrari and Maserati brands. The
Group has expanded its global reach through the alliance with Chrysler Group, whose
product portfolio includes Chrysler, Jeep, Dodge, Ram and SRT brand vehicles. Fiat
Group also operates in the components sector, through Magneti Marelli and Teksid,
and in the production systems sector, through Comau. Following the acquisition of
a majority interest in Chrysler, Fiat has accelerated the integration of the two groups
with the objective of becoming a strong and competitive global automaker.

Here Márcia Naves, Superintendent of ISVOR, Denise Eler, Design Mindset
and Sense Making Consultant and Natalia Ribeiro, ISVOR's Design
Intelligence Manager, share the story of how they have embedded design
within ISVOR's mindset.

Design as an outsourced resource at ISVOR

Competitiveness requires increasingly competent persons. Organizations are looking for education activities that can change behavior and promote the critical competences in order to achieve sustainable results. As a corporate university ISVOR doesn't only deliver traditional education to help organizations achieve their goals, but are focused on developing peoples' capability to imagine the future, so they can create and innovate.

Historically, the general level and quality of education in Brazil is low. In addition to this, a lack of investment in the education sector for a number of years has meant that companies have had to invest in developing their staff. ISVOR's methodology starts with an understanding of the organizational cultures, strategic plans, economics scenarios and changing forces as well as the business model. Until 2009 ISVOR did not have an in-house design team working on this process. They only had the Human Resource team and managers using this methodology. Designers were involved just at the end of the process as an outsourced resource.

Design as a core competency at ISVOR

In 2009 Márcia Naves became the Superintendent of ISVOR. She brought her beliefs on protagonism, andragogy, sustainable knowledge, and cross skilling benefits in order to promote the crucial and strategic changes in organizations. With these aims in mind, Márcia invited Denise Eler, a Design Mindset and Sensemaking consultant, to work with ISVOR on building an e-learning department. Denise began to develop a Design Intelligence Team consisting of 20 designers from different design backgrounds, including graphic design, interaction design and computer science. This team started working on new e-learning materials, processes and practices.

ISVOR began to develop Fiat's e-learning materials in automotive-related technical processes, as well as human organizational development and innovation development skills. These are the services that ISVOR currently offer to Fiat, but this offer is always evolving.

Natalia Ribeiro leads the ISVOR Design Intelligence Team and its approach is to focus on developing a genuine understanding of their clients' problems. "To achieve this we first help clients to reframe their problems, by sharing them within the Design Intelligence Team in order to develop a process we can use to arrive at a solution. Usually we invite clients to co-create with us. For instance, a client within Fiat organization wanted to teach the car development process through e-learning material. We initially had to work

We encourage engagement through our designs for both the physical experience and the process of learning, ensuring that people have a pleasurable learning experience.

with them to develop an understanding of the car development process, and then find ways to teach that process in an engaging way that would be relevant to an audience from a diverse range of backgrounds."

But the key challenge in this work was actually to create and nurture a culture of e-learning within that target audience. "We always try to involve clients in the process from the start, if we can. This means making them aware of the design process, and the testing and prototyping of solutions. We find it really helps to get lots of people from across the company together to do this, as collaboration increases our chances of coming up with the right solution."

In the process of developing new e-learning materials, ISVOR also generate many different insights into how learning can be improved. "We encourage engagement through our designs for both the physical experience and the process of learning, ensuring that people have a pleasurable learning experience. We also realized that we could offer different types of products beyond e-learning materials, and began considering how we might improve learner engagement using different kinds

of media and methodologies. Over time we found ourselves not just delivering training material, but developing design processes to help our clients share their own information and come up with new innovative ideas."

The results brought by Design Thinking to the educational processes motivated Marcia to invite Denise to share this mindset with the ISVOR's leaders, its stakeholders, clients and partners. And so, in 2009, ISVOR made the conscious choice to become a design-driven company focused on embedding visual language, co-creation, sensemaking, prototyping and experience design into the creative process as a way of solving educational and organizational problems. From this point, they encouraged people to be more creative, adopt an open mindset and to solve problems from different perspectives. As a result, ISVOR has started to offer new methodologies to encourage this to happen and help people face current challenges. This approach can be seen in action at the entrance to the ISVOR offices where art installations have been installed to encourage staff, customers, students, partners and visitors to question their surroundings.

Art installations at the entrance to the ISVOR offices

Design as a business mindset at Fiat: the story so far

In 2010 ISVOR's new design-driven approach captured the attention of Paulo Matos, the Innovation and Methodology supervisor at Fiat Automóveis. Paulo is responsible for leveraging innovative culture at Fiat, and he knew that it was important to engage staff in co-creating approaches to implement Fiat's strategic vision. Paulo believes in more than technical innovation – he also considers learning and communication to be key to innovation. In order to realize his strategic vision Paulo wanted to find new ways of building connections between the people within Fiat, rather than taking the usual innovation approach of connecting Fiat with external suppliers, universities and government agencies. The aim was for ISVOR's Team to co-create an Innovation strategy with Fiat's management team, to maintain the company's competitiveness in the growing Brazilian market. Paulo felt that strategic conversations were required around 3 key areas: (a) Current challenges and opportunities, (b) How Fiat could be better structured to enable innovation, and (c) Internal culture.

Discussions between Paulo Matos and Denise Eler centred around co-creation and the concept of 'sensemaking' – a critical skill that precedes strategy – and ultimately led us to communicate Fiat's vision internally through Design Thinking workshops. From a Design Thinking viewpoint, strategy is work in progress. Corporate education is a living system that can train people to further their careers, and to perform the transformations necessary to support the viability of business strategies in a sustainable manner. ISVOR believes in a process of continuous training, which exposes people to new knowledge and experiences. Denise's highlights this by

Corporate education is a living system that can train people to further their careers, and to perform the transformations necessary to support the viability of business strategies in a sustainable manner.

commenting "design is a mental model that enables us to realize a vision of the future, and provides us with the tools to make sense of chaos. Sensemaking and imagination are the key design skills that can lead to improvement in leadership and business results" (refer to ISVOR's Design Process diagram).

For ISVOR's Design Intelligence Team, moving into the Design Thinking space meant a transition away from the design of e-training programmes delivered to individuals, and towards the design of experiences and processes that support collaboration and aid conversations at a strategic level. Their team are still using the same approach, but the customers and partners have become much more involved and they are now co-creating with them. "Finding ways to communicate a concept and make it come alive is an important part of our role. For example, if we wanted to explore new market forces we would get everyone in the workshop to think about how those market forces are going to impact Brazil as a country. We would then facilitate conversations around how Fiat might respond to these challenges, by drawing out the company's strengths and looking for new opportunities. Finally, we analyze the learning derived from this process and communicate the outcomes back to our client."

The Design Thinking workshops format engages a diverse range of people to understand a current situation, be open-minded and think differently about the future. ISVOR have been central to the development and communication of Fiat's Innovation strategy across the company in Brazil, as well as the engagement of the company's staff in important strategic conversations.

In addition to supporting Paulo Matos in the development and dissemination of Fiat's Innovation strategy, ISVOR's Design Intelligence Team were involved in translating that vision into action. This involved exploring new approaches to business modelling and cultural development. To achieve this they created a new educational experience called the Da Vinci programme (www.programadavinci.com.br). This is a

series of products and services designed to promote a culture of innovation within the company. Specifically, they were designed to help people be more creative and support them in developing an open mindset, and take responsibility for innovation. The core of the Da Vinci programme is design, which brings with it a unique capability to explore human needs. "For example, we improved on Fiat's existing Innovation Workshops by offering Da Vinci Open Mind experiences such as Da Vinci Convida, where renowned creatives like Deborah Colker, (a Brazilian choreographer, founder and creator of the OVO spectacles of the Cirque du Soleil) share their vision of the creative process with ISVOR customers and partners. By adopting a design mindset people are encouraged to ask different kinds of questions, which are more relevant to a growing economy. We can already see a difference in the Fiat staff who have participated in the Da Vinci programme – they are much more likely to consider future issues, and to seek out collaboration across different departments."

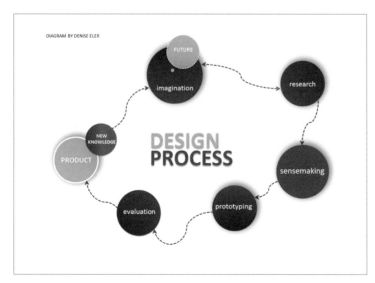

DIAGRAM BY DENISE ELER

FUTURE
imagination
research
NEW KNOWLEDGE
PRODUCT
DESIGN PROCESS
sensemaking
evaluation
prototyping

ISVOR's Design Process

ISVOR has learnt (and are still learning) how to spot new opportunities, and build new skills and knowledge in order to improve its offerings. The main challenge is to share the design mindset and innovation across Fiat Group.

The ISVOR Team has also worked with Paulo to explore future opportunities for Fiat, through designing and hosting two-hour workshops with small groups from across the plant. They designed the process and experience of the workshop, and also facilitated

people to engage in conversations around selected topics, leading to the generation of a lot of new ideas. In essence, they designed an innovation methodology to systemise the creative process. "We always include fun and relaxing activities within our workshops, as a way of getting people to step outside their comfort zone. For example, in one workshop we asked a top chef to demonstrate the process of creating his food as an icebreaker activity. We find that unusual activities like this can become platforms for great conversation."

As well as teaching ISVOR how to design a network inside Fiat, the workshops have also led to the team designing networks between Fiat and the outside world. In 2012 they created an inspirational event at ISVOR to engage Fiat leadership in a dialogue around the Fiat MIO project. Fiat MIO (which translates to My Fiat) is the first ever crowdsourced car, created using an open design process.

The Da Vinci Programme is aimed at promoting a culture of innovation in Fiat

Fiat Mio team

The future of ISVOR and Fiat

ISVOR has learnt (and are still learning) how to spot new opportunities, and build new skills and knowledge in order to improve its offerings. The main challenge is to share the design mindset and innovation across Fiat Group.

In 2012 ISVOR won the Premio Qualitas award, for being Fiat's best supplier based on the work they have done to date. ISVOR were recognized for helping Fiat staff to think differently about the future, and for supporting them to take responsibility for their actions. This is a prestigious award, and difficult to obtain – further proof of the impact ISVOR's Design Thinking approach has made at Fiat. "We have seen firsthand how design approaches can result in the generation of greater sales and profit, but our work is really about helping Fiat to innovate. With digital technologies improving at an exponential rate, cycles of industrial innovation will become shorter and innovation itself will become a commodity. Innovation is not just about product; it's about how you prepare your people to be innovators. At the moment the focus is on quality, but this does not allow room for failure and making mistakes. To innovate you must fail often but learn quickly from it; and to change mindsets you must

Innovation is not just about product; it's about how you prepare your people to be innovators.

embed a culture of innovation. This is a big challenge, and to meet it you need people who view problems holistically and are able to ask lots of new and challenging questions. This takes a lot of effort but, in the long term, will prove worthwhile." ~end~

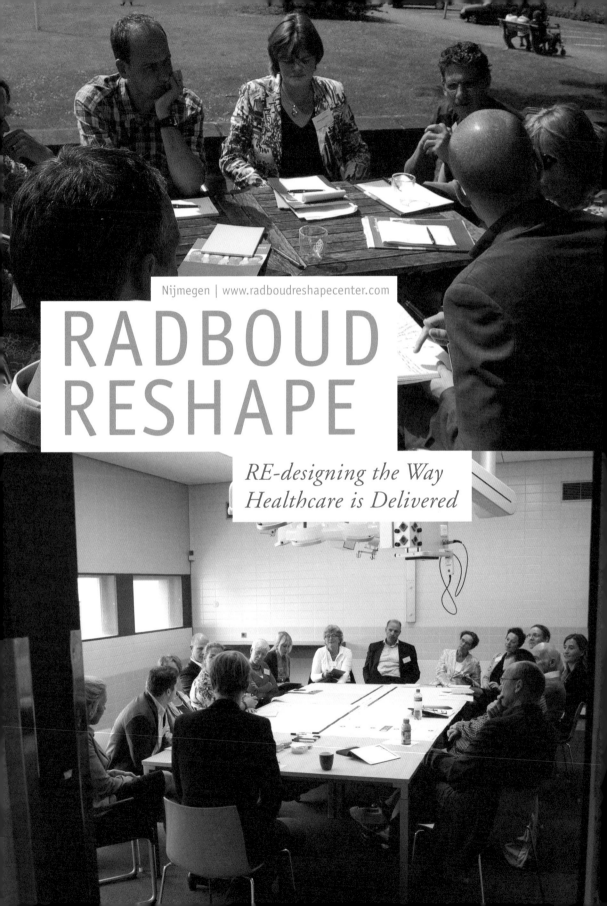

Nijmegen | www.radboudreshapecenter.com

RADBOUD RESHAPE

RE-designing the Way Healthcare is Delivered

Radboud REshape's Transitions

The REshape
Programme

Co-creating easy
to use products

Patients as Partners

Radboud University Medical Centre (RUMC) is one of The Netherland's largest medical university with over 11,000 researchers, doctors and nurses, located in the city of Nijmegen. The REshape programme was set up in 2010 as part of RUMC, in order to change the way healthcare is delivered by focusing on patient-centred care and bringing healthcare innovations into practice. Following this, the Radboud REshape & Innovation Center was then set up to bring together projects and initiatives happening through the REshape programme. We spoke with Lucien Engelen, the centre's founding director about REshape's aims, and the challenges of 'redesigning' healthcare and promoting a patient-centred focus.

A vision of a patient-centred healthcare

I became involved with Radboud University Medical Centre (RUMC) after I was appointed the Head of Regional Emergency Healthcare Networks and Advisory to the executive board in 2007, as part of the organizational restructuring that was happening at RUMC at the time. The intention of the reorganization was to enact a cultural shift that would involve the voice of the patient, and my role at that time was to help realize that vision of creating patient-centred healthcare.

I often talk to researchers in our facility and ask them why they do what they do. Their answers tend to be: 'Because I am a researcher'. They have completely lost their connection to the larger aim of improving healthcare for people, which is what Radboud was set up to do as an academic medical centre. Somehow we have lost our connection to people. This is not just the case with researchers, but also with doctors, nurses and other frontline staff. Of course there are exceptions, and although some of my colleagues have not completely lost this connection, many do not see the 'human' in the patients – only the diseases that they carry. The patient's voice gets lost in amongst bureaucracy and budgetary constraints, which lead to time limitations for each consultation. All these factors reinforce the current culture, and reduce the chances of us doing things differently. It is always going to be easier to comply with the current system than to change it. This is the reason we feel it is important to create project champions, who can provide a platform from which to bring in new patient-centric practices.

The REshape programme

My first few years at RUMC were spent focussing on developing new innovations for the Acute Healthcare area, and getting to know the organization. During that time I started to discover how we might use new technology to change things, if we could find a win-win situation for both healthcare professionals and patients. A lot of the projects that we set up at that time became successful, and this convinced us that a more structural approach was needed. As a result an embedded REshape programme was proposed in October 2010, with a strategic plan that uses innovation to introduce a patient-focused mindset throughout the different departments of RUMC.

Initially there were three strands to this plan. Firstly, we would make and implement products. And so, as a vehicle for our healthcare reforms we are scouting, inventing and sharing innovations at an international level, and creating a network around this area. So far we have successfully developed and launched four projects that are available for the public to use through our website at www.radboudreshapecenter.com/portfolio.

The second strand of our plan involved educating our students and staff. As part of this work we have started the Radboud REshape Academy, consisting of eight

Almost 90 per cent of e-health innovations fail due to usability problems, because the user (or patient) is rarely consulted.

One of the REshape Masterclasses session

Masterclass courses that touch upon all the different aspects of the changing face of healthcare. These courses are open for anyone to attend, and the Academy was set up to accelerate the development of participatory healthcare with the mission of 'Patient as Partner'. The topics of the Masterclasses are based on knowledge, experiences, discussions, and questions that arise in our everyday work, and from people in our network. We ran eight Masterclasses in 2012 on topics including Patients as Partners, E-heath = Empowered Health, ICT for Healthcare and Participatory Health Education. These events served as a prelude to the curriculum revision of the Bachelors degree delivered by our Medical School, and also the subsequent revision of our Masters programme.

The third strand of our plan involved setting up events and conferences to bring people together and share ideas. These include the annual REshape conferences, which began in 2009 and are focused on the topic of Health 2.0. These conferences then led to much larger international conferences, such as TEDx Maastricht and Medicine 2.0 and others (TEDxRadboudU and TEDxNijmegen). At a smaller level, we also organized PechaKucha™ events every few months to share insights and make connections locally.

We have now grown the REshape programme to include several extra strands running concurrently, such as our research section, an incubator which acts as a meeting place for innovation, and also a games lab.

Co-creating easy to use products

What we are trying to do with our innovation programme is develop products that use everyday technology in an easy way. A lot of products invented in the healthcare field are far too complicated. One of the best examples of a good product – which I am currently using myself – is a weighing scale with a built-in transmitter. Whenever I weigh myself, it sends my weight for the day to my personal webpage via wifi. My GP can then access the information via my webpage, to monitor how well I am looking after my weight. My data is also automatically added to his patient system database, as he has chosen to subscribe to it. This seamless transfer of data on a daily basis is happening automatically, without any additional action on my part. We currently ask our patients in the cardiology department to come in once a week to have their weight and blood pressure taken. By making these devices, easy to use, we have the opportunity to engage our patients by offering them more control over their own life – as well as reducing

TEDx Maastrict Conference

the number of visits they have to make to the hospital. If we want to we can offer lots of this type of technology, but we have to make it incredibly simple to use. Almost 90 per cent of e-health innovations fail due to usability problems, because the user (or patient) is rarely consulted. That is the reason why, for every project that we embark on, we always ensure that there is an identifiable patient need for that product, rather than blindly following a false premise.

All of our projects are based on co-creation. We have now run over 25 projects, and up to 75 per cent of those project outcomes have been completely different from the original idea put forward by the medical staff, due to consultation with patients. These projects have been highly appreciated and used by patients and their families, as well as their informal carers. Every project starts with a 'pitch' from someone who had identified a problem or found a possible solution. Firstly we have to decide if there is a problem and, if so, whether it is worth investigating. Then we involve different stakeholders, which might include patients, their carers, family members, our medical staff, IT staff and finance people coming together to define the problem.

Patients are incorporated into the process from the beginning, and are involved throughout as stakeholders experiencing the process.

One of our project examples is *AED4.US*, a crowdsourced website and smartphone application that shows the exact locations of defibrillators in the Netherlands. It is important to get the heart back to a rhythm within the first six minutes of a cardiac arrest in order to improve the chances of survival. Although there are an estimated 20,000 defibrillator devices (AED) in use in the Netherlands, there is no way of finding out where these devices are located locally. The aim of the website is to enable a global overview of where these devices are located and available to use, if needed. Anyone is able to add the location of a publicly available device, whether there are trained volunteers on location and, if so, how to contact them. Since its launch in 2009 there have been 18,500 registered AED devices added to the platform, and the app have been downloaded over 250,000 times.

Patients as partners
Healthcare has been delivered in the same way for the past two hundred years. Nothing has changed apart from the doctors, nurses and medication. The only aspect that has changed significantly is that we no longer deliver healthcare to people in their homes. A hundred years ago we had a network of doctors visiting patients in their houses. Over time, healthcare has moved out of the home to being delivered through institutions. This is what I call an 'ego' system, where patients have to place themselves in hospitals to receive care. We are trying to reverse this situation, and over the next ten years we hope to bring healthcare back into the home by using technology as part of the healthcare eco-system. E-health is one example of this, using social media to

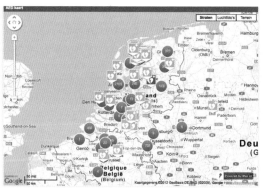

AED4.US is a crowdsourced website and smartphone application that collects the exact location of publicly available defibrillators throughout The Netherlands

provide a channel of communication that is helping us to remobilize healthcare.

I like to use the analogy of the banking service. We have become 'employees' of the bank, taking on activities that 20 years ago they would have been doing for us. In the past banks provided services such as money transfer and cash withdrawal. Now we are the ones enacting the money transfer, checking bank balances and organizing transfers via the internet. I expect that healthcare will move along the same lines. This might mean that, in ten or fifteen years time, patients and their carers may be able to do even more for themselves.

Healthcare has been delivered in the same way for the past two hundred years. Nothing has changed apart from the doctors, nurses and medication.

Our goal is to treat patients as our partners, and we would like to be partners to our patients. This means that we are no longer trying to change the workflow of patients to suit our system. It is not simply about changing the doctor's processes to suit the patient, rather that we need to design a process that will benefit both sides. For example, my weighing machine example saves time for the GP but also helps the patient to have more control over their own care. This is a process of co-production.

We are trying to bring healthcare services back to peoples' communities and neighbourhoods. We are starting with outpatient clinics opening up in different towns and neighbourhood. To achieve this vision requires planning, scheduling, technology, different communication but – most importantly – a mind shift. This is our long-term vision, and we believe it will be the saviour of healthcare. To reflect this, we have changed our tagline and incorporated our most mission statement of 'Patients as Partners' in all of our strategic plans.

The way our projects and programme are being run and implemented is what I would define as 'service design'. Service design is a toolbox that comes with different techniques and different people that you can bring into your process. The analogy I would use is that service design is one of the tools in our Swiss army knife. We may be using design tools in an implicit rather than explicit manner, but the toolset will vary over time and is dependent on which stage the project is at. We aim to train our staff in using this service design toolbox, and we are trying to upscale that model but our biggest current challenge is to try to shift the organizational mindset.

The most important thing we do at the start of our projects is listen to the patient. Although that may seem obvious, it has never been done in healthcare. In 2010, I appointed our first CLO, or Chief Listening Officer, and we have recently won the 2012 Hostmanship Award, meaning that eight thousand medical professionals deemed our work to be 'groundbreaking'. Of course we are proud, but I also found this to be very bizzare. At Radboud we just assume that talking to patients is part of the process, and I would not really describe what we do as being distinct from service design. To me, it is just the way that services should always be considered and designed. It still amazes me at how uncommon the practice of talking to patients is when developing healthcare services. That is the reason why I set up the Patient Included Act, which enables conference organizers to self-certify the fact they actually have patients included in their programme. For us including the patient is normal practice, but throughout healthcare our approach actually seems to be the exception rather than the norm. That's why it is great to see how worldwide healthcare conferences are now following our example.

Challenges in delivering patient-centred healthcare

We are currently nowhere near our goal of creating a patient-centric organizational shift. Depending on which research you refer to, changes in healthcare take at least seven and up to seventeen years to enact. We are trying to first raise awareness before attempting to REshape our organizational mindset. What we observe and feel is that there is a force of patients wanting to be included in the development of their healthcare, and this is driving a lot of our initiatives in unexpected ways. The growth of exponential technology has helped move our project forward. For example, we now have the ability for patients to be actively involved in their recovery by enabling them to monitor their own data.

However, the resistance from a lot of the medical staff has been stronger than we initially anticipated. This opposing force somewhat neutralizes the progress we make through the other factors of patient support and technological growth. We will never achieve 100 per cent buy-in from all of the staff, but if you were to ask me when we would have more than 50 per cent of the staff moving with us towards this aim? I would say we are three to five years away. Although there are a lot of departments completely aligned with this aim, and many others heading in the right direction, the main indicator of a successful shift to patient-centred healthcare will come from the patients. They have to actually see and experience the shift before we know if we have achieved what we set out to do.

At present I estimate that we have achieved buy-in with only 10 per cent of the staff, so there is still a lot of work to do. For example, e-Health (in which the 'e' is not electronic but empowered) will take us longer to implement,

The most important thing we do at the start of our projects is listen to the patient. Although that may seem obvious, it has never been done in healthcare.

but the impact will be much higher. The speed of acceptance is often overestimated, but the impact it can make is enormously underestimated, as it will completely change the way healthcare is delivered.

When we started the REshape programme, the most important aspect was to consider what we were trying to achieve and why. It seems to be the one question that is not asked often enough. It made sense that in my first TEDx conference in April 2011, I delivered my talk right after Simon Sinek's opening speech in which he described his Golden Circle framework. In the talk he described how the Golden Circle framework (which he developed) is entirely focused on understanding the 'why', and why trust has to be in place if we actually want to do something. This focus on the 'why', along with our use of Design Thinking and our interactions with Arne van Oosterom of DesignThinkers Group (see their story on page 92), has helped us define our vision of doing things differently in healthcare.

So far we have been successful in setting up our strategic plan for Radboud, and describing what we would like to achieve and why. We now need to work out how to scale this approach. Our first challenge is to shift the mindset of our 11,000 organizational colleagues, but we recognize that this will take time and cannot be achieved overnight. As part of this continuing effort we have been working with four healthcare chains during 2013, to re-design their services from a patient's point of view. We are doing this by applying Design Thinking and common sense and, most importantly for us, by consulting with patients – since they are the real experts in managing and living with their conditions.

-end-

Adelaide | www.tacsi.org.au

INWITHFOR
&TACSI

Co-designing Social Solutions in Australia

INWITHFOR & TACSI's Transitions

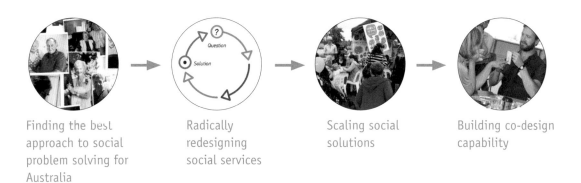

Finding the best approach to social problem solving for Australia

Radically redesigning social services

Scaling social solutions

Building co-design capability

Social design has been used in the UK since the early 2000s (for example see thinkpublic's case study on page 52 and Uscreates snapshot on page 72). This has contributed to a growing evidence base that design can add value to social problem solving, creating new solutions to seemingly intractable problems. The Australian Centre for Social Innovation (TACSI) has been pioneering the use of co-design alongside a number of other disciplines since 2010, bringing a new approach to social problem solving by finding bold ideas that lead to better lives. Chris Vanstone is Director of Co-design at TACSI, Co-founder of InWithFor, and was formerly a member of the RED team at the UK Design Council and London-based social business Participle. Chris speaks to us about TACSI's co-design approach, and how it addresses social challenges to create meaningful value for people, communities, service providers and the government in Australia.

The coming together of TACSI and InWithFor

InWithFor was founded in 2009 to develop new kinds of solutions to big social challenges like educational disengagement, repeat offending, unemployment, chronic disease and ageing. From the outset we wanted to develop a hybrid process for solving social problems, a process that would blend design practice with the rigour and knowledge of social science. Prior to co-founding InWithFor I'd been part of too many design-led projects that engaged people but did not fit within existing policy contexts. Meanwhile Sarah Schulman, my co-founder, had been involved in many projects which created new policies that did little to impact upon people's lives.

As we were starting InWithFor in London UK, TACSI (then led by Brenton Caffin) was starting up in Adelaide, Australia. Brenton was looking to build a team to 'Radically Redesign' social services in Australia. This aligned really well with InWithFor's aims – and so I ended up in Australia working at TACSI, and I now lead a team that co-designs radical new social solutions and builds organizations' capabilities to adopt the co-design approach.

Finding the best approach to social problem solving for Australia

In its early years, TACSI was weighing up alternative approaches to creating social change. We ran the million dollar *Bold Ideas, Better Lives* challenge, which identified and supported promising social innovations in Australia. We also explored the potential for adopting innovations from other countries for application in Australia, and started our first Radical Redesign project, *The Family Project*.

The Family Project started with the question, 'How can we enable more families to thrive, and fewer to come into contact with child

Design brings a repeatable process to social problem solving at scale. As a process it provides the scaffolding for diverse disciplines, as well as users, providers and policy makers, to come together and collaborate.

protection services?' We were joined by a secondee from child protection services, Carolyn Curtis, who now runs *Family by Family* and is Acting CEO of TACSI. We undertook 12 months of work with over 100 families to co-design and develop *Family by Family*, a new peer-to-peer solution that supports families who have been through tough times to make the changes they want in their lives. These changes may be getting out of the house more, making new friends, getting on better as a family or, for migrant families, getting a better understanding of Australian culture. *Family by Family* is open to any and all families who want to make a change.

It has been three years since we started *The Family Project* and it has been very successful. In our first year over 90 per cent of families reached the goals they set themselves, and our initial cost-benefit analysis suggests that every dollar invested in *Family by Family* saves between seven and nine dollars, by preventing children being removed from their families. Due to the success of *Family by Family* as a solution that was co-designed with families, the enthusiasm for this approach has placed co-design at the core of TACSI's work.

Design brings a repeatable process to social problem solving at scale. As a process it provides the scaffolding for diverse disciplines, as well as users, providers and policy makers, to come together and collaborate. As a good design approach is grounded in reality, the bullshit does not last long. You can have amazing theories, beautiful frameworks, elegantly designed things and great business ideas, but when you try them out in context you quickly learn that they may not be as promising as they once seemed. It is a humbling process, because it forces all of us to recognize that, when it comes to what creates change, we are more often wrong than right.

Radically redesigning social services

We often talk about our co-design approach as 'working backwards'. Our projects work in the opposite direction to most policy development, because we start by understanding people. We work out what would create change for people, and only then do we go on to create systems and structures that can allow new solutions to spread. Our process has four stages, that are currently called Look, Create, Prototype and Grow.

In the Look phase we spend time with people experiencing social challenges, and those who have come through those challenges. We call this second group the 'positive deviants', and we use ethnographic methods and guided interviews to learn from them what is already enabling change in their particular communities. Our solutions are then often inspired by creating similar kinds of enablers for people who do not already have them in place. So, this first phase is really about redefining the starting question and getting some hunches around potential solutions.

The second phase, Create, is about developing ideas for new solutions that could enable change at scale. We try to co-design at every stage of the process, developing our ideas with people in the situation, practitioners who might be working in that area, policy makers and leaders. Everyone comes on the journey, and by the end of it we have a pretty good idea about who would be involved in the solution, how to make it attractive to them, how resources would flow and how that solution would scale.

The third Prototyping phase is about trying out a small version of the solution in real life with real people. Prototyping helps us

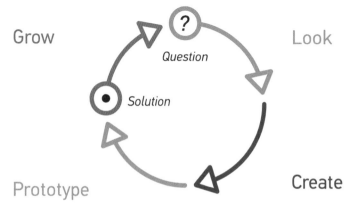

Grow

? Question

Look

Solution

Prototype

Create

TACSI's Co-design approach

Family by Family programme recruitment, measurement and programme website

refine our hunches about what works for people. It can be a really frustrating stage of the process, as most of what we try out doesn't work well at first. We prioritize the prototyping of interactions that create change for people, before prototyping the systems that are needed to support those interactions at scale – like training and policies. At the end of the prototype we develop a Runbook for the solution. This is an interactive blueprint that documents how the new solution works, scene by scene, touchpoint by touchpoint. Typically our solutions consist of over a hundred scenes and over a hundred touchpoints. For each of these we document how to run or use it, and also the hunches that have informed its development.

Another important part of prototyping is the case for growth. Using our initial hunches about the change, we can calculate the cost of running the solution to create a financial case for investment. We also use documentary films that capture user and practitioner experiences of the prototype, and these create more of an emotional case for investing in something different.

The fourth phase of our process, Grow, is about getting the solution into the real world, usually in partnership with other organizations. In the case of *Family by Family*, the Grow phase meant starting a new enterprise, which TACSI currently incubates.

We are continuing to iterate the parts of the solution that still need development, but now that the model is less in a state of flux we can start to measure the social impact it is creating. Measuring this is often key to further growth.

Our approach to measuring the social impact of a solution is dependent on its context. As much as we can, we build measurement into the core of the solution so we do not have to create too many extra evaluation scenes. As with everything else, we prototype our evaluation to be sure that it makes sense and has value to people. In *Family by Family*, our prototype involved the families naming their goals and then using stickers to measure progress. Alongside this we do a follow-up evaluation to get a more objective view on the change we have created.

Scaling social solutions

When it comes to co-designing for social impact, two things are really important to get right: the stuff that creates the change, and the stuff that enables that change to spread in and beyond a particular community. Our ambition with *Family by Family* has always been vast. The aim is to enable more Australian families to thrive, and there are a lot more families that we still want to reach. The challenge is to spread the solution to new communities without losing any of its fidelity. That is a challenge we expect to face in a very real way, given that we expect to start *Family by Family* in another state in the next year. *Family by Family* is not the first family support programme, but what makes it different is the details of the interaction – those hundreds of scenes and touchpoints that have been designed. Whilst it is tempting to grow faster, we really need to grow at a pace that will allow us to prototype the scoping processes, training, support and quality assurance systems. This will enable us to deliver *Family by Family* in different states as well as in South Australia, keeping the most important elements of that solution in place so that the programme continues to create good outcomes for families.

The important thing is to design into the solution a means to adapt to local context. We have seen the importance of that when spreading *Family by Family* within Adelaide. The first *Family by Family* site was based in the south of Adelaide and our second site is in the north, just a 45 minute drive away. Through spending time with families in the North before we started the programme, we quickly realized that copying what we had done in the south wasn't going to work for them. The geographical and cultural differences were too significant, even in a relatively homogenous city like Adelaide. By using this same kind of adaptation process we hope that one day *Family by Family* could even grow beyond Australia.

Building co-design capability

A conundrum for TACSI in the early years was whether to focus on developing solutions, or scaling the co-design approach behind those solutions. Initially we focused on developing and scaling the solutions. Now, after increasing interest from organizations who want to use co-design, we are focusing on both spreading our solutions and building the capabilities of other organizations through workshops and mentoring. We recognize that TACSI alone cannot address all the social challenges facing Australia, so we want to see other organizations adopting the co-design approach and enabling more Australians to thrive.

We have tried out bits of capability building in the past, but didn't always have the best experiences. We did a project with a government department and, whilst we were able to build the co-design capability of the people on the ground to do things like ethnography, the bureaucracy of the organization was focused on systems outcomes around efficiency. So although we were able to build capability in the methodology, the bigger ideology was not aligned. The result was an on-the-ground team unable to put their new capabilities into practice, a senior team that had a project that did not fit with its overall strategy, and lots of useful learning about opportunities to enable outcomes for families that still remains unpublished.

We prioritize the prototyping of interactions that create change for people, before prototyping the systems that are needed to support those interactions at scale – like training and policies.

Now we are taking a much more rigorous approach to the development of training and support services for organizations. That means being more realistic about what it takes to build capability, being more intentional with our curriculum, recognizing that to adopt a new approach requires change at all levels of an organization, simplifying how we talk about our work and developing ways to measure the change we create, as well as getting better at spotting organizations ready to adopt and sustain a co-design approach.

Embracing co-design requires organizations to make a shift in culture, and not all of them are ready to make that shift doing things to people to doing things with them, from providing answers to asking questions, and from ensuring success at all cost to embracing failure. Spreading co-design will mean supporting organizations to make a fundamental shift in how their decision making is driven.

You can see the beginnings of this shift in the proliferation of strategies with names like 'customer first' and 'people at the centre' – but organizational practice rarely matches intent. Surveys and consultations, the tools most typically employed to put people at the centre, simply do not achieve this. Most of the people I meet through in-home interviews or ethnographic studies do not complete surveys or go to public consultations. They have more pressing things in their lives, and literacy, cultural or self-esteem issues often get in the way. If someone does not have the confidence

to leave their home, how can they be expected to turn up to a town hall meeting and make their point in a crowded room?

For organizations with a culture of avoiding risk, the idea of deliberately embracing failure (albeit at a small scale) can seem perverse, unprofessional, and a wasteful public relations challenge. The reality is that prototyping can save time and money by identifying what does not work at a small scale, before things that do work are scaled and spread. Because of the emphasis on meeting people and trying things out in their context, co-design can give a voice to the people who stand to benefit most from innovation in services, and provide a way for them to work with professionals to influence the shape of their services.

Alongside the principles, project stages, methods and tools, we also need to create team and organizational cultures that support co-design. One of the most important aspects of our work is the diversity within our teams. The members of our 'design' team are drawn from very different backgrounds in design, social science, business, and community development, and each brings their own unique perspective. Social science is good at helping us to understand what creates change. Design is good at developing things that are attractive to people and work for them. Business thinking helps us develop solutions that are sustainable and have a model for growth, and community development expertise helps us engage people in the first place. As

Workshops to build participants' capabilities in the use of co-design

Care Reflect project

Weavers project: Volunteers with caring experience training to become weavers

well as this, we deliberately draw on diverse experts and sources of inspiration in order to supplement our learning. Such diversity can bring challenging questions, such as: How do you strive for highest quality outputs, but still get things done within time and on budget? How do you create a culture that believes in rigour, but also where it is acceptable to fail? How do you find a way for people from very different disciplines and with different world views to share, communicate and recognize what each can bring to the table? At TACSI we have worked hard to develop a common view of what great work looks like and to build some common skills, such as basic visualizing, and to provide opportunities for people to teach classes or run sessions that draw on their particular expertise.

Where next for TACSI?

As a centre of innovation TACSI will keep searching for new approaches that can improve outcomes for Australians, but right now we are focused on co-design. This means focussing on the co-design of new peer-to-peer solutions, and using co-design to continually adapt and improve them. It also includes building the capability of other organizations to do co-design, and strengthening the co-design and social innovation community within Australia.

Since prototyping *Family by Family* we have gone on to apply our co-design approach in the areas of ageing and caring, developing six new solutions – two of which, *Weavers* and *Care Reflect*, we have taken into prototype. *Weavers* aims to spread a new type of volunteer role, a kind of midwife for caring – whilst *Care Reflect* is an in-system solution that enabled a new kind of peer support between paid care workers. We are now trying to take *Weavers* and *Care Reflect* into a start-up phase. Now that *Family by Family* has been at start-up stage for a couple of years and has some proven outcomes, we are looking at growing it within South Australia and spreading it to other states. For me, in my new role as Director of Co-design, I will be overseeing our design activities in start-ups and projects and helping to develop a new suite of offers to help organizations build their co-design capability. One day, I hope to be taking the co-design approach and learning experiences we have honed at TACSI in Australia, back to the UK and Europe. *-end-*

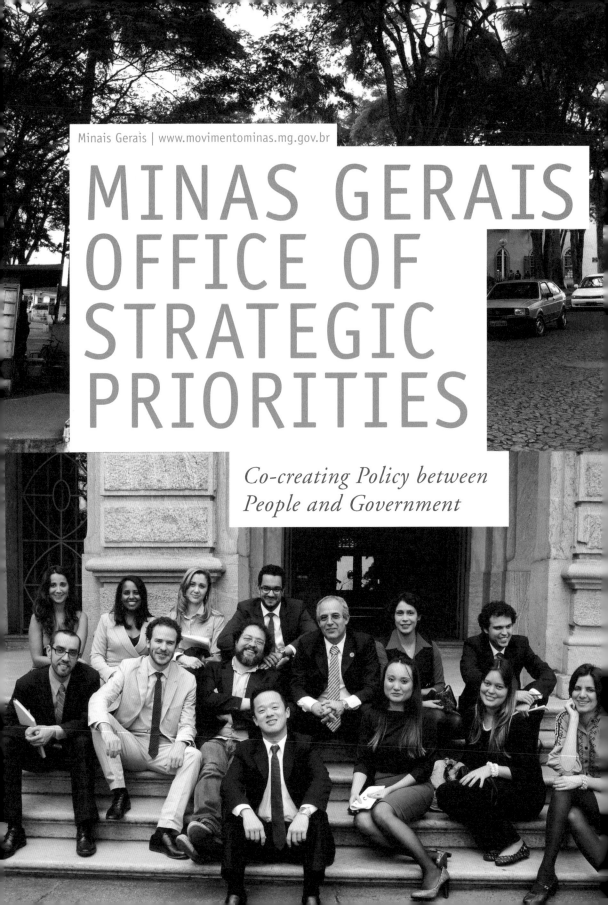

Minais Gerais | www.movimentominas.mg.gov.br

MINAS GERAIS OFFICE OF STRATEGIC PRIORITIES

Co-creating Policy between People and Government

Minas Gerais OSP's Transitions

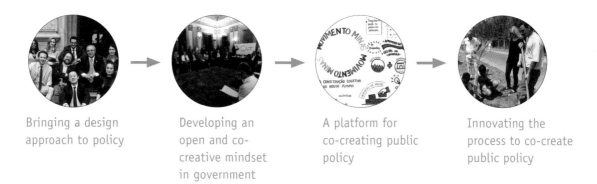

Bringing a design approach to policy

Developing an open and co-creative mindset in government

A platform for co-creating public policy

Innovating the process to co-create public policy

Minas Gerais is the second most populated state in Brazil, contributing the third largest GDP for the country. The Minas Gerais Office of Strategic Priorities is located in the state's capital city of Belo Horizonte, and in July 2011 they formed *Movimento Minas* or the 'Minas Movement'. The programme is focused on using open innovation and policy crowdsourcing to foster a more collaborative government, and draws on design and systems thinking approaches to co-create public policy. We interviewed André Barrence, Director and CEO of the Office, who has a background in economics, law and public administration; and Caio Werneck, Public Manager, who has a background in evaluation and monitoring of public projects. André and Caio gave us insights into the work of *Movimento Minas* and how it is bringing people and government together.

Bringing a design approach to policy

We work in the office of Strategic Priorities in the Minas Gerais government. The main role and purpose of our department is to cooperate with other governmental agencies to deliver better results, by providing information, innovative management tools and human resources.

Although André and I do not come from a design background, we have come to admire how design can place things into different perspectives for different people and be used for something far beyond the making of desirable objects. We agreed that a lot of the problems in the Minas Gerais government should be approached like a blank canvas, rather than being hampered by existing structures. We saw a need to merge disciplines and approaches to solve the complex social problems we were seeing, and wanted to create a new shape for our professions. We were interested in design, and started to investigate how it could be used to help us find different solutions. This led us to starting the *Movimento Minas* programme, as a collaborative way of building solutions to societal challenges (see the *Shaped by Us* project in our interview with Andrea Siodmok on page 220).

Brazil is a young nation, with civilians only returning to power with a democratically elected representatives in 1985. We are still trying to build a sense of citizenship through the ways people interact with government, and we face the challenge of being a huge country. We see Design Thinking as a great way of customizing policy, rather then making it universal from the beginning.

Governments mostly work through linear and rigid processes, which start and end inside the bureaucracy. Governments also have a habit of thinking that they know it all, and it has been like this here for many, many years. In the past couple of years there has been a global movement of new initiatives aimed at opening up government to citizens and participants, and we see the introduction of Design Thinking as another step to achieving an open government in Minas Gerais. Governments are still struggling to make information publicly available. To adopt an open innovation model is to develop a mindset of failing and having resilience, testing, failing again and finally succeeding. Governments do not work this way. They always tend to think there is a best solution for each and every problem, rather than multiple possible solutions. In our government you are not allowed to fail, so giving people permission to fail before reaching success is a critical step. Adopting a Design Thinking approach goes a step beyond simply making information available to the public, and into the realms of social innovation, making the government more open by encouraging the public to share their insights.

Developing an open and co-creative mindset in government

We believe at least two things are likely to change through the introduction of a Design Thinking approach into the policy cycle.

The first potential change relates to the fact that government are the institutions most likely to face the challenge of delivering effective and efficient policies to their citizens. To achieve this ourselves, it is crucial that we try to be as open as possible with what we are developing and delivering. As well as delivering services, the government also has a responsibility to deliver public value. In that regard we do not think that the government can be the only judge of what is defined as public value. The whole approach of Design Thinking and systems thinking can help us

Adopting a Design Thinking approach goes a step beyond simply making information available to the public, and into the realms of social innovation, making the government more open by encouraging the public to share their insights.

to become more effective in our actions as a government. If we can come up with an idea and test a public policy at low cost, before it is too big to fail, that will certainly add value. Furthermore, the notion of convergent and divergent thinking – improving the way we deal with uncertainty by bringing flexibility to the process – also has the potential to add value and lead to more innovation-driven initiatives.

The second point is related to a change in the orientation of public action. When a service does not fit the real needs of the public, then it is not well designed. This seems obvious but, if governments could be more citizen-oriented when designing policies, we would definitely see an increase in societal benefit. When more people are interested in receiving better value from their services, then there will be higher public value. However the government cannot achieve this alone. It needs to be more open to different ideas and perspectives if it truly wants to achieve public value by co-creating with citizens. Design Thinking and its tools can open up the possibilities of government, developing effective policies and creating real public value.

It is truly a challenge to introduce a different mindset that is open and co-creative in the government. It is not a short-term objective, as it can only really be achieved in the long term. The key challenge is convincing our stakeholders and sponsors in government that adopting a Design Thinking approach is a good idea. To overcome these barriers we need to have good leadership support and sponsorship. We can see that the Design Thinking approach, and the overall experience of bringing in people and ideas, creates political capital. But to achieve this we will need support from the top, and from the very beginning, because we will probably fail a few times before succeeding. We do not expect to immediately transplant the mindset of a designer into a civil servant, and so we view this as an ongoing process. There is a tendency in government to focus overtly on tools rather than on changing mindsets. At present we see that there are people here who are interested in Design Thinking, however they are still only focusing on the tools. Furthermore, we do not use the term 'Design Thinking' in government. It is impossible to say that there is a whole design approach at work here, and so we think that the term 'co-creation' is more appropriate, as it says a lot and delivers the core idea.

A platform for co-creating public policy
Movimento Minas (www.movimentominas. mg.gov.br) was launched in July 2011, with the aim of bringing the public and government of Minas Gerais together. It started as an online platform to enable citizens to participate by gathering ideas concerning ten

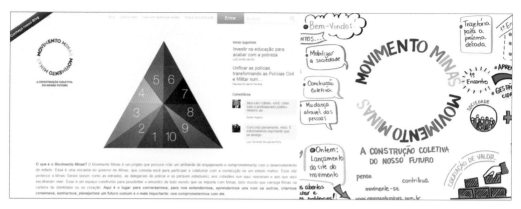

The *Movimento Minas* website and programme

long term challenges faced by the government, such as changing society through culture and education, reducing poverty and inequalities, and increasing security. These areas formed the guidelines to the state's strategic planning. At first our aim was to bring transparency into government, to start building shared values with society. But soon we realized that, through more specific challenges and a clear participation process, the online platform could better connect with real action. This led us to design a new version of the platform, and also to introduce a design approach into the process.

Throughout the project, we thought about how we could bring the online participatory experience into the real world, to look at where problems were occurring and test out solutions to see if they would work. We are trying to bring a fresh approach to the problems facing government, by prototyping public policy. However we know there will be limits, as we are unable to prototype every policy due to time and cost factors. As a starting point we created an event and invited 21 Minas citizens, all very accomplished in their fields – scientists, professors and business people – to contribute ideas around the topic of environmental policy. Their expectation was that we would

implement and build new policies for government straight away. However, if we did this we would be reinforcing the historical transactional relationship between the people and the government, in which the government is the provider of education and healthcare and in return the people pay taxes. We believe there should be a shift in the way government and society interact, and we wanted to encourage a new approach of co-creating public value by working collaboratively with society to identify problems and take them right through to the implementation of solutions. This is the change we believe in, and this is our goal.

The ideas gained from the first event were quite general, so we took one idea about planting trees to make the roadsides more pleasant, and explored which actors we could work with to deliver not only environmental but also social value. During this process we drew on design and systems thinking to transform the idea.

The *Tree Planting* project became a pilot of our prototyping process. Our first step was to map initiatives already running in the state. We talked to the State Roads Department, the Environmental Department and to other offices within the government. From these conversations we came up with the idea of using the labour force of prisoners, which had never been used before for such purposes. Our main challenge was to convince the actors involved that the prototype, if successful, would be a good start for a broader project. But before we could grow this idea, it would be necessary to collect some practical feedback. We tried out this model in a city called Teofilo Otoni in November 2011, and this provided us with useful information about the technical and political challenges of running such a project. The logistics of the maintenance of the plants proved to be the most critical point. In early 2012 we redesigned the experience based on what we had learnt, and prototyped one more time in another town, Ponte Nova. This time around, one of the areas we wanted to explore was the possibility of building a partnership with the Environmental Department, including more activities to build up the capacities of the prisoners, maintaining the plants while also helping to combat fires. From that prototype we collected other insights and learnings for the design of the project, which was then given to the Environmental Department to be developed. The result of this project was the rehabilitation of prisoners, so that when they are released

from prison they have skills that they can use in the outside world. However, there was also other social value to be gained. The prisoners enjoyed teaching their knowledge to other people, which increased their self-esteem and self-worth. It was only our first prototype, but we expect this project to become an initiative that is sustainable for the prisoners while also producing the environmental and social value we had hoped for.

We shared the outcomes of this project with the policy makers, not knowing how they would respond to our approach – as the government is generally a closed organization and often view themselves as 'the experts'. Telling them that we had adopted a co-creative process to develop and implement the idea was not an easy task. But, based on the success of the project, we were able to demonstrate the value of the Design Thinking approach and achieved high buy-in from all the different parties involved.

Our second project was the *Teenage Mother* project, which came about very differently from the *Tree Planting* project. The Chief of the State Department for Health invited us to contribute to an initiative aimed at reducing

The *Tree Planting* project in progress, with inmates from a local prison planting and maintaining trees on the roadside

risks in pregnancy. We chose to work in the challenging area of teenage pregnancy, as it demanded more engagement with society. We chose a specific group of teenage mothers located in remote areas, who had difficulty accessing appropriate medical monitoring. Due to these difficulties, a high proportion of these girls suffered from miscarriages or delivered babies with health problems. We divided our working process into three steps: Challenge, Ideation, and Prototyping. We facilitated collaboration in the first two steps by using the online platform, and also by organizing face-to-face meetings. One of the end results of this project was an improvement of our online platform, to allow for more exchange of ideas and to encourage collaboration.

Innovating the process to co-create public policy

We have taken our inspiration from Nesta's open innovation programme, and from organizations like Participle and the Design Council's RED team in the UK. We also work with the design school at Universidade do Estado de Minas Gerais (UEMG), and research public value with Fundação Dom Cabral, a business school focused on innovation. Although we are constantly finding relevant new approaches to our project through our exposure to work in other places, we are also building our own co-creative process. We are applying some of the principles of Design Thinking, but generally what we do is use the experience we have gained from our projects to understand what will be most valuable to our context. We are only just beginning to figure out how Design Thinking approaches can help us achieve our goals; still testing a lot of the principles and tools, and have yet to figure out what really works and what does not.

For example, in the *Tree Planting* project we had three steps: Listening, Co-creating with actors and Implementation. We started by explaining what our core idea, and then we developed the strategy with the actors based on this starting point. We prototyped the idea in a specific city. At the end of this prototyping phase, we then used the method of storytelling (a more informal approach than would normally be used in government) to communicate the different paths that we had taken to the government's policy makers. To make the idea sustainable we also had to consider the structure, offices and policies that already exist. For this purpose we used the Business Model Canvas[1] with stakeholders, to build a business model for the project. Normally we would use planning and legal instruments for planning laws, but we see a limitation in these as these instruments are more focused on enforcing stricter control than fostering better planning. Using the business model tool helped stakeholders to think more broadly, and to consider how the project could be resolved.

As we go on, we will try out more tools and develop our own toolbox that we are capable of re-using. Eventually we will develop and deliver our own methods of Design Thinking in government. We also have to consider how we will introduce this type of thinking, because there are a lot of traditional structures within government. As we begin to see results in our department, it will become easier to spread the approach of Design Thinking.

Challenges in sustaining a design approach in government

Local governments are pretty autonomous from state government. Of course there are shared policies at the federal level, but we have our own space to implement new

Consultations and public forums held during the *Teenage Mother* project

policies. We are not sure how this will spread to other states, unless we can show clear political gains and personal recognition from a political leader, such as the Governor. Minas is probably the most innovative state government in Brazil, as we have truly forward-thinking leadership, so this is the right place for a design approach to flourish. However in the next five to ten years it is likely it will only spread to local government in Brazil, due to the leadership and environment required for it to be effectively adopted at federal level.

Even within what we consider to be the most forward-thinking state leadership, we still had a lot of convincing to do to make our projects happen. Part of our approach is to build the right partnerships, rather than trying to build a big team. When we were first developing our business model we wanted to anchor our projects outside of government, to ensure that they did not rely on the stability of the political situation. In Brazil, any new government will always end up reinventing the wheel because they tend to disregard any progress made by their predecessors. The first four years of this cycle involves deconstructing and reconstructing before we can even move to an implementation stage – and so we have to develop a programme that can be functional

outside of different political scenarios.

To convince government to change their approach, we need to deliver solid results. The overall approach of government is based on an economic model, and so they look for two things: a measurable improvement in results, or a reduction in spending. We are convinced that there is more to achieve than just being efficient and delivering better value for money. Co-created value is the true value, but government works to a different logic and so Design Thinking must prove itself against that logic by delivering better or cheaper results. We can see design achieving way beyond these deliverables, but we need to find better social indicators because we do not see a way back now – we believe that Design Thinking is the only way to solve the tough problems that the government of Minas Gerais is facing today. *-end-*

Notes

1. The Business Model Canvas is a strategic management and entrepreneurial method that allows companies to describe, design, challenge and reinvent their business model. It has been developed by Alex Osterwalder and Yves Pigneur in their 2010 book, The Business Model Generation.

SECTION III

VIEWPOINTS

Design experts reflect and share their views on the future of design

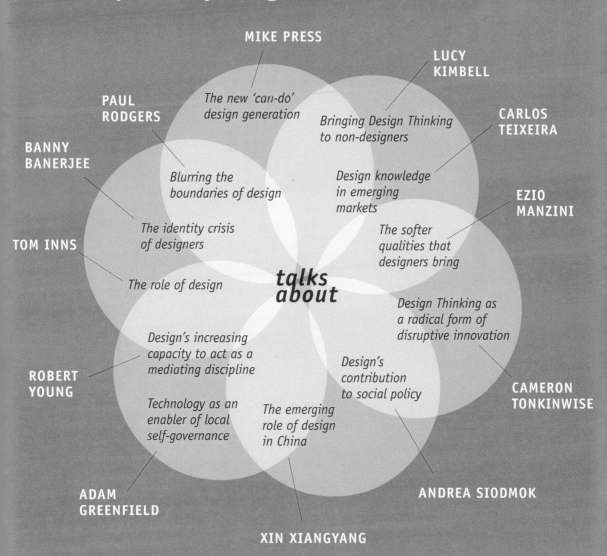

MIKE PRESS
The new 'can-do' design generation

LUCY KIMBELL
Bringing Design Thinking to non-designers

PAUL RODGERS
Blurring the boundaries of design

CARLOS TEIXEIRA
Design knowledge in emerging markets

BANNY BANERJEE
The identity crisis of designers

EZIO MANZINI
The softer qualities that designers bring

TOM INNS
The role of design

talks about

Design Thinking as a radical form of disruptive innovation

Design's increasing capacity to act as a mediating discipline

ROBERT YOUNG

Design's contribution to social policy

Technology as an enabler of local self-governance

The emerging role of design in China

CAMERON TONKINWISE

ADAM GREENFIELD

XIN XIANGYANG

ANDREA SIODMOK

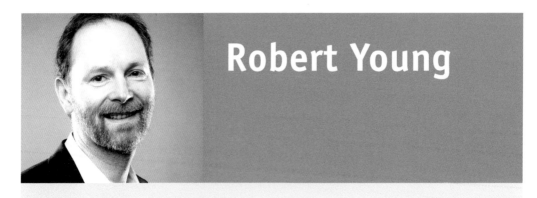

Robert Young

Robert Young is Professor of Design Practice at Northumbria University, UK. Originally trained as an industrial designer, he has worked in the furniture, engineering and manufacturing industries and also as a design researcher with the Home Office of the UK government and the emergency services. His research and consultancy interests explore the future of design practice, complex systems design, social innovation and service design theory and practice. In our interview, Robert spoke about design's increasing capacity to act as a mediating discipline, and the challenges this brings to existing design education and practice models.

Can you tell us what your current role involves, and what drives you in your work?
I am the Professor of Design Practice at Northumbria University Design School. My role is to develop research related to design practice, and I believe it is one of the most important roles in a school whose ethos has always concerned the practice of design. In this sense it differentiates from research and learning around design, where design is treated as an object of enquiry rather than a process and practice of doing. The challenge of the role is to get design practice academics to reflect on their interventions, and to ask questions about the intellectual and professional challenges this poses – particularly how implicit practices can be made explicit in order to celebrate the new knowledge and understanding they contain.

What excites you about design at the moment?
The thing that has always excited me about design is the creative oeuvre that lies at the heart of a designer's practice; that part of their DNA that is fundamental to their creativity. It gets them out of bed in the morning and drives them through the hardest of projects. In a paper written by Davies and Talbot 25 years ago for the *Design Studies Journal* titled 'Experiencing ideas: identity, insight and the image', they studied the nature of design and creativity and identified that there is something distinctive about the creative gene – that being creative is a natural form of adrenalin in designers, and one of the core things that drives them. For me, that aspect of creativity is not limited to products or artefacts, but pervades every aspect of life. It is the facility to work with people and introduce creative opportunities at every twist and turn. The relevance of creativity now is the same as it has always been – that fundamental capacity for humanity to make change in the world, and to imagine an increasingly better construct for ourselves.

What are the current trends in design practices, and what are the factors driving them?

We have always rubbed shoulders with technology, and latterly with other disciplines that bring technology to the marketplace. But technology on its own, for its own sake, can be blind to the social and cultural needs of people. It needs disciplines like design, that are fuelled by creative intent, in order to translate its capacity. Design has embraced the digital world, and that has emancipated our exploration of the application of design thinking across traditional design practices. Designers are increasingly moving across disciplines to confront the possibility of the new, and this has refreshed the capacity of designers to work in ways that have a greater impact on society. The mediation of graphic and industrial design through to interaction, user-centred and service design represents that increasing capacity to interface with the social and hard sciences in a way that matters – generating new opportunities and a greater relevance within contemporary society.

The opportunity of technological development itself is perhaps the main driver for change. We rarely see situations where artefacts are discrete; they have increasingly become part of an evanescent, ubiquitous and interconnected system. Hence, designers have had to understand the complexity of these 'things' in relation to behaviour and systems that may have always been present in more discrete forms. Technology has enabled these things to come together in a more fluid way, and designers have had to become more aware of this fact – and part of that process is to develop an understanding of how to work with other disciplines and specialists. One of the more contemporary roles of design is to act as a mediating discipline between different branches of the social sciences and hard sciences: an 'inter-discipline', in a way that

the reductionist approach of those disciplines might not allow. Whilst design may not be the only discipline taking this role, it is still a very important one due to its command of creativity and inherent ability to see patterns and negotiate problems and solutions. There is a kind of vitality and fierceness in design's capacity to do this that a lot of the other disciplines lack. Perhaps it comes from the fundamental philosophy and purpose of those disciplines, which is primarily to understand the world; as opposed to design's purpose to change the world. Design is a way of 'being' as much as it is a way of 'doing'.

Are these the same trends that will drive design education?

Design has to understand that its traditional evolved role in terms of artisan practices should no longer be the singular offering in design education. This model still has an important role to play, as the fundamental skills that we associate with design, creativity and making (referring to the process of acquiring skills described by Richard Sennett in his 2008 book *The Craftsman*). The challenge for design education is to take into account how it relates to other disciplines, and we face even more massive challenges in addressing these issues – for example, how to enable people to live and work together successfully in an intense urban environment. A lot of the current issues and problems that we encounter have come about because we must live in high-density conurbation areas, revealing new problems relating to these living contexts. How do we provide people with the natural resources they require? How do we address the unique bond that people still want to have with their environment? Design education has to take its lead from the way we contend with such issues. What this means for design education is that it cannot exist in isolation, purely as a process of art and design learning. Instead it must confront the reality of how designers work with other disciplines.

In terms of the curriculum, the problem is what to leave out. Design education has always had concerns about what to put into its 'pot of learning', particularly as traditional design skills – like learning to see through drawing, or proving a concept through making prototypes – are extremely time consuming. This aspect of 'learning through doing' cannot suddenly be reduced as, according to Sennett, there is an acknowledged wisdom that an individual requires around 10,000 hours of practice in order to become proficient. Sennett's argument is that, until the learning of basic skills is time-served, you do not actually see the nature of the problem that you are dealing with, because you do not have the capacity to think beyond the act of 'learning to do'.

I think we are at a point now where we have to seriously re-think the evolution of the design profession, and the role of design in society. Design needs to equip itself much better in order to work with people from different walks of life. To do that, it needs to address the relationship between different types of knowledge – between 'know-how' and 'know-that' (as described by Nigel Cross in his 2007 book *Designerly Ways of Knowing*) and also between tacit, implicit and explicit forms of knowledge. We cannot have much credibility with other disciplines if we are not able to articulate our knowledge and skills fluently. Designers believe that if they are allowed to work on a problem, they can demonstrate value through their engagement in a project. This expectation is increasingly naïve, particularly when the process of commissioning and establishing a brief is based on a discourse of intent rather than a portfolio review. Designers need to be

articulate, and confident in their capacity to explain the value they can bring to a situation upfront. Therefore, one of the big challenges in design education is helping our students to understand the competencies and values they bring to these kinds of situation. They need to be taken through a process of learning not only those competencies and values, but also an appreciation of the knowledge and skills inherent to other disciplines, to help them understand how to interact with them. It is about introducing them to threshold knowledge and translation mechanisms that allow them to collaborate in multi-disciplinary teams.

This is a massive challenge for design schools all around the world. Each school has its own heritage, which can work in their favour but at the same time can be the limiting factor. The fact is that most current design educators in the UK have come from a craft-based educational tradition, which is great for producing designers of desirable products and artefacts – but not that great for producing designers who can co-create the interconnected products, services and systems of the future. We still have educators that think about the future by drawing too much from the past. The purpose of design education is to release the design potential of the student group, not to hinder it. In that respect, the design educator's role should be more about facilitation to learn than direction in how to do. Astute staff know how to balance the two and enable new ways of thinking to emerge.

What do you think the future of design practice will look like, and what factors do you think will shape it?
The best way to interpret this question is to ask ourselves where, how and by whom will design be done in the future. Who will be

the producers and the consumers, and how will these roles merge with the advent of proactive communities in society, additive manufacture, connected mobility and the 'internet of things'? In the short-term we know that only one company can win on price, and all the others must use design to sustain value. What we are seeing is that professionals are increasingly portfolio-oriented in their career pattern, meaning that they rarely stay in one organization over a long period of time. The designer's portfolio therefore must expand, to show not only their traditional core design skills of creativity, analysis, synthesis and representation, but also their capacity to engage with other disciplines, professionals, clients, users, stakeholders, contexts and problems. There is a kind of dialectical element here, as well as a dialogical element. I do not think we are currently equipping students in the best possible ways for this future pattern of work.

There are also questions as to whether design is best practiced in manufacturing, service or communication organizations that serve a consumer society. The nature of big business is changing. The fundamental approach has changed, and this inevitably changes the way designers work with them. It is no longer sufficient to have a narrow range of core products, and businesses are increasingly recognizing the need to be viral in their operation, and to appreciate the wider ecology of the product and service systems they provide. That ability to be viral is seen as a means of deferring risk in cases of reduction in demand, or a sudden crisis in a social, economic or environmental context. How designers relate to this change is interesting. Having portfolio capacity is important, in terms of solving current problems but also in demonstrating the

capacity to frame and narrate convincing representations of future problems and their likely solutions. This is where I see the real potential growth area for design education, and for designers: to act as interpolators for commercial companies, second and third sector organizations, managing the cross-fertilization of disciplines in order to connect the dots, and bring products and services into being. This takes them into realms from which they have traditionally been excluded, and enables them to operate at a more strategic level in companies and organizations. In the future design and design education must become more proactive in leading the exploration of major issues in society. At a more prosaic level, this will see designers initiating products and service concepts for licensed exploitation by organizations, rather than the traditional mode of reactive designing commissioned by industry.

The traditional role of design consultancies must also change. Products and services have become interconnected, and behaviours have become more complex. There are only one or two consultancies that can act as the purveyor of iconic product specification, and so everyone else has to use design as a means of identifying and leveraging different positions in the marketplace. This is a great opportunity for design. In the last few years we have seen a significant growth in strategic design thinking practices. I would link these to innovation practices, but design-led rather than business-led. It is about offering a better quality of service and creating more memorable experiences, and design has a massive part to play in delivering this. The real challenge for design at the moment is successfully articulating its value in this evolving space. *-end-*

Tom Inns

Professor Tom Inns is Director of Glasgow School of Art (GSA), Scotland's specialist university-level institution for art, design and architecture. Tom studied Engineering at Bristol University, and completed a Masters in Industrial Design at the Royal College of Art. In 1990 he was a co-founder of the Design Research Centre at Brunel University, becoming its Director in 1996. In 2004 he was appointed Director of the AHRC/EPSRC funded *Designing for the 21st Century* research initiative, and in 2010 joined Duncan of Jordanstone College of Art and Design (DJCAD) as Dean before moving to GSA in September 2013. Tom regularly delivers knowledge-sharing events and workshops with innovation agencies across Europe, and here he speaks of the changes he has seen in design, including the context in which design operates, its emerging leadership and the new roles of the designer.

Can you tell us what your current role involves, and what drives you in your work?
There are several parts to my role as the Dean of Duncan of Jordanstone College of Art & Design. The first is a management role, looking after 1000 students and 150 staff. The second is more strategic and involves leading this whole portfolio of activity forward, keeping it up to date, ensuring programmes are viable in the market place and identifying new directions for DJCAD's research activity. The external context in which art and design operates is changing so much, and one of the results is the emergence of new roles for artists and designers. This has a direct impact on teaching and research, and one of my specific personal research interests is in how design can be used in interdisciplinary spaces to bring different teams together, to help them understand and resolve complex problems.

What excites you about design at the moment?
For me it is the whole notion of Silent Design in a 21st Century context. The term Silent Design was coined by Angelas Dumas in the 1980s, and it can be used when you come across a situation or organization which has clearly been 'designed' but does not necessarily foreground itself as a designed entity. When I see this is, it excites me because I wonder who has done it, and how the organization has achieved it. Have they worked with professional designers, or do they have inherent design abilities within their organization?

An interesting example of this is Innocent Drinks, a UK based company which has become known for their smoothie juices. Their brand is known for its no-nonsense honesty and down-to-earth communication with customers and retailers. Although the founders of the company are not designers, I consider them to be a 'design' organization in the way they develop the product, market themselves and position their brand. The company is very entrepreneurial and although it is based upon physical products, it has a strong web presence and really understands consumer behaviour, advertising and marketing trends. For me, this demonstrates the application of Design Thinking in a commercial organization. There are of course many classic examples from the public sector, like London's transport infrastructure and the way it continues to evolve with an incredible design quality through the Transport for London (TfL) brand.

Another area that currently fascinates me is how design emerges at different points of time, and in different parts of the world. To me, what lies at the core of design is constant but how it manifests itself changes all the time as contexts shift. If Josiah Wedgwood[1] was alive today, he would not be setting up a ceramics company – he would be Steve Jobs setting up Apple. But because he lived in a particular time, where things manifested themselves in a particular way, he ended up doing what he did. China is a good example of somewhere you can see the role of design changing as contexts change. On a recent visit to Shanghai I visited an exhibition in the newly-established Shanghai Design Museum. The exhibition illustrated how the economy of Shanghai has evolved over the last 100 years. During this period it has been largely based on manufacturing, and specifically on the meticulous copying of existing products, but with an added twist. It is often a very subtle but significant little twist which offers consumers the best features of a competitor's products, but better. Chinese firms have been very successful with this model, and it is fascinating to observe how they are now using

design to do more, and to really innovate. One of the core challenges for China is going to be how they adapt their educational system to respond to business demands for design to be used in these new spaces.

Brazil's model contrasts with this because their society and culture is different. It is entrepreneurial but in a totally different way, because in Brazil design has more of a social function rather than just a business function. My DJCAD colleagues Mike Press and Frances Stevenson have recently been doing some work in Rwanda where, although there is no formal art and design education, there is still a great interest in what design can offer both business and society, and although the context there is so different they are also grappling with the question of 'what design is'. I would argue that, here in the UK, we are in a post-industrial economy that is finding its own new roles for design.

What do changing contexts mean for designers and design students?
Often expectations are built into our students that they are going to be working in the same way as their predecessors. When that does not happen, they feel they have lost their identity as a designer. We should build different expectations about what design is, and also emphasize the changing context that designers have to operate in.

There are two sides to this story. Education (particularly Higher Education) obviously pays a key role in the development of a designer, but they are only in formal university education for a three to four-year period before they enter the professional context, which might span 30 years. I believe that the design profession itself is sometimes the biggest barrier to moving the discipline forward. It is very challenging for any profession that is forced to morph and adapt to new situations, and although the design profession is in some ways very creative and adapts well to change, in other ways it is still very conservative.

What are the main factors influencing the design profession today?
These factors are linked to the context that the profession operates within. The type and range of clients in the corporate sector is changing enormously, what they commission is changing, and our conventional notion of design existing in silos (product, communication, fashion) is also changing. The drivers of change are different because the power base in the global economy is shifting. It is affected by technology, societal needs and environmental concerns, which are all high level issues. You only have to extrapolate them two to three times before you see a direct effect on a professional designer.

Tell us about the Archipelago of Design diagram, and how it maps different territories of design.
The map came out of the *Designing for the 21st Century* project funded by the UK's Arts and Humanities Research Council (AHRC) and the Engineering and Physical

Sciences Research Council (EPSRC). I used it to help me make sense of the 41 different research projects that were running under this initiative. Some projects were very technological, some social, some were focused on a particular stage of design process and others were based on co-design – but none of them were confined to a specific subject area of design, such as industrial design or communication design. The map uses the shape of an archipelago to describe where design came from and how it is now developing into different areas. Historically, design emerged from the industrial revolution and was informed by Victorian ideas of invention. The archipelago starts very narrow but becomes broader and broader as you move along, illustrating how design is influenced by other factors. The 'islands' of product, fashion and communication design emerged in the 1960s. The digital world comes on-stream between the 1990s and 2000, and Design Thinking begins to emerge in the 2000s – leading us to where we are now, which I term the 'ocean of uncertainty'. This diagram emphasizes my earlier point about the core of design remaining the same, but the context changing.

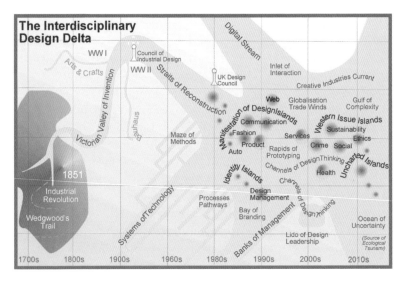

Archipelago of Design diagram

Where will design be in the future?
Let's take the UK as a starting point. The reason product design is no longer so important in the UK is due to the fact that the manufacturing industry has shrunk. There is still massive growth in the digital design area but product design for UK-made manufactured goods is becoming less important. This is partly due to the way manufacturing has shifted, and where design is sourced for that manufacturing. Another reason is the financial pressure on public services to find efficiencies, and the potential that design can play in providing greater value there. These are the contexts that are changing from a UK point of view, which tells us why perceptions of design are the way they are.

Are UK institutions capable of educating students for this changing context?
There is still something unique in the UK design education model. My recent trip to Shanghai cemented this viewpoint. I visited the Shanghai Institute of Visual Arts, which has expanded enormously over the course of the last five years, with thousands of students focused entirely on the visual arts. They have the most amazing facilities in terms of space, workshops and technical support. However, their students are finding it difficult to think creatively and abstractly due to the educational model they work within. UK design institutions like the Royal College of Arts (RCA) have been around for over 175 years, and their way of learning and working has been hardwired into the culture of UK design education.

There are three markets that design education can focus on: delivering the existing design educational model to firstly, the local and secondly, the international markets. The third market is to deliver Design Thinking. We are comfortable delivering to the first market. The second, international market is notoriously complex to reach, mainly because of a fundamental lack of cultural understanding. And the third market of Design Thinking is very complex and difficult, because it demands that we develop an understanding of other disciplines – and design is generally not very good at doing that.

What do you think design practices will look like in the future?
I think ultimately design practices could come from quite different places, other than design schools. The Innocent Drinks is an interesting example, where three bankers set up a company that is very design-led. IDEO is another example, as probably only 20% of their staff are designers. Design practices are not the total preserve of design schools, particularly if they are slightly prehistoric and do not adapt to changes quickly enough. I teach in the management school in St Andrews University to marketing students, and most of the students really understand brands. They might not be able to design a beautiful new product but they are very capable of mapping and facilitating a complex situation, and generating solutions using Design Thinking approaches. I can envisage the next generation of design practices coming from quite broad spaces. Design has to be up for that challenge by really understanding its attributes and the value it brings. *-end-*

The authors congratulate Tom Inns on his appointment as Director of Glasgow School of Art shortly after this interview was completed.

Notes
1. Josiah Wedgewood is generally credited with setting up one of the world's first innovative manufacturing companies in the 18th Century.

Banny Banerjee

Banny Banerjee is Founder and Director of Stanford ChangeLabs, a new initiative at Stanford University that aims to create rapid, large-scale and sustainable transformation around complex issues such as water provision and social inequity. Banny originally trained as an architect, and also holds graduate degrees in mechanical engineering and design. In India he worked in the fields of architecture, structural engineering, and low embodied energy building systems. Prior to joining Stanford University, Banny worked at Xerox PARC on ambient media and physical computing, and at IDEO as a designer and design strategist creating novel experiences and crafting futures for leading technology companies. Here, Banny shares the story of his shifting identity as a designer as he reflects on the changes in the design discipline, and the deep transformations that design can enact if changes are embraced.

What changes have you seen in the discipline of design over the last ten years?
In order to depict how design has changed, I'll first give a brief overview of my own journey. First and foremost I was a bit of an anomaly, in the sense that a lot of the my fellow designers had gone through design school and had very sharp identities as specific types of designers – product designers, industrial designers, interaction designers while I saw myself drawn into any area that needed design intervention.

My own journey has been a little convoluted. I studied architecture at undergraduate level and, since I grew up in a family with engineers and artists, I had an equal interest in the engineering as well as the more artistic aspects of architecture. I had my first crisis when I left architecture school. Upon graduating, I realized that while I loved the field of

architecture I was deeply at odds with the way it was being practiced. In reaction to this, I moved to rural India and spent two and a half years working on a housing project that used earth as a building material, conducting research on ultra low-cost structural systems. All that I had learnt in architecture school seemed relatively inconsequential in the context of a rural development framework. I was dealing with large social forces, and it wasn't about building beautiful houses or controlling material. It was about deep involvement with people's lives, understanding sociological and economic forces, and dealing with massive resource issues, political feedback loops and landholding patterns.

After coming to the US and completing a graduate degree in architecture, I worked in the energy industry conducting computer simulations of energy systems and then, after that, as a software engineer. My plans to keep my artistic practice alive were only partially successful, and I missed being a designer. Then I heard about the unique design program at Stanford, and made the decision to go back to graduate school. I enrolled into the Stanford design programme in 2006. At the time it was very much a hands-on program about making 'stuff'. I was always covered in sawdust and smelling of machine oil but, although we made a lot of things, there was also a lot of emphasis on being human-centred.

After my degree I worked for a brief period at Xerox PARC doing research on ubiquitous computing, and then I joined IDEO, back when it was mainly a product design company with engineers and electrical engineers building physical artefacts. Fast-forward to ten years later, and the range of projects we were designing had undergone a radical change. We were in the midst of an evolving discipline, and this was reflected in the different types of projects that were coming through the door. We were still working on product innovation projects, but we also had an increasing number of more complex strategic projects. Designers became better at articulating the process of Design Thinking, and using techniques such as ethnography and structured brainstorming to tackle increasingly diverse problems. While Design Thinking may have been experiencing its moment in the spotlight, to my mind, the design community lacked the collective ability to objectively evaluate whether the current form of Design Thinking could meet the requirements of these new territories. The general assumption seemed to be that, since human centred design had proven successful in identifying unmet needs and translating them to business opportunities, those same processes would be equally effective in addressing more

complex issues involving social, cultural, financial, economic and political forces.

At around this time, I was invited to apply for a faculty position at Stanford as Director of the Design Program. I had never considered academia as a career path, because I saw myself as more of a designer than an educator, and when I was offered the position I had to do a great deal of soul-searching about making the switch from industry to academia. My eventual decision was actually born out of a crisis that I saw growing within the design field, and recognition that this was a tremendous moment for design to step up and address a new class of challenge.

Can you expand more on this crisis?
It was, and continues to be, a three-way crisis. Firstly there is the gap between the rubric and the nature of the challenges that designers are asked to work on. Secondly, the stakes that are linked to the new consequences are much larger than any we have faced before. For example, if you made a mistake on a commercial product by specifying a wrong component, that would be a serious business setback. But if you are working with a mining company to prevent a civil war, and you fail? The stakes in these new types of project are much higher, and bring with them a much greater set of social and environmental consequences. The third crisis is that the most critical challenges of the time demand that design, along with the other dominant fields, retools itself to be able to make transformations at a scale that is relevant to the scale of the challenges. Challenges such as climate change, environmental devastation, the energy crisis, the food crisis and the impending water crisis are all complex interlaced problems marked by urgency, scale, and a resistance to improvement. Design needs to do its part by

developing new methodologies to address these challenges.

The deeper crisis playing out alongside all of this is that, as a civilization, we are party to a tragedy of the commons playing out at a grand scale. The way we currently define progress is very much at odds with the health of our society and our planet. Our institutional structures, decision making systems and innovation methodologies fail to earn any confidence in our ability to ensure a sustainable future for our civilization. This creates a need for genuinely scaleable and radical innovation – and this is the need that drew me to Stanford.

Have you observed identity crises, like the one you experienced, happening for other designers?
I see this identity crisis in my students. We have a well-established design program here at Stanford, and our students are graduating with a Masters and Bachelors in Design. We also have a world-famous institute called the d.school, and the two form a continuum. The d.school is exposing graduate students from all disciplines to the power of Design Thinking, while the graduate students in our degree-granting Masters program in design spend two years delving deep into the nature of design activity. Graduate students from every part of the campus, as well as people from industry, are being exposed to design through this program, and essentially being told that they can be design leaders too. They go out and introduce themselves to the students on the design programme and say 'Hello, I'm a d.leader. Who are you?'

There cannot be a clear understanding of what constitutes design expertise in a world where the rudiments of design thinking are becoming as commonplace as basic numeracy,

and that certainly creates the potential for a crisis of identity. Our economics and business students acquire a genuinely powerful toolset through their exposure to design thinking, and yet there are also people here who have spent decades honing the ability to bring their design skills to bear at an entirely different level of expertise.

The fact that Design Thinking is now enjoying widespread adoption and popularity is excellent, as long as the borders of the field expand rather than conflate. A certain amount of tension between the component parts of such a rapidly evolving field is unavoidable, and it would be a mistake to think of that field as being homogenous or advancing at a uniform pace. Design is a very heterogeneous field, and the real game seems to be around how you play with and leverage that heterogeneity.

Despite this crisis in identity this is, to my mind, still an absolutely tremendous moment for designers – because we need them to create the highly innovative solutions that will have a deeply transformative impact on our world.

How do you maintain design expertise when design is being democratized?
At some level every human is a designer, if they are using creativity to transform undesirable situations into preferred ones. And yet there is a huge variation in the degree of expertise that these designers can bring to bear. I like to use the metaphor of sports: everyone can be taught to catch a ball, but not everyone can be an Olympic athlete. Design Thinking is certainly becoming democratized, and people with varying levels of experience, talent, education and skill are using it with different levels of expertise. However, complex challenges or difficult design tasks demand a level of

expertise that only comes with extensive training and experience.

It is possible for individuals with degrees in fields other than design to become expert designers, but it does not happen overnight. I am genuinely happy that there has been a democratization of Design Thinking, but it is currently experiencing a broad application by people with relatively little depth of knowledge in design. This results in a number of different problems. One is that, in the course of design being democratized, the marker of what constitutes expertise is often lowered. Since methodology is being taught as a repeatable process, the design process ironically runs the risk of becoming formulaic, even as the nature of its applications become more diverse. In addition the skill of design, which used to be easily discernable within the quality of the final artefact, is much harder to perceive when it is being applied to more abstract issues. This expansion of design beyond the creation of artefacts means that expertise is harder to achieve, while being easier to claim. Establishing expertise in the face of democratization has become a genuine problem, bringing with it a need to create not only a scaffold upon which individuals can build increased levels of expertise, but also a better way to clearly demarcate the novice from the expert.

One of the recurring themes of our book is the perceived loss of power when non-designers are also considered design thinkers. What are your thoughts on this?
Let's not mistake control for power. If you want to have a lot of control over the details, if that is your definition of power? Then yes you are going to lose power. But you can frame this better using the model proposed by Alain Findeli over a decade ago, in which he used the analogy of a designer being within a stream – where they might influence, but also be influenced by, the rest of the elements in the stream. The situation then becomes focused on the circle of influence that you have in your role as a designer, and power is the degree to which you are able to shift the trajectory of a system into a more desirable direction.

I think that designers are now more powerful than they have ever been before – it's just that power does not look like power in the traditional sense. Our traditional mental models of power and leadership are built around hierarchical and centralized thinking that comes from the military. Now, through design, we are enabling people to exhibit every modality of successful leadership irrespective of their seniority. We are opening doors that allow us to influence the shape of the future in a way we simply could not have imagined ten years ago. A decade is a miniscule period of time in which to have undergone such a profound transformation, and there is a feeling of loss of power. However, the arena of design itself is expanding at an unprecedented rate, and enjoying a new salience in relation to critical issues. The designers who embrace these changes, and who see themselves as being on the cutting-edge of a rapidly changing and expanding field, are using their expertise to create powerful and influential leadership roles for themselves, expanding their skillset and working with people from other disciplines to co-creating transformative propositions within the context of increasingly complex challenges.

In the larger scheme of things, if our goal as designers is to generate frame-changing propositions that bring transformative impact in the context of ill-defined challenges, then there has never been a better time for design as a field to engage in the most complex challenges of our time. *-end-*

Paul Rodgers

Paul Rodgers is Professor of Design Issues at Northumbria University, UK. Prior to joining Northumbria in November 2009, he was Reader in Design at Edinburgh Napier University and a post-doctoral Research Fellow at the University of Cambridge's Engineering Design Centre. Professor Rodgers has published more than 100 papers in book chapters, journals and conferences. His book *Digital Blur*, written with Michael Smyth, was published in 2010 and showcases creative practices at the boundaries of Architecture, Design and Art. Paul speaks here about the fluidity of design boundaries, and the possibilities they present to future designers.

Can you tell us what your current role involves, and what drives you in your work?
I am the Professor of Design Issues at Northumbria University Design School and my current role covers two main areas: teaching and learning, and research. I am involved in first year Industrial Design and Transportation Design teaching and support students with their final year dissertations. I also supervise five PhD students, and will probably be taking on a couple more soon. PhD supervision is an integral part of my practice; I really enjoy nurturing young and talented PhD students. My research at the moment consists mainly of writing with other people from different parts of the world. I would like to spend more time actually doing 'real' research, sitting in design offices like IDEO or somewhere else interesting, understanding what they are doing and asking

them interesting questions. I really enjoy working and collaborating with people.

What gets you excited about design at the moment?
Working with people, which I mentioned before. I seek out interesting collaborations in order to help me drive ideas forward. I am also critical about design; I think you need to be as an educator. However there is a line to be drawn, you cannot be overly critical. You need to be critical of design but also celebrate, acknowledge, explore and push its potential. It is like being a father and telling off one of your kids – you do it to make them better people. So sometimes you criticise design because you want to make it better.

A lot of what is said about design is spurious. There is too much celebration of design, and suggestion that design can 'solve' the world's problem. Designers cannot achieve anything by themselves. However, design can play a central and pivotal role if designers are part of the team that looks at some of these wider issues – whatever this might mean.

No single thing excites me about design at the moment, there are many things going on. It is always easier to see issues and problems. Chris Alexander points out in his book *Notes on the Synthesis of Form* that it is much easier to see 'misfit' than it is to see 'fit'. It is always easy to see the problems and issues with design but there are many, many things that fit well, for example: the iPhone. It fits my life, made my life a lot easier, but has made such an impact. The Facetime function has enabled me to talk to my kids and wife who live 100 miles away. Those little things excite me, and continually excite me. Of course there are downsides to this as well, such as obsession with wanting to own these new products driving consumption. But I would hope that these negative aspects are outweighed by the positive intervention of design.

What are the current trends that you see in design practices, and what factors are driving them?
Designers are certainly struggling for work at the moment due to the economic situation. I think there will be a return to localism (or glocalism, as they call it), if it is not happening already. I see it as a return to local production of goods. For example, there is a furniture designer/maker collective in New York that consists of an artist, a designer and a carpenter. The artist comes up with ideas for hand tools, the designer takes those ideas and turns them into functional hand tools, and the carpenter then uses and manipulates the hand tools to create bespoke furniture. So they have this wonderful system for using hand tools to

create beautiful furniture, all working out of a shed in Brooklyn. I do not think the UK does enough to help young designers and graduates to form collectives and businesses. Look at the way that America funds scientific endeavors, or the way The Netherlands have supported design in the last 10 years. There may well be a move towards localism and the re-establishment of craft as a key part of design.

Are these the same trends that will drive design education?
I think young people now have greater access to higher education. I certainly didn't feel that way when I left school in the early 1980s, but there has been a concerted move to make university education more accessible. I do not disagree with this, but it can bring problems. For example I have encountered students who, when asked, stated that they had no real interest in design but were simply encouraged by their parents to get a university degree.

Current factors driving design education? Numbers and money! It has become a market economy and design education has been commoditized. It is like buying fish fingers; you can find the most beautiful fish fingers if you are willing to pay enough. Similarly, you will find a better place to study if you are willing to pay or work hard enough. I am

You need to be critical of design but also celebrate, acknowledge, explore and push its potential.

also finding that design education is becoming more homogenized. If you try to be too different, you might find it difficult to attract students. As a result design education in the UK is beginning to resemble a typical high street, full of similar-looking chain stores. This can make it hard for students to distinguish between the programmes on offer.

What will future design practices look like, and what factors will shape them?
We are yet to reach the end of the digital revolution, to coin Bruce Sterling's opinion of where design is going. His view is that we are only at the start of that revolution and that it is going to explode. I have sat in demonstrations where, if you want to order a new sofa, you can design it and have it made in three hours. Terms like 'prosumer' have emerged in recent years to reflect the notion that the producer and the consumer can be the same person. On the one hand this is quite exciting but, will it need to be regulated? We have seen the beginning of this trend through work by the likes of Freedom of Creation (a design company specializing in 3D printing), Lionel Dean (a designer specialising in additive manufacture in design research), and the numerous amateur makers and hacker communities utilising cheap and accessible rapid prototyping tools. Some of the outputs are interesting, some are atrocious. It comes down to a question of 'Who has the power to create?', and maybe not everyone should have that power. There are indications that people are producing a lot of stuff that may not be very good. There are obvious parallels – for example, in music. The digitization of music has transformed the music and entertainment industry. Food is another example. 10 years ago, everybody wanted to be a DJ. Now they want to be a chef. Maybe in the next decade it will be a designer.

I am interested in how people manipulate, exploit and shape digital technologies. The practices featured in my book *Digital Blur* are incredibly lean and can react to opportunities really quickly. They are set up in completely different ways from the larger consultancies like IDEO and Seymour Powell. Their reliance on networks can make or break their whole existence. One of the major benefits digitization has brought to these types of studios is that those networks are much easier to develop, to retain, to exploit and to break. That is the power of social media and the digital world. You have the potential to be one of the most creative and interesting practices in the world, just by working from your garden shed, as long as you have a large network of collaborators. Take for example Sense Worldwide (a strategy consultancy), they have a worldwide network of 'associates' they can call upon to help them gain local knowledge of a new place. These types of network are crucial to design companies.

Good designers are always seeing connections, and repurposing for their particular context. We can see this in practices such as Greyworld, Troika, HeHe in Paris and many others. They are inspirational due to the way they work, which is very different from the design consultancies model of the 1980s. The values have changed; HeHe specifically say that they are not driven by money. Helen Evans from HeHe beautifully articulated the view that if you can separate what you do for money, then the freedom it gives you is amazing. There is a real integrity to the way they work, and the network of people they work with is incredible – like laser engineers from Finland for a project based in an incinerator plant in Paris. This clearly illustrates the power of the network, facilitated by the internet and social media. Universities will have difficulty keeping

That is the power of social media and the digital world. You have the potential to be one of the most creative and interesting practices in the world, just by working from your garden shed, as long as you have a large network of collaborators.

up, but we should at least be mindful of what is happening.

Designers' practices are incredibly fluid at the moment. It is difficult to keep track of the pace in practice but it is still important to give our students a good grounding in the core skills of design. A reappraisal of these core skills is necessary, but the important question is 'Have they changed?' I would say yes. Designers need to get a handle on technology, and they need to learn how to develop networks. The tools, media and machinery have changed but the core skills behind design – like communication, empathy and cajoling – remain key. *-end-*

Mike Press

Mike Press is Professor of Design Policy at Duncan of Jordanstone College of Art & Design, at the University of Dundee. Mike has written and researched extensively on design, innovation, contemporary craft and the management of creativity, speaking at conferences worldwide. His extensive publishing record includes authorship of three books, among them *The Design Agenda: A guide to successful design management* and *The Design Experience*. Mike speaks here about the entrepreneurial spirit and social vision of a new generation of designers, and the important role that design educators play in supporting their development.

Can you tell us what your current role involves, and what drives you in your work?
I am Professor of Design Policy, which means that I oversee research in areas where design plays a strategic role and is concerned with policy in a broader sense. Originally this was based around government policy and the *Design Against Crime* project, but now I am interested in its broader strategic dimensions, and how design gets into new territories and forms of practice. I am also responsible for running the Design and Craft subject area at Dundee University, which includes undergraduate and postgraduate studies.

What gets you excited about design at the moment?
Everything really! Currently I am excited by the willingness of people to engage in the challenges and discussions which I see happening in classrooms, workshops,

conferences, on Twitter and even on Facebook. Let me give you an example. I watched the London riots in August 2011 with horror, partly because they were taking place in areas where I used to live. Something is fundamentally wrong if people are so desperate that they will torch the place they live in. If you take away their youth clubs, if you close down the few opportunities they have for training, if all the employment has been taken away, how else do you expect people to express themselves? Unfortunately, in this case, it was through violence and destruction. After a few days of watching this on TV, I decided to set up a Facebook group to ask if anyone was interested in looking at how craft and design contribute to progressive social change, particularly given what we had seen in the riots. Within a day we had 80 people signed up to the group. We now have 300 people, and have had a number of really productive

When I look at what is happening in areas such as service design, social design, public service and start-up culture in design, I can see all these new territories emerging for design. There is real interest, activism and a commitment to explore these new possibilities.

discussions. We have discussed ideas to develop a book and have held a number of meetings in London and Dundee. We are calling it the Change Makers group and it consists of a former student of mine based in London, a colleague in New York and myself. We are trying to get things going by pulling together great exemplars that will inspire people to understand what social design and craft is.

We live in an age now where people get a huge amount of satisfaction, enjoyment and self-esteem from creativity, which we can see illustrated in the rise of DIY culture and knitting culture. A behavioural economist at Harvard University calls this the 'Ikea effect', meaning that people value what they make themselves. The Ikea effect can be seen taking place in communities as well, and there are a number of instances where social craft and design practices have significantly changed the self-esteem of people, old and young, in deprived areas.

When I look at what is happening in areas such as service design, social design, public service and start-up culture in design, I can see all these new territories emerging for design. There is real interest, activism and a commitment to explore these new possibilities.

If we look back, say to the 1990s, design was about self-employed practice, making stuff and designing in the corporate context. We have moved on hugely in the last decade and it is energising to see that happening in the world.

Why do you think this is happening now?
I think because there is a new generation of designers emerging who are naturally entrepreneurial. They do not necessarily 'like' design in its traditional sense, or the way that we are presenting it to them. They respond by making their own model of design practice. Snook is a great example of this (see their story on page 70). They wanted to change the world and make it a better place through service design. I witnessed for myself how Snook founder Lauren Currie started out as a product designer and then did her Masters degree, coming out of it as a different type of designer – a 'service designer'. She used that time for self exploration and professional redefinition. She started Snook with Sarah Drummond to create the type of organization they wanted to work for. They now have a staff of six in their Glasgow office.

There are lots of other people around the world doing the same thing, what I would describe as entrepreneurism linked to a social vision, and that is partly because people have been disengaged from political activism for very good reasons. I was politically active when I was younger, but then I became very cynical about it. Young people do not want to get involved in political parties because they do not see how our political system is actually enacting any change. They have a vision to make the world a better place, and they would rather do it through their own means and using their skills as a designer. Politics have moved on and interwoven with design in a fascinating way. I am looking at organizations like FutureGov (see their story on page 60), Engine and live|work, and observing that not only are they acting like political activists, but also they are doing it in a concrete way. It's not about manifestos, it's about sharing great practices and coming up with solid ideas.

What are the current trends that you see in design practices, and what factors are driving them?
The practice of designing public services is currently very interesting. This area has a political dimension because the challenge is to understand and envision ways of serving less fortunate communities, as that is what most public services are set up to do. It is about understanding how these communities grow, develop and transform their positions.

At the University of Dundee we are doing increasing amounts of work with NHS (National Health Service) Scotland to help them re-engineer their service provision. Additionally, our students on the Masters of Design for Services course worked on a project with Dundee City Council to redesign support and services for young people who have no qualifications or employment. Our students' first job was to figure out how to get these young people to tell their stories. This group can be very difficult and challenging

to work with, so how do you empower them to articulate in that way? Because once their stories are understood a meaningful co-design process can take place; without that understanding, there will only ever be well-meaning social service providers trying to anticipate what young peoples' needs are.

I find the area of entrepreneurialism really exciting, and I am seeing more evidence of this in our students when they get to their degree shows. In the past they would use the degree show to try to get a job, but in reality there are not many jobs available at the moment. So instead they think 'Let me try to get my idea to market!' A great example of that is Joanna Montgomery, who has a product called *Pillow Talk*. She has used social media in a really exciting way to create a fan base for her idea, and has already won around £90,000 from different sources to fund her product – that's a product that does not actually exist as yet. She is right on the verge of making the idea real. Joanna is just one example, but a lot of our students are now very good at exploiting social media to build a market and then using that to build a business, whereas in the past they would have to get support from retailers first before they could commit to manufacturing. We now have technologies that enable designers to make their products themselves, and this has really been key to encouraging the entrepreneurial spirit in our graduates. Crowdfunding sites like Kickstarter and other UK equivalents are also helping our students realize that it is not impossible to realize their dreams. Even finance is not the massive obstacle it once was – it's still very challenging, but in a fair way. You do not have to be rich to make it happen, just excellent at pitching and presenting your ideas. We have a long way to go but we are edging our way towards becoming an entrepreneurial meritocracy. For our recent graduates it is natural to believe themselves capable of bringing an idea to market. The question is no longer 'Am I going to do it?' but 'How am I going to do it?' There is an attitude shift taking place.

How is design education keeping up with all these changes and challenges?
When I look at design education overall, I do not think we serve design students as well as we could. Traditionally we have had this very narrow, restricted vocational model which does not fit with these new territories of practice, which require different skills from our students and demand a different awareness of the world around them. Things are changing, and while some design schools have made exciting and timely changes to their curricula and approaches for others there is still some way to go.

I am trying to keep relevant by asking myself if what I teach now would be useful to people like Lauren and Joanna? There is no point in teaching students knowledge, because knowledge ages fast. Instead it is about giving them the tools to gain and adapt knowledge, and also an attitude of positive thinking, enthusiasm and a belief that anything is possible. Design is the art of the possible. That's our job as design educators: to teach people to understand the art of the possible. People get empowered by education when three things come together: self-confidence, passion and skills. They develop a skill, they have the confidence to apply that skill, and

they also have a passion to use it in their lives. As long as those three things come together, that person's life becomes meaningful. So what do we teach? You learn a skill, but you cannot be taught a skill. So the only two other things that we can teach are self-confidence and passion. We have to help students build their self-confidence, and we have to transmit our passion of the subject and encourage it in them. That is why communication is really important, and why educators need to communicate stories about how passion, self-confidence and skills come together, to encourage our students to go out and use design to change the world. *-end-*

Design is the art of the possible. That's our job as design educators: to teach people to understand the art of the possible.

Lucy Kimbell

Lucy Kimbell is a designer, researcher and educator. She is Associate Fellow at
Saïd Business School, University of Oxford, where she has been teaching design
and design management to MBAs since 2006. Her writing on design includes book
chapters, peer-reviewed journal papers and conference keynotes. She is also a
Fellow at The Young Foundation based in London, where she brings design expertise
to the Foundation's work on social innovation and venturing. In 2012 she published
the *Social Design Methods Menu*, which makes design approaches accessible to
managers and entrepreneurs. Lucy speaks here about bringing Design Thinking
to non-designers, and going beyond design process towards the teaching and
translation of a design culture.

*Can you tell us what your current role involves,
and what drives you in your work?*
I refer to myself as a designer, educator and
researcher working in an expanded field
of design practice. Mostly I try to draw on
academic research and explore through my
own practice ways of thinking about and
'doing' designing. One of my main activities
is teaching a version of Design Thinking to
MBAs. I have written and presented at a
number of conferences, and I sometimes work
for other universities as an external examiner
and on course validations. Through my
consultancy Fieldstudio I help organizations
and entrepreneurs with collaborative research,
problem definition and idea generation that
typically takes the form of large workshops
for up to 100 people. When I was Head of
Social Design at The Young Foundation, my
role was to develop a design capability within

the organization. What's shared across all this
is working slightly outside of what is usually
understood to be design.

How do you define design capability?
I do not think designing is just a set of skills.
I am influenced by Guy Julier's idea of design
culture (see his book *The Culture of Design*
published in 2007 by Sage Publications) where
design is seen as a cultural practice which
includes skills, knowledge and understanding,
and the social processes which shape them. It
is unfair to expect non-designers to be able to
practice Design Thinking simply by teaching
them a few methods. You can expose managers
and executives to some aspects of designerly
approaches (as I do on the Saïd Business
School MBA programme), but that doesn't
give them the same kind of capability as people
who come from a design culture that has been

nurtured through training and practice as a designer.

Culture is complex, and you can't develop it overnight. A design culture is made up of a set of practices that are organized through the institutions, particular design schools and firms which are transformed through discourse in conferences, websites, presentations and what people talk about in bars and emails. I am located within this design culture, and I see my role as being a critic of it, as well as a translator of it to managers and entrepreneurs.

I am interested in some of the things that I see being called Service Design. I am critical of the way it's being discussed, which often is quite naïve and does not learn from directly relevant fields like participatory design, workplace studies or operations management. While I have taught design a lot, my main teaching experience has been in non-design environments where I translate design culture and show people from enormously varied backgrounds and sectors such as technology, finance, the military, law, marketing and healthcare what design can bring to their organizations. They usually find this temporary engagement with design practices and culture productive, challenging and enjoyable.

What is the role of design or Design Thinking in shaping responses to complex social problems?
I am interested in how policy is enacted in strategies and actual organizational capacity to design and deliver services. For example, last year I helped a housing provider who wanted to design a befriending service to support older residents in London, people living in their own homes or in residential care homes; some of whom are active, some of whom cannot get out so much. Current government policy is to encourage older people to stay in their

I am interested in how policy is enacted in strategies and actual organizational capacities to design and deliver services.

homes for longer rather than move into care homes, due to the rising costs of caring for a growing population of older people and those with complex chronic conditions. This is also affected by changes in resource patterns over the next 20 years. My interest is not so much in policy but, in this case, how a provider can support a population of older people and how, by doing so, could also benefit their families, their carers, their neighbours and ultimately the state. For example, the befriending service might reduce a person's admissions to accident and emergency departments, improve their mental health, or reduce stress on carers. So within this one service there are implications for multiple policy areas.

How does design contribute to the development of better services?
The organization that I worked with was already acting as the designer of the service. I provided them with support in its design and implementation. This represents a shift in how designers operate in this space. Design here is an orientation to the social and material in how a service is constituted, including attending to how people behave, how they feel, what they know, what capabilities they have, how they engage with one another, what material or digital artefacts exist within all of this, why things are the way they are,

The terminology I use at the moment is that as designers, we tell stories and we make maps. We bring a strong focus that is both imaginative and analytical into our storytelling about what encounters will or could be within a service.

and how they could be otherwise. A design-ethnographic orientation emphasizes an understanding of how a service might work at human scale. The terminology I use at the moment is that as designers, we tell stories and we make maps. We bring a strong focus that is both imaginative and analytical into our storytelling about what encounters will or could be within a service. We help create service ecology maps that look at how these people, artefacts, organizations and resources are connected together, and explore how things could be different. Without our interventions, managers would be proceeding without close attention to the lived experience of the people they are designing for and with. They would not be attentive to the material artefacts and qualities of people's interactions with them, and they might not put resources together in novel ways. My team and I create what I term 'boundary objects' to help the client begin to rethink what the service they are designing is made up of. 'Boundary object' is a term from sociology, and I use it to refer to things like personas, segmentation models, visualizations of customer journeys and service blueprints. These items are used to help clients and their partners to conceptualize what they are doing, and to have a closer resonance between the trajectories they are trying to create for particular users and the particular outcomes they are working towards.

What implications does the idea of Service Design have for design education?
Service Design is interesting because it cannot avoid the social world in, and for which, designing takes place. The most interesting practitioners are attentive to both the social processes and artefacts that are part of a service. Good designers and students will already be implicitly doing things in their studio practices that show how you can't really separate the social and the material, but it's only recently that design theory has started engaging more with sociology and anthropology – of which there is already a long history in systems design and Human Computer Interaction. Designers need to be much more theoretically informed and have a much clearer understanding of value and impact and how things become operationalized. The methods that I enact in my teaching and in my practice are very much at the intersection of design, the social sciences and management. The context is value creation. Value is not necessarily predefined, it is a result of how a service is configured and enacted and is within the context of organizations and entrepreneurs trying to enact change. In this context the theoretical starting point is not an object, but practices – although objects are absolutely critical to practices. I believe these ideas are relevant to education in all design fields.

What do you think the future of design practice will look like, and what factors do you think will shape it?

I think there will be more designers becoming entrepreneurs, who not only design a venture or service but also decide to run it. Design as a specialism will continue to exist because we still need objects to be realized. However, if we are to consider the use of design in relation to contemporary problems and organizations, this requires designers to have a much better understanding of how different organizational worlds work, and how discrete objects have agency and meaning within social worlds. Design practice now needs the type of concepts and frameworks which cannot be found while running or working in a design-focussed consultancy, or studying at a design school.

It's becoming more crucial to articulate why design or, as I currently think about it, design ethnography as a discipline is important, and how the social and material worlds are entangled: how they come to be, and the roles that designers and designing can play within them. There's been a distinct spread of the ideas of Design Thinking into other fields, such as social venturing. There are entrepreneurs designing services by trying to put the user at the heart of the service and designing artefacts to reduce material use or change behaviours, but they still lack the culture that designers bring with their orientation towards continuous practical experimentation. While Design Thinking may have spread beyond design, the contemporary Western version of the state of design – as evidenced at events like the London Design Festival – is still all about objects. We lack serious and public conversations about the role of design, and this is where I think design researchers have failed to illuminate why and how design and designing matter.

Unfortunately, while design practitioners tell great stories about what they have made and are able to describe their processes, they do not necessarily have the ability to present a convincing argument on a disciplinary level to other fields, or to the wider public. My experience of talking to sociologists and managers is that many of them have not heard much about design, other than about IDEO. Hardly anyone outside our disciplines reads our literature. Only a small minority of managers and entrepreneurs understand what repeated practical experimentation, and an orientation to how things are given shape and form as well as behaviour, can do for them.

Design is still fixated on the pleasure of new ideas while ignoring where those ideas might have come from, what has happened to bring those particular ideas to the surface, and what their future impact might be. Design remains focussed on forms, materials and the idea of authorship. I do not claim to design anything, as often the 'things' that I design are complex organizational artefacts which are difficult to show. Design culture has to change to accommodate this emerging type of design, which could be led by educational institutions, as well as by practitioners and people who don't even think of themselves as designers. Through these changes, the boundaries of what lies inside and outside of design will be reshaped over the next 20 years. *-end-*

Carlos Teixeira

Carlos Teixeira is an Associate Professor at the School of Design Strategies, Parsons The New School for Design in New York. He has a PhD in Design from the Institute of Design, Illinois Institute of Technology. His academic research centres around the transformations occurring in design practice and within the context of knowledge economies. Currently, Carlos's work is focussed on interpreting the growth in demand for design competencies in emerging markets such as Brazil, China and India. As a practitioner, he has professional experience as a communication designer and strategic design consultant in the United States and Brazil. Carlos speaks here about the challenges for designers in a knowledge economy, and the need for new models of design practice to meet the requirements of emerging markets.

Can you tell us what your current role involves, and what drives you in your work?
I was educated at Pontifícia Universidade Católica in Rio de Janeiro, Brazil and worked as a graphic designer for eight years, before completing a PhD at the Institute of Design in Chicago. Following my PhD I joined Parsons The New School for Design, where I continued to research, work and teach to give myself the space to explore new design priorities – such as the knowledge economy, emerging models of design and new markets.

What are your views on the current changes of roles and practices in design?
My understanding right now is that we are changing from an economy that was based on goods, to an economy that is based on innovative ideas and knowledge. We are transitioning into a knowledge economy, and the value in a knowledge economy is

based on capacity to produce and work with information in order to turn knowledge into ideas. Ideas are the core of this new economy. An idea can be anything; it can be a new production system, a new technology, a new drug, a new brand or a new service. Whatever you create comes out of that capacity to understand complex issues, and to transform that understanding into an idea in order to generate economic value. This is the foundation of a knowledge economy.

The question that I have been exploring since my PhD in 1998, is how to understand design's role when we shift the focus from tangible material into a knowledge economy. I do not think this is a major shift away from a design perspective because design, as I define it, is applying knowledge of process in the imagining of new possibilities. I understand design as this experimental, innovative capacity to imagine something beyond what is today, understanding the potential and creating new alternatives. Design is a process, and the know-how of navigating that process. People are trying to understand how ideas are created and that is what designers do all the time – but although there have not been any significant changes in our design process, we have become fixated on the idea that design is defined by its output; for example, in the way we identify our disciplines as industrial design, communication design, product design, interior design and fashion design.

There is a huge potential for design to play a major role in the early and strategic stages of innovation. Historically people did not have the expertise or capacity to innovate systematically in the early stages, but design can contribute to this by providing systematic processes and methods. The opportunities for design to contribute in this way are becoming more common. This is the key change, but it is also very challenging. How do you go from being an industrial designer with a specific expertise in designing products, to employing that expertise in tackling a very complex problem at the front end of an innovation process? Once we start operating at the strategic level the problems are far more complex than what we are used to. This change is not only seen in design practice, but also reflected in society in general. The process of innovating needs to be design-led, but not necessary led by designers. This is the other major shift. Designers are not the only ones 'designing'.

There are claims that designers are already working at the highest strategic level with the CEO of one company, but this is merely a drop in the ocean if you consider the rate of innovation that is going to be required for a knowledge economy. Most designers are not

ready because they are still thinking either 'I am the designer' or 'I am the expert', when in fact designers act as consultants. I have not found many designers who are able to work with an organization and transform it to a point where it becomes design-driven.

What is your interest in design in the emerging markets?
Until 2009, I was researching how multi-national companies and Italian industrial clusters were applying design, and what role design played in that context. I became very familiar with their models but I was not finding out anything new or interesting about design. At the same time, my research was converging into the notion that design is really about knowledge brokering. I use the term 'knowledge brokery' to mean that design has the capacity to transform information into ideas. I was beginning to see this transformation happening in India, China and Brazil, and that is why emerging markets became the focus of my research.

How do you go from being an industrial designer with a specific expertise in designing products, to employing that expertise in tackling a very complex problem at the front end of an innovation process?

From what I know about design and how it is practiced by companies in developed countries, I am certain that these companies do not know how to design for emerging markets. The model of a small design firm with a few design specialists working on a project for three to six months to develop innovation, and asking for an expensive hourly fee, will not work. We are talking about billions of people needing innovation after innovation in the coming years. I started to see this type of transformation and innovation happening as I was travelling around India and China, I saw it everywhere I went and it was happening without the involvement of what you might call the 'established' design firms like IDEO, frog or Design Continuum. This is the reason why I believe that design is happening regardless of whether designers are involved or not, and why I am interested to find out more about this situation.

To give you some context: the entire population of Italy, which is around 61 million people, would fit into the state of Karnataka in South India. This means that if the entire design capacity of Italy was brought into India, it would only serve a small fraction of their population of around 1.2 billion people. What I am trying to highlight with this is that there is a huge need for design, but currently there is a lack of design capacity in emerging markets. Even if I were to use all the design capacity from around the world, it would not be enough to address all of the emerging market's needs. The problem is that we are still trying to sell Design Thinking and design consulting in the same project model, which will not work in this context.

The emerging markets need design to solve problems that are not typical design consulting projects; for example education, healthcare, energy, sanitation, mobility and all the basic infrastructure that governments are supposed to provide but, in the emerging markets, are unable to offer. There are major business opportunities here, but at the moment design is not ready to design education systems or healthcare systems. Even the few current examples, such as applying design to rethink the UK healthcare system, are not transferable to India or China. If you look at the size of the UK's health requirements against those of India, they are not comparable in terms of scale.

The immediate challenge is that design is simply not ready to tackle problems at this speed, scale and diversity – we have never seen them before so all of our processes and methods, such as design ethnography and user-centred design, will have limited impact when we are trying to understand the needs of billions of people. You cannot just conduct a few interviews and assume it will be enough. There are over 300 different languages spoken in India, and if you travel 50 km out of one region into the next you could find people with an entirely different culture, religion and social structure. It then becomes difficult to claim that you can offer user-centred design. How are designers to conduct research within so much diversity and complexity? The speed and scale of change is unprecedented. If you look at the literature relating to know-how in design, what you find is that we simply don't have the know-how for this context.

What new models of design are you seeing?
Currently, the major opportunity that exists for design is in the start-up space. However a big challenge for designers is finding the funding and sponsorship to pay for the initial work. Design is not usually thought of as a valuable asset in the early stages of establishing a business. Start-ups are more focused on their proof of concept, and once they have

The biggest challenge design has to face is that we are still trapped in the old models of 'doing design'. We need to design new organizations, and new types of design.

the money and resource they will then look to scale up and involve design at a later stage. For designers to work with entrepreneurs and investors, they need to be working on the process of creating ideas, and the output of those ideas. I am not saying that industrial design and other traditional disciplines will disappear. We will continue to need that expertise, but strategic design will be needed to frame the ideas. Start-ups will still need to translate their innovative concepts into products, software applications and brands, but design is also needed at the idea definition stage.

I do not see many designers, design schools or design firms that are well-prepared for working in this way. They are still providing expertise to large corporations in a traditional way, acting as their outsourced design arm. Designers already know how to do this, they have many years of experience in working this way. The new model is about design as a collaborative innovation system, practiced by design organizations or companies who are design-driven. There will need to be a completely new way of doing, practising and organizing design at the early stages of an innovation process.

Another way is to work in networks. I have been involved in design projects in Brazil, and when I was working on those projects I created a network of design firms to work with a large company. When I first approached design firms, several of them were reluctant to collaborate with other design firms. I had to convince them that unless they were willing to collaborate, their individual teams would be unable to handle the project on their own.

The biggest challenge design has to face is that we are still trapped in the old models of 'doing design'. We need to design new organizations, and new types of design. I have termed this 'Enterprising Design' and am teaching a Master's level course at Parsons titled Enterprising Design Knowledge. I am educating the students in understanding what design can do, and embedding design capacity into organizations in order to help them to systemically innovate. We also need designers to be able to coach, mentor and structure before they can scale. My point is that if we have a few designers who can transform organizations to become design-driven organizations, then we are able to scale. My suggestion is that we try to get the design community to think about design-driven open innovation systems, and to think of how to mimic what design organizations do – but on a larger scale. *-end-*

Ezio Manzini

For more than two decades Ezio Manzini has been working in the field of design for sustainability. Recently he has broadened his interests to include social innovation and founded DESIS, an international network that supports and promotes design for social innovation and sustainability. Throughout his professional life Ezio has worked at the Politecnico di Milano in Italy. In our interview he talks about his interest in understanding how design changes when operating in a context where 'everybody designs', and calls for design to actively present, articulate and support socially recognized qualities of living that will accelerate the transition towards sustainability.

Can you tell us what your current role involves, and what drives you in your work?
Today, a large part of my time is taken up by DESIS – Design for Social Innovation and Sustainability: a network of design labs, based in design schools, that promote social innovation towards sustainability. These DESIS Labs are teams of professors, researchers and students who orient their didactic and research activities towards starting and/or facilitating social innovation processes (to find out more about this have a look at www.desis-network. org). What I do on a daily basis is a mixture of writing, lecturing and networking that, as a whole, I consider a design activity: the strategic design of a large social enterprise.

Beyond that I am directly involved in some design research programmes. For instance, in the autumn semester of 2011, I have been invited to Parsons the New School for Design in New York as a visiting professor, to develop a research programme based on grassroots social innovation and public service innovation in collaboration with Parsons DESIS Lab.

What gets you excited about design at the moment?
Globally, our societies are in the middle of a dramatic transition towards a (hopefully) more socially and environmentally sustainable world – a transition from which large and brand new challenges emerge, and in which, in my view, design could have an important role to play. Given this very general framework, I am particularly interested in understanding how design changes when operating in a context where 'everybody designs'. That is, when a design approach is adopted by every actor involved in the process, and even beyond that, when it is adopted by society, by individuals and communities trying to solve the problems they encounter in their daily lives.

Let me say something more on that last point. The starting consideration is that every human being is naturally endowed with the capability to focus on a problem and imagine a solution, while recognising constraints and opportunities. This mixture of creativity, realism, dreams and entrepreneurship is a natural human design capability, but it can be enhanced or reduced by the society in which those humans live.

My idea is that the improvement of this diffuse design capability plays an important part in increasing people's (perceived) quality of life and, at the same time, accelerates the transition towards sustainability. In fact, for human beings, satisfaction in life means having dreams, concrete capabilities and the possibility of realising them (that is, in our terminology, to have the possibility and opportunity to design their own life). At the same time we can observe that in a small, densely populated and highly connected planet, people's sensitivity, knowledge, creativity and entrepreneurial capabilities are our some of our most abundant resources. Therefore, the most promising sustainability strategy is to consider these things an asset and create the conditions to catalyse them, transforming their potential into actual action for large-scale systemic change.

Given that higher design capabilities are (or should be) diffused between everyone, we have to develop a better understanding of what the professional designer's role needs to become. To do this we have to improve our language, and make a clear distinction between professional designers (design experts) and all the other actors participating in the co-design process (design amateurs).

Let us refer back to design history. Traditionally designers have been seen, and have seen themselves, as the only creative participants in interdisciplinary design processes. But today, due to all the reasons I've mentioned so far, this clear distinction blurs and they become professional designers among many non-professionals. But even when this distinction blurs, it does not mean that the role of design experts is becoming less important. On the contrary, in this new context design experts have the crucial function of bringing very specific design competencies to the co-design process – they become a particular kind of process facilitator, using specific design skills to enable the other actors to become good designers themselves. In short: they are enabling people to design their own lives.

...I am particularly interested in understanding how design changes when operating in a context where 'everybody designs'. That is, when a design approach is adopted by every actor involved in the process...

What do you think designers bring to the story?
A phenomenological way to answer this question is to look at what happens when designers (i.e. design experts) participate in a multi-disciplinary design team. Experience suggests that one of the first contributions to be recognized will be their capability to visualize and prototype. 'Visualizing' means to make the ideas under discussion clear and visible through drawing, videos or storytelling. 'Prototyping' means to make those ideas tangible and testable. When the ideas that have been visualized and prototyped are translated into systems, they become highly complex (and creative) ones.

However, visualizing and prototyping are only the first of the contributions that designers can make to new design processes. The most important and delicate step involves a move from visualizing to visioning. 'Visioning' means to bring the designers' ideas into the design process, making them visible and using them to feed other partners' conversations. Therefore I am suggesting that our understanding of design should move from a domain of 'design as tool' to one of 'design as content', considering the designers' ability to deal with the soft qualities of artefacts, referring for example to qualities such as as meaning and beauty that cannot be measured in quantitative terms, but have a deep impact on social acceptability. These design-specific contents are the second and, in my view, most important contribution designers make to the new design processes.

If we assume that we are already delivering the technical toolkit in our current education, how do we begin to teach and make explicit these s oft qualities?
The design of soft qualities cannot be taught in a direct way, as we would for technical,

ergonomic and economic features. But what we can do is teach it in an indirect way, through design experiences and continuous socialized discussion. This approach has always been a pillar of teaching in architecture and design schools, where the ability to deal with soft qualities has been developed mainly through 'design studios' – that is, by inviting students to develop ideas and discuss them collectively. This helps to develop the sensitivity and language that produces these qualities.

The problem now is that in many design schools, when new artefacts such as services and organizations are being developed this kind of cultural discussion seems to be lost, overwhelmed as it is by technical, economic and managerial considerations. Of course designers should understand those languages and contents, but they must also develop their own design contents. These contents should be related to artefacts' soft qualities, and use design languages that permit them to start, and then deepen, the social conversation around those artefacts. The importance of these soft qualities, and consequently of their specific design contribution, is particularly clear when we consider the biggest challenges of our age. Today, more and more people recognize that the present crises (environmental, social and economic) will bring radical changes to people's behaviours, and that ways of living will have to change in response. From this perspective, if we want to maximize people's ability to change by choice (that is, to re-orient their ways of living, and to change because they choose to and not because they have to), the main issue is about sustainability. This relates to the development of socially-recognized approaches to living that require more sustainable behaviours, and could be attractive to a growing number of people.

To present, support and articulate these sustainable qualities is, in my view, the most specific and original contribution designers can make to the facilitation and acceleration of our transition towards sustainability.

What do you think the future of design practice will look like, and what factors do you think will shape it?
Everything is changing fast, including design and design practices. At the beginning of design's history a century ago, it was always described in relation to the object to be designed. Today, with the artefact's evolution from simple material products to complex hybrid, material and immaterial systems (the new artefacts), design is defined less and less by its objects, and more and more by its processes and its ability to be applied to different kinds of artefacts (such as tables, chairs, services and organizations). Of course this evolution affects design as a whole: its theory, methods, practices and – in particular – the architecture of the design process and the designers' role within it.

A particularly deep and interesting change is happening. This can be summarised as the shift from (mainly) linear processes towards (mainly) networked and open-ended processes. To make this statement clearer, let's go back to a traditional design manual. What it normally tells us is that a design process starts with research, continues into concept generation and concludes with the development of the final solution. Today the new artefacts emerge from a designing network, where each node is a design initiative developed by different teams of designers and experts. These design initiatives can involve ethnographic research, the realization of simulations and prototypes, scenario building or final solution co-development. But all of them are conceived

...I am suggesting that our understanding of design should move from a domain of 'design as tool' to one of 'design as content', considering the designers' ability to deal with the soft qualities of artefacts...

and developed as self-standing projects: autonomous design initiatives with their design programmes and final results. These design initiatives are mutually connected, creating a flexible mesh capable of producing results that can always be updated, upgraded and re-oriented.

In the face of these new products, professional designers are changing their position and role within the design process. They become part of a growing number of actors who work together to generate wide and flexible networks that collaboratively conceive, develop and manage new solutions. And hopefully, these will be sustainable solutions. *~end~*

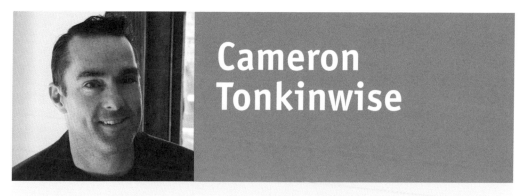

Cameron Tonkinwise

Cameron Tonkinwise was recently appointed Director of Design Studies at Carnegie Mellon University (CMU) and Chair of the Doctoral Studies Committee. Prior to this, Cameron was the Associate Dean for Sustainability at Parsons The New School for Design in New York. Before moving to the USA, Cameron held positions as Director of Design Studies at the University of Technology, Sydney and as Executive Officer of Change Design (formerly EcoDesign Foundation), a not-for-profit independent research organization in Australia. In this interview Cameron makes a case for Design Thinking as a radical form of disruptive innovation, and discusses what that means for design education.

Can you tell us what your current role involves, and what drives you in your work?
Primarily my job is about working with faculty at CMU to renovate Richard Buchanan's existing PhD programme. There are very few PhD programmes in America, and none that are wholly focused on design and understanding design. Instead they are normally based around social science in relation to design, such as the programmes at North Eastern and at North Carolina State University. Illinois Institute of Technology (IIT) has a DDes programme, but this kind of doctorate for non-architectural designers has not taken off yet in the USA. So that's 60 per cent of my job, and the other 40 per cent is creating a new design studies curriculum for the undergraduate programmes. It's also part of my job to create a new vertical core for the product, interaction and visual communication designers.

How do you define Design Thinking?
I would define it in two ways. Firstly, I consider Design Thinking to be the type of thinking that designers do during the act of designing, which is a combination of:
a) Material thinking – about what materials can and cannot do
b) Visual thinking – testing sketched forms for buildability, operability and usability in imagined contexts
c) Empathy – an ethnographic sensibility toward not just what people say they are doing, or even what they are actually doing, but what they would do, if only they could.

The second way I define Design Thinking refers to how it is used by designers (or non-designers) to solve problems beyond what would normally be considered the realm of design. In this context, normal designing concerns the making of things that people buy to make their lives more efficient, productive or pleasurable. The beyond-the-norm problems (often mischaracterized as 'wicked problems') to which Design Thinking is now being applied are more often to do with strategy and systems. For example, these may be in areas such as commercial innovation (increasing market-share or creating new markets) and social innovation (helping people to change their lifestyle to improve health and employability).

Innovations that result from the second definition remain, to my mind, innovative within 'as-usual' circumstances. No matter how innovative the new strategic direction that comes from a design thinking consultancy, the proposition still involves a business, with employees, charging customers for a product or service. The mere fact that social innovations are distinct from commercial innovations is an indication that social innovations are not yet disrupting the larger organization of society – or worse, that social innovations allow the commercialization of the social, rather than the socialization of commerce. To put it more starkly, what is often innovative about social innovations is how they enable people to cope with their situations rather than change them. For instance, I might need to use a design toolkit to 'DIY' my healthcare, food provision or education because I am excluded from mainstream commercial provision of those goods and services. But my DIYing actually perpetuates my exclusion. I can continue, and the goods and services can continue, without either being changed.

This is where Design Thinking starts to head towards service design thinking, sustainability strategy and generally making society less materials-intense. You will naturally have to start thinking about more revolutionary propositions for the decoupling of use and ownership. You do not need to own what you use, and so you could start thinking about the kind of business models and service systems associated with car share schemes, tool sharing or co-housing. This application of Design Thinking is really about looking at new business models that do not bear any relation to current forms of profit and loss, valuation and customer relation management.

This is why I believe there is a third, radically disruptive and innovative potential within Design Thinking, linked to the three characteristics I mentioned previously of material thinking, visual thinking and empathy. Our societies are unsustainable because we are good modernists, which means that we are thoroughly ambivalent. We think that well-being comes from material things, but we pay no heed to the materiality of those things. As James Twitchell (Professor of English and Advertising at the University of Florida) once said, the problem with consumerism is that, in the end, it is not materialist enough – it does not behave as if it really values material things. Only this double-bind explains how our houses end up stuffed with so many things, and yet our systems of value cannot account for the ongoing social and ecological cost of those things. The only people in our society who truly understand the materiality of all the things that fill up our homes, are designers. Good designers know the value of materials: what they can and cannot do, why they are good for one device and not another, where they come from and where they go. Within the material thinking of Design Thinking lies a way out of our unsustainable modernist ambivalence – a radical, Copernican potential to really valorize the products of design, putting materiality at the centre of value production with circular economies of product take-back and material recovery structured into how society resources itself.

Our societies are unsustainable because they are hopeless at imagining the future, let alone factoring those futures into present value systems. Designers work in the realm of futuring: they visualize rich pictures of future scenarios where both material environments and lifestyles co-evolve. They not only fantasize about these futures, but also critically evaluate their feasibility and argue for their preferability. Unfortunately, designers must do all of this within the short-termism of market economies, which is precisely why designing must break free from the professional service of design consultancies – hence the radical potential of design(erly) thinking.

And finally, our societies are unsustainable because we do not practice what we preach. We claim to be modern products of the Enlightenment engaged in humanist enterprises, and yet we have created economic structures and organizations that are dehumanizing. We need households filled with comforts and toys because, for most people, employment is unsatisfying; and when employment is satisfying it is mostly because it involves the successful production of even more stuff. Our material unsustainability is dependent upon our fundamentally non-empathetic society. You have to wonder, why do businesses consider the creative empathetic research aspects of Design Thinking to be such a radical breakthrough? Social researchers will listen to what people say in order to understand their values. Designerly empathy is innovative by comparison, because designers are empathetic with people engaged in habitual practices that are fused with all of the things that make up their material environment.

I am alluding here to what has been called 'the practice turn' in sociology and anthropology: the recognition that a fundamental unit of social analysis is a practice, which is comprised of 1) devices and infrastructures, 2) skills, habits and know-how, and 3) meanings and identities. Social researchers usually focus on 3, sometimes 2, but only designers bring 1 into the mix operationally. This more comprehensive form of empathy has radical potential, because it offers a more accurate account of the way we live. For example, we may intend to be sustainable (3), and know how to be sustainable (2), but we might not have the material opportunity to actually be sustainable (1). Real social change requires all three of these elements, and this is where design is at its most powerful.

How is Design Thinking perceived at the moment?
In the US there is quite a concerted backlash against it, and I am seeing a significant trend of leading professional organizations 'jumping on the grave' of Design Thinking and reasserting the importance of a traditional disciplinary practice and craft-based expertise. Recently, there has been growing support for a point of view put forth by a leading voice in the field of visual identity, who derided the latest American Institute of Graphic Arts (AIGA) competition. The competition focused on the design process rather than its outcome, in her words 'completely missing out on the beauty and affect of the design' while perfectly illustrating her view on what is wrong with the strategic approach to design and Design Thinking. It indicates to me that lots of people think the pendulum has swung too far toward strategic design and client/customer-centredness. There are a number of firms that have established consultancies in the Design Thinking and strategic design space. All the major companies, like frog, Smart, Continuum and IDEO, clearly offer strategic advice but lots of other more established firms are now reasserting the importance of a craft-based version of design. It is the same

kind of backlash that we saw against science in relation to global warming. To attempt a return to design fundamentalism is to search for something that experts are less able to control. In a weird way, Design Thinking gets coded here as a loss of control, and an excessive democratization of expert designing.

How does the changing role of design impact design education, in light of this shift from 'design of things for people' to 'design of people'? I think there are two big consequences of Design Thinking for the undergraduate education of designers, and both concern design moving away from the fine arts to become more integrated with the liberal arts, and vice versa. As design has evolved from the application of fine art to products, into the practice of enhancing the efficiency, productivity and enjoyability of human-product (or human-built environment) interactions, designers have progressively had to do more social research. This is a bit schematic, if not mythical, but let's say that designers originally conducted research only around materials. And then, following a typology suggested by Liz Sanders (a design researcher focused on participatory, human-centred design thinking and co-creation practices – see 'Design Research in 2006' in *Design Research Quarterly* vol.1 no.1, September 2006), designers start to ask customers what they might want, using market research via surveys and focus groups. For the purposes of this type of research, a person is just a bundle of semi-rational consumer desires. But then, in order to make products more helpful and innovative, designers start observing people and realize that they actually do things differently to what they self-report. At this point, a person becomes a more complicated ecosystem of semi-conscious practices. In Sanders' typology, the designer then begins to undertake generative design

research – which means engaging in co-creative activities and participatory design. At this stage in the design research, the person under study now has a history and a future; they are an ensemble of trajectories and latencies. Design Thinking, and the more strategic new design practices like service design, therefore require designers to have much richer perspectives on the people for whom, and with whom, they are designing. They need to understand psychology, not just consumer psychology but social psychology and perhaps even psychoanalysis (which recognizes that people are also comprised of unconscious aspects). Designers also need to understand sociology, not just statistical analysis but also social, political and economic history. They need to understand anthropology, not just ethnography but material cultural studies and technology studies. They of course need to know much more about living systems, about (co-)evolution and resilience. And they also need to be highly honed observers and interviewers, which means they need to understand performance: improvization, character, expressiveness and self-awareness. Design Thinking is, in fact, a performing art.

My argument is best conveyed by the popular saying that 'in service design, humans are your material'. This is in fact a very dangerous idea, but it does contain a warning not to treat people like inert materials. Designers should instead try and discern what – like a material – a person can be reasonably made to do or not do, via persuasion or design-enabled facilitation. What we need now is a design education that studies the human as well as the white space, serif type, moulded plastic and organic textile drape. *-end-*

Andrea Siodmok

Andrea Siodmok is an independent design consultant involved in a number of innovation projects in the public and private sector. She was Chief Designer at Cornwall Council and Programme Director for the Designs of the Time (Dott) Cornwall programme between 2009-2013. Prior to this Andrea was Chief Design Officer at the UK Design Council, helping to set up new design strategies for a range of government departments including the Department of Health and the Home Office. As design approaches are increasingly being used to develop transformational solutions, Andrea shares her viewpoints on the role design can play in public sector innovation.

Can you tell us what your current role involves, and what drives you in your work?
As Chief Designer at Cornwall Council my role has been to use design approaches to tackle some of the complicated challenges that we face in local government. Cornwall recognized design as an approach that would enable them to get close to users, be creative and develop transformational solutions. Over the past few years my role has also been to increase the capacity of the council to innovate, by applying creative approaches such as design. This role was created as a result of the work and legacy delivered by the Dott programme.

What was the role of Dott Cornwall, and what impact has it had on social innovation in public services?
The Design of the Times (Dott) programme was initiated by the Design Council in the UK as a series of community projects, events and exhibitions based in the North East of England in 2007, and its aim was to demonstrate how design as a process could help make life better. The second Dott programme was located in Cornwall, South-West England and had a similar aim of bringing together local communities and world-class designers to work on projects that improve how we live, work and play. Dott Cornwall ran from 2009 to 2011, and its role was not only about working with designers, but about bringing together different actors and parts of the system to create change in regional development, public sector and government.

Dott's success has contributed to a debate around redesigning public services at the regional, national and European level. Cornwall Council is looking at its £1.2 billion budget responsibility regionally, and aims to become more efficient and effective whilst exploring new ways of working with citizens. Dott and

Cornwall Council's work in innovation has contributed to the UK's Design Commission[1] report *Restarting Britain 2* around design in the public sector. Additionally, the European Design Leadership Board published the *Design for Growth and Prosperity* report in 2012, which identified levers that can be used to create growth through design.

Who else is working in the social innovation space, and can you share a project example?
At both national and European levels, there is a broader trend around using social innovation to look at where capacity can be built within government systems. Dott is not the only programme working towards this goal of creating positive change through design approaches. There are people like Good for Nothing (www.goodfornothing.com) who work with local councils arranging camps, jams and hack days. There are organizations like Innovation Lab and the Young Foundation in the UK, and Red Associates and MindLab in Copenhagen who are also doing similar work. There is a huge untapped market for the delivery of design intervention, potentially through start-ups, because it can immediately start to confront the existing consultancy models of design practice. The most notable example of this is FutureGov, a creative agency which is a mixture of designers, policy and technical experts (see the FutureGov case study on page 60). Another example is Capita, a leading UK business management company that is also looking to set up a social innovation service design capacity inside their organization.

We started the *Shaped by Us* (www.shapedbyus. org) project at Cornwall Council in 2012, as a way to test the viability of the Dott results and spread their impact to a wider national level. *Shaped by Us* is a new online community tool that helps movers and shapers to tackle issues within their community. Challenges are set up by individuals or organizations from within the community, and are open for anyone to join in and contribute. The online platform also offers toolkits and useful guides as well as opportunities for funding and sponsorship, and access to local expertise. This support will enable a project team to develop their favourite idea, while other members can also contribute possible solutions. With help from the Local Government Association and Nesta we are planning to launch the programme nationwide in 2013.

The UK is often seen as a model for how to use design to drive social innovation in public services. Why do you think this is the case?
There is a simple, and also a complex, reason for this. I spent time advising parts of the Brazilian government, and one of the observations they made was that in Brazil, design is a noun – a 'thing' and not a process or an approach. Much of European design culture is based around the design of objects, so the notion of design as an approach does not have a vocabulary. In the UK we are quite comfortable with the idea that design is a way of doing things, as opposed to the outcome of doing them. That is partly grounded in UK research history but also in philosophy.

The more complex reason is to do with the emergence of the UK service economy, due to government policy in the late 1970s and 1980s, which forged a market for services and consultancies. This greatly benefitted design, which is associated with the consultancy model on a global scale. The irony is that the UK design sector is one of the best in the world, because UK industry is so bad at buying design. Many of our leading UK agencies have spent years without any UK clients. When there is no local market, designers have to up their game to become world-class and build strong consultancy models. This lack of a domestic market has enabled UK designers to develop the art of selling design as a process rather than an object; because if you are selling design to Hong Kong or Dubai, you are not selling stuff. You are selling strategy, and an approach where delivery happens elsewhere. It was not long before these consultancies began to apply this approach to new sectors, which has led to work with big global corporations on service design thinking. The Design Council should also be credited, as they recognized the domestic market failures and responded to the potential in service design by creating new platforms for design exploration, such as the Red Unit[2], Dott programme and Design Challenges.

Despite these advances the digital industries remain preeminent in the UK, and service design has not scaled as we expected for two reasons. The first reason is that the value design brings to the table is not being recognized. The public sector does not have market contestability and, without a market, there is less demand for design. The biggest driver for design in the UK public sector is the recent budget cuts, which have meant the old ways of doing things are untenable and people have no other option but to innovate. However, with a lack of funds, the question is: can a time of cuts be turned into a time of investment in design? This will really make or break the UK economy. Cornwall Council sees design as the best option, but I still need to demonstrate the true value of design by prototyping and delivering projects that result in better services for less money.

I believe that Generation Y can change things for us. They have a whole new mindset, and when they join the private and public sector workforces they expect to be creative and are prepared to take risks. It is more intuitive for them to take on the role of an innovator using a design approach, than to act as a traditional civil servant whose responsibility is to be a guardian and controller. I hope within 10 years most parts of the UK economy, in both private and public sectors, will have an expectation to be innovative. By then I hope design will have proven that it has an evidence base, a set of tools and methodologies that are open, not exclusive, and can be deployed to tackle social and economic problems.

What factors will encourage designers and the public sector to work together?
Although a portfolio of work will get you through the door in the private sector, to be a supplier to the public sector you have to meet a baseline of pre-procurement assessment – for example, by demonstrating an equality policy. The procurement process can vary widely between organizations and this tends to discourage service designers from engaging. So there is an argument for removing these barriers, and the simplest way to achieve this would be to set up a national service design panel or framework. This would provide a roster of service design companies which meet the various criteria, making it easier for any public organization to procure services. It would also be a brilliant way to create a joined-up network of what are currently quite disparate individuals and agencies.

Once we get past the credentials phase, councils will expect to be able to see what they are buying. The problem here lies in the fact that it is very hard to buy things that are not defined. Designers can help their clients to innovate during this pre-specification phase by engaging in the shaping and definition of the problem. However, the public sector often wants a precise specification of what the designer will deliver. This can be difficult, because until you are able to define the specification by exploring the issues, a solution cannot be predetermined. For example, with Dott we were required to deliver specific back-to-work interventions and had to be very clear about how we were going to achieve this. But the whole point was that we would not know how to achieve it until we began the process of co-design and co-creation. So for the first three months we failed to meet our targets, because we were too busy working out how to meet those targets. In the last few months we actually exceeded our targets, because you have to go into the unknown before you can project out into the known. Being honest about the ambiguity within design can help us to recognize where we are in the journey, and prevent us from promising outcomes that might prove to be unrealistic or unsuitable.

What do you think the future of design practice will look like, and what factors will shape it?
I get excited by the large-scale design policies that countries like China and Korea have put into place. The UK requires a bold approach, so I agree with the Royal Society of the Arts' (RSA) view of Public Services 2020 (www.2020publicservicestrust.org) and the need for a new enlightenment, a new renaissance. The scale of design has to change. If it doesn't, there's a strong chance that a lot of our skills will end up being outsourced. The UK is rightly criticised for being good at coming up with new ways of working, but failing to take advantage of them at any significant scale. Other countries watch what the UK is doing then do it better and faster themselves. As a result, the UK gets left behind.

Design is an evolutionary discipline, and it has always evolved to meet the requirements of different markets, from private to public sector. The market shapes the design profession, which is why we have graphic, fashion and now service designers. Governments can have early-stage involvement in those markets and, by doing so, create confidence. In times of recession government probably has more of a role to play in giving direction, and shaping policy conditions to help grow new markets. The way that we reconcile our needs with environmental and social concerns will be the biggest driver of design in the next 10 years. Design will explore the possibility of doing more for less by partaking in the circular economy, recycling and extension of product longevity. On the social side we have other massive global challenges, such as providing support for an ageing population.

One positive thing about Europe is that it lives quite well with its own contradictions, particularly in the UK. There will always be a market for designed objects, especially at the luxury end. A significant proportion of UK design is focused on luxury and I see no end to this market. I recently attended a meeting at the European Design Leadership Board, and their argument was that Europe should lead on the quality of designed luxury, drawing on our history to push the idea of a new craft developed through localized manufacturing. There will also be a big move towards design in the social space. These two drivers will be good for innovation and quite healthy for the design sector as a whole, as the tension between social and luxury will catalyse change in unpredictable ways. *-end-*

Notes
1. The Design Commission is an industry-led research group, which sits alongside the UK's Associate Parliamentary Design and Innovation Group. The report can be downloaded from www.policyconnect.org.uk/apdig/design-commission.
2. The Red Unit was set up by the UK Design Council from 2004–6 to tackle social and economic issues through design-led innovation.

Xin Xiangyang

Xin Xiangyang is Professor and Dean of the School of Design at Jiangnan University in Wuxi, China. He holds a PhD in Design from Carnegie Mellon University, and his research interests lie within interaction and service design, cultural studies and product development. He has lectured internationally, conducted workshops on interaction design and cultural innovation, and has served as a guest professor in China. Xiangyang shares with us his five-year plan to reform the Chinese design education system, in response to the extending scope and evolving principles of design.

Can you tell us what your current role involves, and what drives you in your work?

I took up the position of Professor and Dean at the School of Design at Jiangnan University in 2011. The design programme here was started in the 1960s, and is considered to be one of the first such programmes in China. As a result we have over half a century of design history and design education experience in the school. After working abroad for a number of years, I decided to return to mainland China in 2011 because I felt that the country was ready to transform and reform design education and design practice at national policy level.

Can you provide some context to Chinese design education?

Two major inspirations for Chinese design education were Germany and Japan. China in the 1960s did not have many private companies, or much in the way of light industry. We had the traditional silk and tea

industries, which had been around for 200 years, but the government wanted to expand its export market and so they invited six or seven schools linked to the National Light Industry bureau to take up the challenge of building a light industries sector in China – and our school started its design programme in 1960 in response to this call. Two educators from Tsinghua University and two from our university were sent to Germany and Japan to study design. When they returned to China in the 1980s they started the first Bachelor level degree programmes, with postgraduate degrees introduced in the 1990s. So for a very long time, these two schools acted as a window between China, the west and the rest of the world in terms of design education.

The shift of design as a discipline from its orientation as a decorative art towards a more contextualized professional emphasis has been a pattern recognized in most of the world, but China has always been a couple of years behind. This began to change as the Chinese economy expanded and we became the 'world's factory'. The Chinese government soon realized that design's role is not only to decorate, and that it can also be used as a key competitive element in the economy – for instance, in identifying and realizing product opportunities that are innovative and respond to the emotional needs of the consumer. Our former Chinese Premier Wen Jia Bao has said that we now have to respect industrial design and consider it a major part of innovation. As a result, in 2011 the Chinese National Higher Education bureau finally recognized design as an independent discipline – which might seem like a strange concept for people outside of China. Here we have subjects that are identified as first, second or third class. First class disciplines includes chemistry, physics, engineering and architecture. Previously design was part of the school of engineering, and everything within it had to follow the national regulations – which define how students are recruited to colleges and how the National Education Bureau validates their degrees. When design was recognized as an independent first class discipline, many schools saw the opportunity to reform design education. When national policies are changed, the government offers huge grants to help support the implementation of those changes. This also created opportunities for non-leading institutions to leapfrog the leading schools, because they are not hampered by weight of their history.

But these opportunities also present challenges, as a lot of schools do not actually know how to transform what they are teaching into a first class discipline. Design is traditionally defined using a prefix before the word 'design', for example graphic design, industrial design or interior design. Now it is thought of more as a

profession, and so we have to think about the scope of design – especially now, when design can be used not only to support the day-to-day needs of consumers, but also as a social reform tool. Design can do many things, which is good, but at the same time people are getting confused about who designers are and what we do. This is very challenging but also presents even more opportunities, and I have realized that the next three to five years is going to be the window for design to be reformed as an academic field, and as a profession at national policy level.

Tell us about your five-year plan
I chose to go to Jiangnan because it presents, in my opinion, the best opportunity for educational reform. Unlike in other Chinese universities, design has been a key component of Jiangnan University for decades and so it has been very well supported and respected at both the university and national level. Jiangnan is also located near Wuxi, a regional city. This is unusual, since most good universities are generally located in capital cities. Wuxi has the seventh highest economic output in China, but only has one comprehensive university – which is Jiangnan. This gave me the platform to do things not only at a university level, but at a national level. In order to achieve this I have a five-year plan to establish a progressive and continuous platform for reform through a series of educational and professional forums and conferences. The first conference was held in May 2012, and focused on Scope, Methods and Principles. We asked professors and researchers from all over China to reflect on what has changed in design, and to consider whether our current tools, methods and principles are still appropriate for design. If design is no longer just for the people, then its principles have to be reviewed. Even though design research has moved on and become 'design with people' and 'design by people',

China is still based on the original model of 'design for people'. About 99 per cent of the design school curriculum is still based on this because the educational system was set up using this model – which had to be approved by national government. This is the reason why reform takes a long time in China, and it is why we need a conference to reflect on what the core of design education is.

I believe we are trapped in the concept of modernity. Modernity is not only a concept for art, it is also a social concept. It is a call for people from all kinds of disciplines to think of the purpose of the artificial, the purpose of production and the purpose of making. When we talked about the post-modern we talked about Universal Design, design with people, design by people. We should no longer be trapped in the concept of what we are doing but the problem is that when we look at our design education model, it is still based on Bauhaus ideals and principles. The focus on formal aspects of design is important, but there are also different perspectives on what is good. It is a simple argument, but one that is not seen in much of the design discussion in China. The purpose of our first education conference was to break the current system and beliefs, and the goal for the next conference in 2014 is to identify and review the key philosophical concepts that are shared across different sub-disciplines of design, in light of its new extended scope. Once we have identified those concepts we can then spend two years creating a framework for them, which will then hopefully become the basis for a new form of design education.

We have planned three major educational conferences in total, along with two professional conferences and smaller forums and seminars happening inbetween. The two additional professional conferences were needed because this reform should not only happen within the academic world, but should also change how we practice. The first professional conference will be in 2013, and will focus on reflection and finding new ways to design. By 2015 we should hopefully have a much clearer understanding of how design can move into the service industry and support innovation. Design is currently seen by the Chinese government as a service industry to support our heavy and light industries. Personally I believe that design not only supports those traditional industries but, in many places, can become their leading force. Although this concept is not that new in other parts of the world, we still need to publicize and develop these strategies in China by publishing papers and getting more designers to become Vice Presidents of corporations, so that design can become a leading profession.

What changes to the design programme have you introduced since you started in your role?
I have already started converting some of my ideas into curriculum changes at the undergraduate and postgraduate level. The programmes are still delivered under the traditional areas of design such as industrial design, interior and architecture, visual communication – so it is difficult for me to enact changes immediately. However I have started some experimental classes, and one of these is focused on integrated innovation at undergraduate level. Design and non-design students can join this class after finishing their first year. We have completely redesigned the curriculum to allow students with different capabilities to explore holistic problem solving in order to prepare them for different applications of design. Students can also learn from each other, and will develop specific capabilities like communication and collaborative skills in the class.

We have also recently established the Open Innovation Research Institute. This is a way to share resources between professors, disciplines, faculties and universities. We have five main areas of research: health, business innovation, social innovation for design, information and service and, finally, lifestyle innovation. We are trying to break down the traditional barriers and encourage students from different disciplines to participate in projects. We are also setting up partnerships with Case Western Reserve University's business school, and the research lab at the Rochester Institute of Technology in the United States.

Can you share with us some examples of how design is expanding into other territories in China?

I have two examples from my own experience. Changhong Electric Co. is a consumer electronics manufacturer based in Mianyang, China. Like many other manufacturers in China they are trying to move from a manufacturing base, to become based on service and brand. In 2004 Changhong established a new branch of the business and, as a result, three existing centres were re-established as software engineering, technology and design centres. The aim is to use these three centres as key components of their future research and development (R&D). In 2008 I was appointed as a strategic consultant to the company, and my role has been to build their design competencies and integrate the design team with the other teams within the business. Changhong are well known in China and have been invited by the Sichuan government to be the province's leading organization for the design profession, so we are organising a Design Thinking conference for the area that will not only give the company exposure to different perspectives of design, but also introduce them to examples of how Design Thinking can be adapted and adopted within the company.

Another project example is my work with the Hong Kong Applied Science and Technology Research Institute. The Hong Kong government employs over six hundred people in this Institute and, since it is a governmental body, they offer R&D services to small and medium size enterprises (SMEs) who do not have the resources to engage in this type of work. I was invited to help develop their design team, which is small but has already made quite an impressive contribution to the company, with many of their products already available on the market.

What vision do you have for design's role in China at the end of your five-year plan?

I hope that, by that time, my message about design education reform will have been accepted by at least 60 per cent of Chinese design students – and, more importantly, by the younger students because it is their future and their career. If I can accomplish 50 per cent of my goal, then I would deem it a success. I am optimistic that this can happen, and having a government that is stable and able to plan long-term is really important in achieving it. Some people suggest that this can make government systems difficult to change, but I have shown them that things can be done differently from the bottom up – without violating government principles or putting people at risk. I urge people not to use the political system as an excuse. I consider it my job, and my aim, to transform Chinese design education as my next major design project.

~end~

Adam Greenfield

Adam Greenfield is a New York City-based writer and urbanist. He is the author of *Everyware: The Dawning Age of Ubiquitous Computing* (2006), *Urban Computing and Its Discontents* (2007, with Mark Shepard) and the forthcoming *The City Is Here For You To Use*. In 2010 Adam established Urbanscale, a practice that aims to bring a human-centred perspective to the design of products, services, and spatial interventions wherever networked information technology intersects the urban condition. Adam speaks here about his vision of a networked city, and the potential for technology to help the world evolve towards local self-governance and self-organization.

Can you tell us what your current role involves, and what drives you in your work?

My background is in information architecture and web development. I was Head of Design Direction for Service and User Interface at Nokia between 2008–10, and prior to that I was Lead Information Architect for the Tokyo office of Razorfish, which was then a prominent internet services consultancy. As far as user experience goes, my primary concern is with the human adaptation to, and interaction with, relatively high-technology products, services and systems. I founded Urbanscale to bring the human-centred perspective I have found to be lacking in the design of services and systems for the urban environment. The practice has been extremely well received, and we have been offered the opportunity to work on some profoundly interesting projects.

From early 2012, despite the generous reception and all the goodwill our work has

generated, I decided to take the risk of putting the practice on hold while I focused on finishing a book I have been working on for a very long time. The strong likelihood is that we will fire the practice up again once the book has shipped, but I cannot in good conscience do both things at once – and I worry that if this book does not come out this year, it will not be relevant or useful to anyone.

The book is called *The City Is Here For You To Use,* and the premise is that everything we know and have learnt about cities in the seven to eight-thousand year history of human habitation in urban environments is undergoing some fairly rapid transformation. In particular there are things that we rely upon cities to do for us, for free, that contemporary information technology tends to cut against. Contemporary cities are decisively networked environments where digital, networked, information-gathering, sensing and actuation technologies become a part of every object, surface, relation and interaction. I am hoping to explore some alternative pathways for their development, attempting to find a way forward for networked information technology that enhances and amplifies what cities do and what they are for. I am interested in the most expedient way to get these ideas into currency, and to challenge some of the incredibly weak and inapposite things that are being done with urban technology at this moment in time.

What is the future of the networked city?
Five or ten years ago, most of the technical pieces were already in place. But the consciousness of the ordinary person on the street was not quite ready for this new idea of a networked city. Now though, around 30 per cent of people in the major urban centres of the developed world have a smartphone. The experience of everyday life is something we engage in increasingly via a networked device. As a result, all of the arguments I am making are so much easier to sell. There are a lot of people out there who already have a visceral sense of what I am referring to. But it also means that we are already on a path towards developing new habits in the way we act and how we use what the city has to offer, and in places where we have gone down a different path it may be hard to recover from that.

I do see hopeful signs, and some of them are in fairly unexpected places. For example, one of the most effective urban technologies I have come across is Foursquare, a location-based social networking website for mobile devices which allows users to post their location to their friends. Foursquare uses an incentive mechanism to encourage users to explore the city in two different modes: the 'Badge' device drives exploration of new places, while the 'Mayor' device encourages a deepened investment of time in familiar places. In the

version current to early 2012, we could see that specific decisions in the design of the Foursquare experience and interaction are influencing user behaviour in some pretty wonderful ways. By helping networked citizens to explore and develop a deeper feel for the places they live in, Foursquare is a fabulous driver of just the kind of habits I would want to encourage, and exactly the kind of interaction that I would prefer to see emerge from the opportunities offered by networked devices.

More broadly I am interested in asking what kind of ensembles a given technology can enter into, and what kind of experiences does it give rise to? In order to understand how Foursquare works, and how it drives observable behaviour, we have to compare it at a fairly granular level to other social location services. It is particularly interesting to contrast it with the way in which Facebook handles location. Facebook does not have any incentive mechanics, and as a result it does not drive the same kind of manifest behaviour. Designers need to understand how even the relatively small decisions that they make about functionality, interface or even nomenclature can have a disproportionate impact on the way someone using their product or service engages with the world.

What are your views on current contemporary design practice?
Firstly, I want to stress that I do not know what 'contemporary design practice' means, or what any such thing would look like. But based on my interactions in industry and with educational institutions around the world over the last 15 years, I find the contemporary design discourse a little claustrophobic.

My own perception is that this has a lot to do with how interaction designers are trained, and

I tend to find the curricula they are exposed to both ahistorical and apolitical. From my experience of teaching across different cultures and institutions, I have found that the majority of students I encounter in design programs have a relatively narrow exposure to ideas. When I first handed out my course reading list I assumed that most of the students would at least have heard of Latour or Foucault, and would be thoroughly conversant with the ideas of Dieter Rams, Jane Jacobs and Victor Papanek. I was shocked, frankly to find that, with a few exceptions, these names and the bodies of thought they represented were completely unfamiliar to my students. Which, in a way, is kind of great because it means I have the enormous privilege of introducing them to these foundational thinkers and doers. But it also means they don't get much time for that introduction, since we only have fourteen weeks in a semester and they are already working themselves to the point of exhaustion on their projects.

As far as the interaction design students I have encountered are concerned, their historical memory goes back only so far as the early 1990s and, with all due respect to them, they have tended to have a very superficial awareness and understanding of historical events. They tend not to be aware of how problems have been defined and solution spaces articulated by the various design disciplines, never mind in parallel areas of human enquiry. Part of my job then, is to help ground them in the history of expression in their own field.

What startles me more than the lack of historical knowledge is the apolitical nature of contemporary design culture, although there are certainly exceptions. There are designers who weigh the human development aspect when designing for emerging markets, and

these types of project at least acknowledge that there are power dynamics and differentials of access in the world. But, specifically with regard to contemporary software development culture, there seems to be an overwhelming urge to design for the 10 per cent of the population who already have access and power, while ignoring the other 90 per cent who do not.

What excites you about design at the moment?
One of the prime drivers of my original interest in ubiquitous computing was the dematerialization of things. My own personal aesthetic is very modernist and minimalist, and I tend to regard most designed objects as *kipple*. This wonderful word, coined by science-fiction writer Philip K Dick in his 1968 novel *Do Androids Dream of Electric Sheep?*, means a kind of rubbish which constantly accumulates, seemingly without human intervention. Well, most things are like that, right? They have a limited lifespan and are not designed with any particular clarity of intention. In naked point of fact, most things are just ugly.

What I love about the present moment is that, due to the ongoing and technologically-driven dematerialization of objects, life is just less cluttered than it used to be. If you are Dieter Rams in the 1960s, the only way you can intervene in the ugliness of the world is to design beautiful things. By contrast, if you happen to be a young interaction design student in 2012, you can design things to *go away*, to dematerialize. A design intervention that might previously have been clumsy, materially wasteful or just ugly can now be made to be evanescent, and literally to disappear from the world. I find that extraordinarily hopeful.

Comparing my apartment space with how it was a few years ago is a good example. It is the same physical space, but it has been utterly transformed by the presence of networked information-processing technologies. I love books and the physical act of reading, but I had five thousand volumes that we had to bring with us from Tokyo to San Francisco, to New York, to Helsinki and then back again to New York. Now we are down to just a thousand, the kinds of books that are lovely as objects or have significant sentimental value. The space itself is no longer about providing scaffolding on which to hang this massive physical presence of our engagement with the world. It has become much more of a platform for conviviality, where people can enjoy food and drink and each other's company.

This is true as a more general principle too: when you convert objects into services, you convert the necessity of owning a vehicle into the opportunity of accessing it on demand. There are now citywide car-sharing services, bicycle-sharing networks, frameworks which enable the temporary and shared use of space. We can live in this very appealing way, dancing lightly on the world and opening up more time and space in our lives for the things that really do matter. But all these services need to be designed, thoughtfully and sensitively. There are incredible opportunities for young designers at the moment, and this fills me with a great degree of hope.

What will design practices look like in the future? I have a fairly long-term utopian view of the future, which becomes possible due to the emergence of a completely different mode of social organization.

One of the most interesting experiences I have had in the last few years happened while I was attending a round table meeting at the Rockefeller Foundation in New York, about the future of networked cities and of networked technologies in cities. There was

a consultant from a global management firm presenting at the event – a very buttoned-down, straitlaced kind of a guy. After he gave his presentation, someone in the crowd asked him if he thought we had collectively arrived at the optimum form of democratic governance and self-management in cities. What he then proceeded to describe was a model of organization where technology is used to facilitate the devolution of power to the local community. I have never been quite sure if he was aware of it or not, but he was essentially describing a form of anarchosyndicalism, something not too dissimilar to what happened when the anarchist CNT-FAI union took over the Barcelona telephone exchange during the Spanish Civil War. These anarchists managed what was then a highly complex, technologically-intensive provision of services for an entire city, and they did so in a self-organized way.

So although it is not a particularly likely outcome, one of the things that gives me hope is the potential inherent in networked technologies of interaction to help the world evolve towards local self-governance and self-organization. If this happens, then the notion of embedded systems thinkers at each stratum in a community of practice – people who facilitate the self-expression and self-organization of those local communities, and harness them into a higher-level and larger scale aggregate of intention – becomes viable. And this notion in turn brings up all sorts of possibilities that I am determined to devote time to explore. At the moment, I have no way of knowing what form these explorations are going to take – but I am reasonably certain that it will not look like work within the neoliberal context of the contemporary client-service model. *-end-*

DESIGN TRANSITIONS
Reflections on our global journey

In these 42 stories we have journeyed through an array of design practices in transition to illustrate how design is moving beyond the traditional boundaries of the field. In this final essay we discuss the four distinct transitions that we have observed during this journey, and share our views on the key challenges and opportunities that design will face in the future.

Shifting sands

Historically design has been a discipline that evolves in direct response to market needs, and in the last decade the accelerated pace of change within those markets has forced businesses to rethink the way they do things. The emerging markets like Brazil, China and India offer exciting new business opportunities – but also the difficult challenge of trying to break into markets already saturated with successful local brands. At the same time the volatility of the more established markets has meant that businesses must learn to deal with more complex consumer expectations, while the growth of service delivery through digital channels means that businesses can no longer compete on price alone. They now have to rethink the way they deliver value to their customers. These changes are not just affecting the commercial sector; they are also impacting upon public and third sector organizations, where financial pressures caused by the recent economic downturn in the USA, UK and Europe have necessitated a rethink of how policies and services are created and delivered. Each of these changes presents the design industry with an opportunity to affect change in new areas.

Advancing technology

Recent technological advances in manufacturing processes and the pervasive use of network technologies have transformed the way that designers operate. They can now take greater control over the manufacturing processes, thanks to improved access to more affordable prototyping tools. This has led to an increasing number of practices producing their own products and services, like BERG with their *Little Printer* (see page 22). The connectivity offered by the internet, mobile applications and social media allows designers to operate beyond the traditional consultancy model, in a much more flexible and fluid manner. This flexibility also enables designers to diversify their practices, moving into new areas such as social entrepreneurship and working with business start-ups.

New layers

While collecting the stories that fill this book, we have seen that design's overwhelming response to change is one of optimism and excitement. Although the way that designers deal with change may not differ very much from the approaches seen in other professions, what is different is how much more often designers experience change at this current moment in time. John Heskett states that the history of design has not followed a linear evolution, but rather a layering one; where the roles and functions of design are continually redefined, and those new definitions placed on top of the old. This constant layering of new approaches slowly transforms the individual designer's practice, and eventually leads to distinct transitions being revealed across the discipline. Through the process of researching this book, we have uncovered what we believe to be the four key transitions happening within design today.

Transition 1: Expanding roles

Today's designers are engaging in a raft of activities that are redefining the discipline's core practices, taking on new roles as facilitators, entrepreneurs and educators.

In our case studies the importance of the facilitator role was frequently discussed, with designers recognized as being the 'translator between all the parties…to bridge the different disciplinary languages and find common ground' (FutureGov). In project work around customer experience, the designer's role as facilitator was particularly important due to the numerous channels through which users and customers can now interact with their service providers, and their increasing demands for consistency and clarity across those channels.

The importance of the designer's role as educator is most clearly demonstrated within the in-house design teams or large corporations, as seen in our stories from the New Territories. For these in-house teams the biggest challenge is not up-skilling their fellow employees on design methodology and toolsets; it is changing the mindset and culture of an entire organization. For the design practices trying to achieve this with their corporate clients, this is often best achieved by letting those clients experience the design process for themselves, showing them 'how it is done, rather than doing the work on their behalf, thus enabling them to replicate the process (for themselves) in future projects'.

The role of the designer as entrepreneur – and more recently, as social design entrepreneur – was also a common theme throughout the case studies. Examples from thinkpublic, Uscreates, FutureGov and Hakuhodo Innovation Lab all suggest a clear move away from the commissioning model, and a new focus on the building of capacity and capability in order to ensure economic sustainability. There is a new wave of activist designers on the rise, leading social change through their pursuit of new business models such as social enterprises. Designers are no longer satisfied with observing from the sidelines – they now want to lead from the front to initiate change.

Transition 2: Greater collaboration

To paraphrase Hakuhodo Innovation Lab: no single institution can address global problems on their own. Those problems are becoming increasingly complex and multifaceted, and in recognition of this designers are seeking out new collaborations with users, professionals from other disciplines, and networks of like-minded individuals.

Designers and users

The realization that the true drivers of change are often the end users, rather than the designer or their client organization, has precipitated a need for designers to develop a better understanding of user and customer contexts. In response to this, designers are actively engaging users in co-designing the solutions to their problems. At Idiom in India, design is used as a catalyst for radical innovation through their DREAM:IN project. thinkpublic's Experience Based Design work with the UK's National Health Service (NHS) has brought co-design practices into the public eye, spreading the tools and language of design into a new field. For thinkpublic, design is not about a methodology – rather it is about 'changing the culture of people in those organizations to embed new ways of thinking'.

Designers and other professionals

The culture change required before design can create genuine value within organizations has triggered recognition of another form of collaboration, between designers and the field of change management. Design practices including Optimal Usability, Claro Partners, STBY, Fjord and thinkpublic, along with IT organization Novabase, described in their stories the need for designers to 'get better at change management' in order to 'influence organizational cultures'. In-house design teams within non-design organizations, such as those working in TACSI, Radboud and Minas Gerais, also emphasized how a change in mindset is needed to allow design to truly flourish. There are several aspects of the professional culture of design that can contribute value to non-design corporations, and an increasing number of those non-design corporations are building their own in-house design teams with the intention of influencing the philosophy and ideology of the organization.

Designers and networks

Designers' influence is spreading, not only within non-design corporations but also around the world. While design practices tend to remain small out of a desire to maintain flexibility and preserve their innovative cultures, they are also seeking out ways to tackle problems on a larger scale by creating collaborations with other practices. DesignThinkers Group, FutureGov, INSITUM, Superflux, STBY and User Studio rely on their global networks of associate designers. STBY call this 'networked collaboration', and their REACH Network is a prime example of this collaboration in action – allowing small local design companies to retain their lean approaches while participating in complex international projects.

Transition 3: Diversifying business models

Almost every design organization presented in this book began as a consultancy model, where design expertise was bought to meet the needs of the client. Almost all of those organizations have since diversified into a range of different business formats designed to respond better to their particular clients' needs and external environmental demands.

Design companies are now launching their own products and services into the marketplace. Optimal Workshop, the product development company born out of Optimal Usability which licenses online user research tools to organizations developed in response to a specific need identified through Optimal Usability's client work. In the social space, FutureGov have transitioned their business model 'away from change consultancy [and towards] a wholehearted commitment to using consultancy to generate ideas for products that can transform the sector at scale'. thinkpublic have launched social enterprises such as *Relative Friends* and the *After Work Club* to tackle the growing challenge of social isolation. All of these design practices have identified, and then responded to, unmet needs in the marketplace and in society.

Increasingly, design practices are developing their own internal R&D departments in order to experiment and test out new ideas. At BERG, Droog, Superflux and User Studio these are distinct areas of the business where their designers can pursue personal projects, creating evidence in support of new product and service ideas while allowing individuals to drive creativity, expand their own horizons and push business boundaries. At PHUNK, commercial and personal work have run side by side since the company was founded with a simultaneous focus on creating new revenue streams for the practice while maintaining a strong personal voice in their work.

The transitions happening within design business models have demonstrated designers' abilities to respond to external forces. They are moving away from being solely consultants, and becoming entrepreneurs, partners and collaborators. This diversification provides designers with fresh opportunities to engage in long-term change projects, while increasing their flexibility and giving them the freedom to explore new business areas in challenging economic times.

Transition 4: Externalizing approaches and demonstrating value

Design is a creative endeavour, where learning happens through doing and critiquing. Experience and intuition play a key role in the work of the designer, but this can make it difficult to see exactly how design happens. People with a limited knowledge of design may perceive its as a black art, but as more of them get the chance to participate in co-creation and collaborate with designers in their own professional contexts, it becomes even more important for designers to externalize the discipline's inner workings and communicate its value.

Many of the practices featured in this book have spoken about changing their approaches in order to demonstrate the value of the design process as quickly as possible. BERG, Fjord and thinkpublic all spoke about an increasing demand from clients for an earlier engagement in prototyping. This has enabled designers and their clients to start 'trying things out rather than imagining' them (Fjord), and to find 'out as fast as possible what works, what does not' (BERG). Design is still a hard sell in many of the emerging markets, as confirmed by the experiences of INSITUM, Idiom, frog Asia, designaffairs Shanghai and live|work Brazil, who have all had to work hard at educating their clients on the value design can bring, and its role in innovating their products, services and systems. In our Viewpoints sections, Ezio Manzini spoke about the importance of a designer's ability to visualize and prototype as part of a multi-disciplinary team. Designers are now developing tools to enable conversations between their project stakeholders from different backgrounds. Lucy Kimbell described the challenges of demonstrating the complex organizational structures that she is involved in designing, compared to the ease with which designed objects can be shared. As practitioners become more engaged in the design of services and systems, so the need to understand context becomes ever more pressing. Current ecosystems must be externalized before the touchpoints of a new service, system or network can be successfully realized, and in each new context value will need to be evidenced through a different type of outcome. As design approaches become more firmly embedded within other disciplines, they also need to be more transparent.

Challenges and opportunities in unexplored territories

Having identified the four key transitions that are driving change in the international design industry, we turn our attention to exploring how these transitions will impact upon three main audiences: designers, design educators, and organizations looking to embed design into their practices.

Designers

A significant challenge faced by today's designers is the need to communicate to external audiences the full range of their skillset, beyond the more obvious and tangible craft skills. The designer's ability to empathize, visualize, synthesize and bring about resolution are the skills that are driving their transition into new and expanded roles. These skills also influence the way they collaborate with their users, partners and peers, and are particularly important in light of the new opportunities being presented for designers to build design capability within organizations by taking on the role of educators. Carlos Teixeira spoke about the scale and diversity of the challenges coming from the emerging markets, and the DREAM:IN project (in the Idiom story on page 100) is an example of how design capability can be successfully scaled and applied in different countries.

Many of the design practices that we encountered were rapidly moving towards, if not already centred on, a deep a sense of social consciousness. Mike Press spoke of the activist and entrepreneurial spirit that he saw emerging from a new generation of designers, pointing to Futuregov and Snook (see their stories page 60 and page 70) as examples of practices who act like political activists, while also using design to turn ideas into concrete outcomes. More opportunities to translate interest in social issues into actionable solutions will emerge, as design gains increased traction by demonstrating its value in the public and third sectors. This value is now being successfully articulated through global happenings like the Service Design and GovJams run by WorkPlayExperience (see page 51).

Design educators

The time has come for design educators to move beyond the educational models previously defined by the industrial revolution. As Robert Young states, 'design has to understand that its traditional evolved role in terms of artisan practices should no longer be the single offering in design education'. In a post-industrial era educators must balance the nurturing of core skills such as sketching, and visualization, with the development of new softer skills and traits such as facilitation, collaboration and empathy. Students need to be able to identify the value they have to offer as designers, and also the value they have to gain through interacting with other disciplines. The challenge for educators is to work out what to include in (and exclude from) the curriculum in order to equip their students to act variously as managers, facilitators, educators, entrepreneurs and communicators. The disciplinary silos that continue to exist within education – while important to the development of the student's identity as a designer – may also prove a hindrance in an age of multi-disciplinary team-working.

Organizations embedding design

For organizations looking to embed design within their processes, the challenge is to see beyond design's toolkit and methods in order to create a sense of ownership over these new approaches, so that they can become accepted as part of the organizational culture. Companies like Novabase has shown that simply applying a prescribed process or method will not work; rather a process of translation and adaptation is required, in order to make those methods relevant to the given context. The successes seen in our five New Territories case studies are all down to the work of strong individuals and teams championing the value of design, in a transparent and simple manner and with the support of senior management.

Surveying new and fertile ground

There are many different conclusions to be drawn about the future of design practice from the stories in this book. It is our hope that by reading those stories you have discovered some fertile new ground to explore as part of your own design journey. We recognize that it would have been impossible to find these stories ten years ago, and that this book is a product of its time – but we believe that this is a time when the opportunities for design's application have become boundless, through an exciting series of transitions that thoroughly deserve to be documented.

And finally, we would like to thank all of our storytellers for their generosity in sharing their experiences and insights with us, enabling us to capture and share so many of the exciting changes that are happening in design right now. We believe design has tremendous power and potential, and throughout our journey we have seen this potential being realized in diverse and inspiring ways – and we hope that these stories will inspire you to seek out and share your own Design Transitions. *~end~*

Joyce Yee, Emma Jefferies & Lauren Tan

IMAGE CREDITS

Cover
Background image – PHUNK

Droog
pg 14 top, pg 15 2nd, 4th image, pg 17 left, pg 18 top left & right – Droog / pg 14 bottom, pg 21 – Kristof Vranken / pg 15 1st image, pg 16 – Gerard van Hees / pg 15 3rd image, pg 17 right – Alexander Moust / pg 18 bottom right – TD Architects / pg 15 5th image, pg 18 bottom left, pg 20 – Thijs Wolzak

BERG
pg 22, 23, 24, 25 – BERG Ltd / pg 23 centre, pg 27 – Courtesy Popular Science

Superflux
pg 30 – Anab Jain

PHUNK
pg 32 – PHUNK

FJORD
pg 34, 35, 38, 39, 41 – FJORD

live|work Brazil
pg 42, 43, 46, 47 – live|work

User Studio
pg 48 – User Studio

WorkPlayExperience
pg 50, left – Kristy Sinclair, right – Beat Schweizer (beatschweizer.com)

thinkPublic
pg 52, 53, 55, 56, 57, 58 – thinkpublic Ltd

FutureGov
pg 60, 61, 62, 63, 64, 65, 66 – FutureGov

We Are What We Do
pg 68 right – Sam Peacock, pg 68 left – We Are What We Do / pg 68 bottom – Antidote

Snook
Pg 70, 71 – Snook

Uscreates
pg 72 left – Alan Boyles / pg 72 right – Mary Rose Cook / pg 73 left – Alan Boyles / pg 72 right – designed by Joanna Choukeir

STBY
pg 74, 75 ,78, 79, 81 – STBY

Hakuhodo Innovation Lab
pg 84 bottom, pg 85 third image, pg 88, pg 90, pg 91 right – Fumiko Ichikawa / pg 87 – Hakuhado Innovation Lab / pg 85 1st and 4th images, pg 91 left, centre images – Aico Shimizu

DesignThinkers Group
pg 92, 93, 95, 96, 97, 98, 99 – DesignThinkers Group

Idiom
pg 100, 101, 103, 106 © Idiom Design and Consulting 2013 / pg 101 second image, 105 © DREAM:IN Social Networks Pvt Ltd.

INSITUM
pg 108 top – Fernando Galdino, bottom – Roberto Holguin / pg 109 left – Mauricio Guadarrama, centre – Fernando Galdino, right– Luis Arnal / pg 110 © INSITUM

DESIGN TRANSITIONS CREDITS

List of contributors:

Luis Alt
Jon Ardern
Luis Arnal
Banny Banerjee
André Barrence
Dominic Campbell
Ravi Chhatpar
Shine Chu
Joanna Choukeir
Lauren Currie
Aldo De Jong
Brandon Edwards
Denise Eler
Lucien Engelen
Tori Flower
Adam Greenfield
Fumiko Ichikawa
Donagh Hargan
Tom Inns
Anab Jain
Matt Jones
Pedro Janeiro
Agata Jaworska
Lucy Kimbell
Lulu Kitololo
Steve Lee
Yoel Lenti
Lidan Liu
Sonia Manchanda
Trent Mankelow
Ezio Manzini
Matthew Marino
Márcia Naves

Mike Press
Rich Radka
Paul Rodgers
Erik Roscam Abbing
Natalia Silva
Andrea Siodmok
Adam StJohn Lawrence
Deborah Szebeko
Jackson Tan
Carlos Teixeira
Cameron Tonkinwise
Geke van Dijk
Arne van Oosterom
Chris Vanstone
Abbie Walsh
Caio Werneck
Robert Young
Xin Xiangyang

Concept, authors & editorial direction
Joyce Yee, Emma Jefferies & Lauren Tan

Creative direction & book design
Joyce Yee

Editing
Louise Taylor

www.design-transitions.com

Joyce: jsheau@gmail.com – @jsheau
Emma: emma.jefferies@gmail.com – @dremmajefferies
Lauren: laurentan@mail.com – @laurentan